PERSPECTIVES ON WELFARE

Perspectives on Welfare

The experience of minority ethnic groups in Scotland

Edited by
ALISON BOWES
DUNCAN SIM

Ashgate

Aldershot · Brookfield USA · Singapore · Sydney

Published by
Ashgate Publishing Ltd
Gower House
Croft Road
Aldershot
Hants GU11 3HR
England

Ashgate Publishing Company
Old Post Road
Brookfield
Vermont 05036
USA

British Library Cataloguing in Publication Data

Perspectives on welfare : the experience of minority ethnic
        groups in Scotland. - (Research in ethnic relations)
        1. Minorities - Services for - Scotland 2. Social service and
        race relations - Scotland
        I. Bowes, Alison II. Sims, Duncan
        362.8 ' 4 ' 009411

Library of Congress Catalog Card Number: 97-71720

ISBN 1 85972 415 9

Printed and bound by Athenaeum Press, Ltd.,
Gateshead, Tyne & Wear.

Contents

Figures and tables

List of contributors

Irene Anderson is an independent researcher.

Nick Bailey is Research Fellow in the Housing Policy and Practice Unit, Department of Applied Social Science at the University of Stirling.

Alison Bowes is Senior Lecturer in the Department of Applied Social Science at the University of Stirling.

Julie Brownlie is a Social Worker with Falkirk Council Social Work Department.

Mel Cadman is Lecturer in Social Work at the University of Strathclyde.

Helen Carlin is Housing and Policy Manager at Age Concern Scotland, Edinburgh.

Mono Chakrabarti is Reader in Social Work at the University of Strathclyde.

Naira Dar is Research Fellow in the Department of Applied Social Science at the University of Stirling.

Teresa Meehan Domokos was Research Fellow in the Department of Applied Social Science at the University of Stirling from 1994 to 1996.

Eddie Donaghy is Research Fellow in the Department of Public Health Sciences at the University of Edinburgh.

Martin MacEwen is Director of the Scottish Ethnic Minorities Research Unit and Vice Principal at Edinburgh College of Art.

Gina Netto is Research Associate in the School of Planning and Housing at Edinburgh College of Art/Heriot-Watt University.

Sheila Paul is Senior Research Officer, Sheffield Health.

Duncan Sim is Senior Lecturer in the Housing Policy and Practice Unit, Department of Applied Social Science at the University of Stirling.

Hilary Third is Research Associate in the School of Planning and Housing at Edinburgh College of Art/Heriot-Watt University.

Acknowledgements

We would like to thank various community groups, the minority ethnic communities and professionals in housing, social work and health for their support for the research projects reported in this book.

We are also grateful to all the contributors for agreeing to participate and for the timely submission of their work.

Typing and secretarial support was provided by Sarah Pugh and Sally Armstrong-Payne of the University of Stirling and to them go our grateful thanks.

We would also like to thank staff at Ashgate for their helpful advice and assistance.

Alison Bowes
Duncan Sim   Stirling 1997

1. The changing policy context

Alison Bowes and Duncan Sim

Introduction

For service users, and other members of minority ethnic communities, questions are often asked as to why there appears to be an endless stream of research, and, in their eyes, no action. Services appear not to change, and the point of continuous investigation is not clear. We will argue in this book, on the basis of research, that progress, albeit slow and often regrettably slow, is being made in the development of health and social care services for clients from minority ethnic groups, and that it is part of the responsibility of researchers to continue their work, as part of a process of maintaining, perhaps increasing, the momentum of change, and its continuous scrutiny. Of course, no one project or one collection of projects can itself bring about major change of the kind that users may demand: the contribution of research must rather be a slow chipping away at the received wisdom of those who feel that services are equally accessible to all, that they are colourblind, and that they need no change.

All the researchers who contribute to this book are critical of current provision. Some are primarily academic researchers, some are practitioners; some belong to minority ethnic groups, some do not; some are specialists in work on minority ethnic groups, some are more generalist in their experience. These contributors offer different perspectives on the interpretation of their research findings, but all use these findings to make practical recommendations for policy and practice in health and social services, which they believe will aid the process of improving minority access. Throughout their work, there is an emphasis on a wider range of perspectives, those of service professionals, policy makers, and, most particularly, users and potential users of services. There is a major emphasis on people's own views of their own needs, and on the validity and importance of these views, which have so often remained unheeded.

We bring together in the book work on housing, health and social work services. Nationally, as Ahmad and Atkin (1996) show, the discussion about minority ethnic groups and community care has barely begun: their edited collection of readings reveals rather a thin research record addressing the issues for minority ethnic groups raised by the move towards the contract economy of care. Furthermore, more general research on community care has tended not to address questions relating to minority ethnic groups: Petch et al's (1996) major recent study for example identifies no specific issues. By including work on the three areas of service, we hope to begin to provide the basis for a more focused discussion of issues in community care.

The literature strongly suggests that there are distinct issues for clients from minority ethnic groups using the three services. These are linked with racism, cultural factors, and some identifiably distinctive needs and wants, all of which vary between and within minority groups. The contributors focus on these differences, and also on ways in which minority ethnic groups do not differ very much in their needs from the rest of the population, where such needs and wants are shared, and where the spotlight needs to be turned on the problematic nature of the services, rather than the characteristics of the clients.

All the research in this book has been conducted in Scotland, and focuses primarily on the South Asian minority population. It therefore has some dimensions which are locally influenced, and especially locally relevant, as does research conducted in any other area of the United Kingdom. But the major issues we discuss are of national relevance, and draw on and complement research findings and discussion originating in other areas.

In this introductory chapter, we begin by outlining recent policy developments in Scotland, focusing on the opportunities, as well as the difficulties raised by current changes. To introduce the contributors, we then identify some of the particular themes they address.

Policy background

There is now a small but rapidly expanding body of work on minority ethnic groups in Scotland but this is only the second attempt to bring the rather disparate contributions together. In 1991, Bowes and Sim's edited collection not only provided a focus for Scottish minority ethnic research but also contributed to comparative literature in the field. The book dealt with the distinctive features of the Scottish minority ethnic experience, while enabling productive comparisons to be made (Bowes and Sim 1991).

It is important to stress that, in comparison with England and Wales, Scotland has a different institutional and legal structure, a different migration history and ideology about migrants (Miles 1980, Miles and Muirhead 1986) and, as shown by the 1991 Census, a different set of minorities.

Housing and social work services in Scotland are organised within a legal framework quite different from that for England and Wales. Social housing is the responsibility of local authorities, housing associations and Scottish Homes, which was established in April 1989. Housing associations in Scotland tend to be much smaller than in England and tend to be locally-based. Scottish Homes, although mainly the funding and monitoring body for housing associations, equivalent to the Housing Corporation in England or Tai Cymru in Wales, still has a landlord function inherited from the former Scottish Special Housing Association. The structure of housing tenure in Scotland is also distinctive with a traditionally dominant rented sector. The level of public renting in Scotland, at 33.1 per cent, is the highest in the United Kingdom; the level of owner-occupation, at 57.0 per cent, is the lowest (*Housing Finance* 1996).

Social work services were delivered by Regional authorities until April 1996, when local government was reorganised; they are now delivered by single tier authorities. Social work departments in Scotland have somewhat wider powers than those in England and Wales, the relevant legislation being more generally phrased. Furthermore, social work services in Scotland include work with juvenile offenders, particularly significantly in children's hearings. In England and Wales, social work and probation services are separate.

The legislative framework for health provision within Scotland is not different from the rest of the U.K., although there are some differences in organisation. The delivery of health services is the responsibility of fifteen Health Boards, established under the 1972 National Health Service (Scotland) Act, to take over the functions of the former regional hospital boards and local health authorities. As with housing and social work, Ministerial responsibility for the work of the Health Boards lies with the Secretary of State for Scotland. For various historical reasons associated with high levels of deprivation and ill health, as well as geographical remoteness in the west and north of the country, Scotland has enjoyed higher spending per head on the NHS and reliance on the Health Service is greater in Scotland than elsewhere in the United Kingdom (R. Ford 1988).

Changes in service delivery in Scotland

Within Scotland, there is no doubt that the most visible change, to the public eye, has been the recent reorganisation of local government. Prior to April 1996,

3

Scotland had essentially a two-tier local government structure, consisting of nine Regional Councils and 53 District Councils; there were also three single tier Islands Councils covering Orkney, Shetland and the Western Isles. As a result of the Local Government Etc. (Scotland) Act 1994, the country's system of local government was reorganised into 29 unitary authorities; the three Islands Councils were unaffected. Many of the pre-1996 District Council Housing Departments were affected by changing boundaries, whether by merging with other neighbouring Districts or through incorporation of previously Regional Council functions such as Social Work.

Some of the new authorities have seen important opportunities, within the unitary structure, for Housing and Social Work Departments to work together more closely, and this has implications for the delivery of community care. In a number of authorities, namely Stirling, Clackmannanshire, East Lothian, Midlothian, West Lothian, Moray and South Ayrshire, housing and social work services have been combined within the same department; West Dunbartonshire seems likely to follow suit.

For many users of local government services, reorganisation may have resulted in a change in the Council's letterhead but service delivery has been relatively unchanged. There is no doubt, however, that policies have changed and will eventually have an impact on services, and funding levels in the new authorities appear to have been significantly reduced. This clearly has implications for the more disadvantaged users of services, who include minority ethnic groups.

At the time of writing, further changes affecting welfare services within Scotland are possible. A Labour government with an overall majority would aim to introduce legislation, within its first year of office, establishing a Scottish Parliament. While the details of the legislation will not be known until after the Election, it is certain that housing, health and social work services would fall within a Scottish Parliament's remit. It is likely that local authorities' roles would be strengthened, particularly in relation to strategic planning and enabling, and a Parliament would be faced with issues of regeneration, renewal and historic underinvestment within the public services.

At a political level, there are now a small number of local Councillors from minority ethnic groups and both the Labour and Scottish National Parties have adopted minority ethnic candidates for the forthcoming General Election. A Scottish Parliament would present another opportunity for individuals to enter the political arena and minority ethnic Members could help draw the attention of a Scottish Parliament to minority ethnic needs and raise the profile of minority groups.

Changes in housing policy

Housing organisations in Scotland are facing a period of intense change. In addition to dealing with the continuing effects of reorganisation, local authorities are now preparing for the Compulsory Competitive Tendering (CCT) of the housing management service. In the housing association sector, new associations have been created as a result of stock transfer, and associations and local authorities have competed for New Town houses, as Development Corporations are wound up. Scottish Homes, the national housing agency, is now funding a minority ethnic led housing organisation. And all housing, social work and health agencies are grappling with the complexities of community care.

The change which is likely to have an impact on most tenants is probably the introduction of CCT for housing management in 1998. Housing maintenance Direct Labour Organisations have had to compete for contracts with the private sector since 1980 but it was not until 1992 that the Government announced its intention to extend Compulsory Competitive Tendering (CCT) to 'white collar' services. Defined management services, which are now to be put out to tender, include rent collection, housing allocations, tenancy management, the administration of repairs and maintenance, and caretaking and cleaning. Strategic policy work on housing remains exempt from CCT and Councils will continue to assess housing need and homelessness applications.

The Scottish Office has required that all defined activities with a value in excess of £500,000 must be tendered. The first 30 per cent of defined activity must be let by April 1998, with the remaining 70 per cent by April 1999. This is two years later than England and one year later than Wales, the delay taking account of local government reorganisation.

Another major change affecting Scottish housing is tenure change. Such changes have taken place elsewhere but are especially significant in Scotland, because of the wind-up of the Scottish New Towns - several years after the process took place in England - and because of the transfer of Scottish Homes housing stock. In the case of New Town wind-up, the five Scottish New Towns collectively owned and managed almost 30,000 houses in 1994 and, as a result of tenants' ballots, around two-thirds of this has now passed to local authorities, the remainder to housing associations. There is no doubt that the Government had hoped for a greater diversity of local ownership in the New Towns but this has simply not materialised (Muirhead, 1996).

In the case of Scottish Homes, the organisation owned 46,000 houses at April 1995, substantially reduced from the 75,000 it inherited from the former Scottish Special Housing Association. It has pursued a policy of transferring its stock to housing associations, as it seeks to divest itself of its landlord role. Ultimately, it will become solely a funding and monitoring organisation, like the Housing Corporation and Tai Cymru.

All of these changes are significant, yet have not perhaps had a great impact on Scotland's minority ethnic population. There are still relatively few minority ethnic households within the Council sector, as discussed in Chapter 2, and many of the changes described above have not, so far, affected services which are in great demand within minority families.

Much more significant, from a minority ethnic point of view, has been the shift in Scottish Homes policy towards black and minority-ethnic led housing associations. Scottish Homes began to take an active stance on racial issues in housing in 1993, with the production of a Consultation Document on Ethnic Minority Housing (Scottish Homes 1993). In it, Scottish Homes recognised that, as the statutory body funding and monitoring housing associations in Scotland, they should be seen to set an example to the housing movement. In compiling the document, Scottish Homes commissioned research, firstly utilising the data contained within the 1991 Census and secondly, using qualitative interviews to examine some of the housing experiences of minority ethnic households.

The research also explored the strategy employed by the Housing Corporation in England, of promoting new black and minority ethnic led housing associations, and of ring-fencing funding specifically to support housing for minority ethnic groups. Scottish Homes suggested in its Consultation Paper that such a strategy would probably be inappropriate for Scotland because the numbers and proportion of minorities in the Scottish population were so much lower than in England. A 'flexible' approach was therefore advocated, which would take account of local circumstances but, in the main, Scottish Homes saw the objective of increasing minority ethnic participation in the housing association movement as best achieved through existing associations. They indicated that they would prefer to avoid a system of separate designated funding for minority ethnic housing.

While welcoming the initial progress being made by Scottish Homes in this area, there is no doubt that many Scottish minority ethnic groups were disappointed by the Consultation Paper. The organisation was accused of playing a 'numbers game', by arguing that the English strategy of ring-fenced funding was justified by the larger numbers of minority ethnic people in England; such a view, it was claimed, took no account of the historical disadvantage faced by minorities north of the border. In addition, Scottish Homes were severely criticised by many groups for holding consultation meetings during a period which included the Chinese New Year, Ramadan and Eid-ul-Fitr. This was felt to demonstrate a lack of awareness of minority cultures (Julienne 1995).

Following the consultation period, Scottish Homes published its policy document in October 1994 (Scottish Homes 1994). The organisation reaffirmed its preference for locally-responsive, flexible approaches to meeting minority ethnic needs, while setting various targets in relation to access, funding, monitoring and evaluation. Specifically, Scottish Homes set an overall target such that, within three years, at least 1.25 per cent of resources would be benefiting minority ethnic households. The figure was derived from the fact that 1.25 per cent of the Scottish population was from black and minority ethnic groups. This again led to criticism that Scottish Homes was playing a 'numbers game' and not looking in detail at the needs which actually existed (Julienne

1995).

The Scottish Federation of Housing Associations had, for some time, within its structure a Housing Equality Action Unit which campaigned on minority ethnic issues. In June 1995, this was relaunched as Positive Action in Housing - the Scottish Ethnic Minorities Housing Agency, and it has continued to campaign, in particular for the establishment of minority ethnic led housing associations within Scotland. Scottish Homes responded by examining, for Glasgow, the relationship between areas of minority settlement and the areas of operation of existing associations. They also examined in some detail the performance of those associations in satisfying minority needs (Dowie 1995). Scottish Homes argued that minority needs would be met through three basic mechanisms, namely targeted Housing Association Grant for minority ethnic housing, the establishment of an Ethnic Minority Forum to allow for effective networking and information exchange, and a requirement for associations to undertake an assessment of minority needs as part of their Business Planning process.

Within a very short period, however, Scottish Homes retreated from its previous stance. At a conference in Glasgow in February 1996, Peter McKinlay, the Chief Executive announced, firstly that Scottish Homes would be committing £8 million for minority ethnic housing projects in Glasgow over a three year period and, secondly, that the organisation would be supporting the Ethnic Minority Led Housing Initiative (EMLHI) which had been established in Glasgow the previous year and which had already attempted to register as a housing association. The allocation of resources was generally welcomed by minority ethnic groups, although there must be some concerns about the decision to focus exclusively on Glasgow. The Chartered Institute of Housing pointed out (*Inside Housing*, 1 March 1996, p.3) that many other parts of Scotland had minority communities in need of resources. The support for the EMLHI is also not clearcut and there is confusion as to how Scottish Homes expects it to operate.

Essentially, Scottish Homes has suggested that the EMLHI would take the form of a management only organisation, whereby several Glasgow housing associations would make available houses for use by the organisation. Other landlords such as Glasgow City Council and Scottish Homes itself could also contribute to the organisation's housing stock, and landlord associations could acquire and develop property specifically for use by the EMLHI. The precise terms of the relationship between the landlord association and the EMLHI would be contained within a standard management/lease agreement. However, it would be expected that property ownership, and maintenance and repair responsibilities would remain with the associations, as landlords. The EMLHI would have control over the allocation of the houses, rent collection and general tenancy management issues.

The proposal seems, on the face of it, to be cumbersome and the division of management responsibilities not entirely satisfactory. It raises the prospect of some associations having minority ethnic tenants of their own, while leasing some of their housing stock for the EMLHI to allocate to other minority ethnic tenants. That the proposal is potentially flawed is demonstrated by the fact that Scottish Homes has commissioned further research into the viability of the EMLHI as a housing provider. The results of the study are expected late in 1996 and will have an important role in shaping the future provision of minority ethnic housing.

Certainly there is a growing acceptance that minority ethnic groups have not been well served by the present system. The paper by Third and MacEwen within this book shows clearly how, at both national and local level, minorities have experienced difficulties in accessing services, while Bowes, Dar and Sim's research demonstrates how one minority group - the Pakistanis - have devised strategies for overcoming such barriers to access. For particular groups within the minority ethnic communities, there is a double disadvantage and this is explored, in relation to the minority ethnic elderly, in Carlin's paper.

Social work and community care policy

Social work departments in Scotland have their origins in the Social Work (Scotland) Act, 1968. Prior to this legislation, specialised departments existed, dealing with different aspects of social welfare and these were criticised because of their segregation and limited conception of their respective responsibilities (Ford 1988). The Act therefore represented a considerable step towards unification of the personal social services, well ahead of England and Wales.

The objective of the departments was expressed in wide terms in the Act, 'to promote social welfare by making available advice, guidance and assistance on such a scale as may be appropriate for their area'. Departments were responsible for personal, professional involvement with individuals and families ('fieldwork'), and also for a wide range of other services, including residential services for various groups, from children to the elderly, day care services, and domiciliary services, such as home helps (J. Ford 1988). These remain the core responsibilities of departments today.

Unlike housing and health services, social work services directly affect only a minority of the population, comprising the poorest and most vulnerable people within our society:

> If social workers often seem overly passionate advocates of their clients' cause, it is partly because they know that such people do not elicit a great deal of sympathy from within the community at large and command virtually no social or economic power. The personal social services, which grew rapidly in a time of economic expansion and tolerant, liberal attitudes, are particularly vulnerable when the political context

changes, public expenditure is closely scrutinised and the level of social generosity may decline (J. Ford 1988, p.136).

Despite these pressures on public expenditure, the need for social services .. probably expanding. Rising unemployment in the 1980s and increased family pressures have led to expansion of the social security budget, at a time when central government is attempting to reduce public spending. Demographic changes too are exerting pressures on the social work service, as the population ages and requires greater levels of support. Prospects for expansion within the social work service, however, look remote.

Within the area of social work, perhaps the most significant changes have been in relation to other services. Although social work was always a broadly defined area, links with housing were sometimes problematic because the two services were delivered by different tiers of local government; health service provision was of course outwith local government completely. More recently, social work and housing have become linked together in some local authorities, following the creation of a single tier system of local government. Further links between housing, social work and health care have resulted from the development of community care, one of the most significant policy changes of recent years.

Present community care policy is generally seen to have its origins in the Griffiths Report (Griffiths 1988). The Report was critical of central government for failing to link the objectives of community care policy to adequate resources. It also found that the division of responsibilities between agencies at the local level was unclear and poorly co-ordinated, and that private and voluntary sector provision, for example in nursing homes, was not properly tied into the overall subsidy system. Griffiths recommended that a mixed economy approach should be used to stimulate choice and efficiency by requiring the public, private and voluntary sectors to compete to provide services on an equal footing (Means and Smith 1994).

The Griffiths Report formed the basis of a Government White Paper on community care, entitled 'Caring for People', but one significant change introduced by the Government concerned the role of housing. Griffiths had viewed the role of housing authorities in community care as being merely the providers of bricks and mortar and not the actual support. The White Paper, on the other hand, stated:

> Suitable good quality housing is seen as essential to social care packages...... Social service authorities will need to work closely with housing authorities, housing associations and other providers of housing of all types in developing plans for a full and flexible range of housing ('Caring for People' 1989, p.9 and 25).

The Government therefore saw Housing, Social Work and Health authorities as having a more equal and co-operative role to play within community care policy.

Joint working between housing and social work, as an objective of local government, is not a new idea. After the previous reorganisation of local government in 1975, the Morris Committee, established by the Scottish Development Department to examine the links between the two services, concluded that co-operation would only be successful if a number of issues were resolved. These included the need for an understanding of the demarcation of respective responsibilities, formal administrative structures established at member and management team level, and joint training for housing and social work staff (Scottish Development Department 1975).

Joint working at a strategic level between housing and social work, however, has generally been ineffective. Clapham, Kemp and Smith (1990) suggest that attempts to implement community care policies have been characterised by inconsistency, confusion and conflict between different services and the organisations who deliver them. They also argue that the levels of resources available have not proved adequate. Such difficulties particularly affect disadvantaged groups and their families, and Clapham, Kemp and Smith's work focuses on the elderly and those with learning difficulties. Minority ethnic groups are not identified specifically, either by Clapham, Kemp and Smith or by Petch et al (1996), as suffering from inadequate community care policies and practices, but they represent another disadvantaged group.

Most recently, the Scottish Office view has been that effective community care must be provided on an inter-agency basis and must be related to the needs and wishes of the users (Scottish Office 1994). In regard to the roles of the different agencies, the function of the social work service is to take the lead in planning and arranging the provision of community care and to secure the provision of social care. Although Health Boards are involved in community care, their current role will be reduced with the closure of long-stay institutions and the requirement to hand over their social care function to social workers. Their main remaining function will be in the development of community health structures. The main role of housing is to provide accommodation which meets the needs of community care users and to allocate and manage that accommodation. Thus, in order to be effective, community care must be a relatively equal partnership between these three sectors.

Six months after the implementation of community care legislation, the Chartered Institute of Housing in Scotland undertook a short survey to establish what the early experience had been. One of the major difficulties identified by local authorities was a shortfall in funding, which resulted in many needs not being met. The availability of community care was therefore becoming restricted:

> At a practical level, the system can create difficulties for
> people seeking access to services. The client groups who
> have best representation and better support mechanisms will

inevitably find it easier to access the system. Those clients perceived as more 'difficult' may also be discriminated against by a bureaucratic process which includes form filling, the need to keep appointments etc. The assessment process can therefore lead people to self-select themselves out of the system (Chartered Institute of Housing 1994: 7).

It is extremely likely that minority ethnic groups would be amongst those failing to achieve access to the system, because of a lack of representation, a lack of knowledge and possible difficulties with form-filling.

Minority ethnic groups have also been affected by local government reorganisation, referred to earlier. A potential problem, especially in social work, is that initiatives aimed at improving services to minority ethnic groups have been reduced or disappeared, as their staff have been dispersed to the new authorities and their resources cut. For example, specialist staff from the former Strathclyde Region Social Work Department are now dispersed over twelve authorities, with new duties, and Central Region's Interpreting Service has been closed down. It may be the case that the smaller authorities within which social work services are now based will find it even more difficult to devote resources to work with minority ethnic groups than did the old authorities. The 'numbers game' may become significant, as it did in housing, with authorities arguing that a small minority ethnic population does not merit dedicated resources.

A number of authors within this book have specifically shown how individuals within minority communities, particularly those with special social work needs, have suffered from a dual disadvantage. Chakrabarti and Cadman show how minority ethnic elders have not been able to make full use of social work services and this is a theme which also runs through Netto's study in Lothian. The low uptake of social work and community care services cannot be attributed to lack of interest or need on the part of carers of older people; rather there are gaps in service provision which need to be filled. Anderson and Brownlie's paper on minority ethnic elders with dementia, and Bowes and Dar's research on elderly Pakistanis also identify problems in accessing and making use of social work services.

The provision of adequate care services to people with special needs calls for a range of strategies to meet their special requirements. While funding levels remain problematic and this adds to uncertainties regarding long term provision, there is a danger that inadequate support will lead to cycles of crisis and instability affecting particular groups of users.

Changing health policies

The Report of the Royal Commission on the National Health Service (1979) had

11

aimed to reach a degree of consensus regarding the funding and delivery of the British NHS, but in the event, the election of the Conservative Government in that year has led to substantial moves away from that consensus. The Commission had argued for government action to prevent illness and poor health, particularly where this could produce identifiable results, for example in relation to smoking and road safety. But this approach was rejected subsequently by the Government which viewed prevention in terms of individual lifestyle choices. Significantly, in its White Paper, 'The Health of the Nation' (Department of Health 1992), the Government made no reference to the impacts of social structure or social inequalities on health differentials, emphasising that lifestyles were largely a matter of individual choice. This approach ignored the findings of previous research, such as the Black Report (DHSS 1980) and is important in the context of access to adequate health service provision for certain groups, including the minority ethnic communities.

Although the Government has sought to introduce a greater involvement by the private sector, within the NHS, this has been limited. Private hospitals and health care have been encouraged, charges for certain services such as dental and eyesight tests have been introduced, and private health insurance has expanded. But the Health Service has remained essentially funded through the tax system.

In the absence of major funding changes, organisational reforms have perhaps assumed greater significance. Within health authorities, an internal market was created by separating out their purchaser and provider roles; it was hoped that this would lead to greater efficiencies. General practitioners were also able to apply for fundholding status, allowing them to draw up their own contracts with hospitals, regarding the provision of medical and surgical services. Hospitals themselves would have an incentive therefore to minimise costs and price their activities competitively and, in order to improve efficiency still further, they could opt out of health authority control, becoming instead NHS Trusts, controlled by separate boards. Finally, within the NHS, there have been significant changes in management structures, with former administrators being replaced by General Managers, with wide powers of financial control, again an attempt to increase efficiency and cut out what was seen as unnecessary bureaucracy.

It is well beyond the scope of this book to debate the effectiveness of these NHS reforms. Nevertheless, it is fair to say that the reforms have generated public disquiet, particularly in relation to specific changes, for example charging for dental tests. In addition, there has been considerable discussion, often in the popular press, about the length of waiting lists and about inequalities in health care. A number of commentators have referred to the difficulties faced by working class families and the unemployed, as well as women and minority ethnic groups in accessing appropriate health service provision. Good health has therefore become an issue affected by class, gender and ethnicity (Jones 1994).

Such inequalities may also be seen in terms of those working within the Health Service. Most consultants, even in areas such as obstetrics and gynaecology, are men and Oakley (1986), for example, has argued that medical technology has been used to remove women's control over reproduction. Similarly, minority ethnic groups have little power within the NHS because, although there are many black and Asian people employed, they tend to occupy lower paid and lower status posts. There are few individuals from minority ethnic groups in senior consultant or managerial positions and those that are tend to be confined to particular specialities, such as genito-urinary medicine or geriatrics.

In addition to these inequalities, the establishment of individual hospital trusts and the development of contracts between such trusts and individual fund-holding G.P.s suggests that we may be moving away slowly from a national health system and towards a collection of local systems. This would make it more difficult for inequalities to be addressed in an effective way. Additionally, the emphasis on individual choice has led to some individuals buying their own private health arrangements, as they do in housing, education and transport (Mohan 1995). This may fragment support for the NHS, since many people will not be exposed to it.

Within Scotland, it is rather difficult to assess the extent of this process. Mohan (1995, p.160) shows that in 1987, only 4 per cent of persons in Scotland had private medical insurance, which along with Wales and the North of England, was one of the lowest figures in the UK. In 1992, there were only four acute hospitals in Scotland in the commercial sector (excluding private charitable establishments). This suggests that Scots have not tended, as yet, to opt out of the National Health Service.

What is true, however, is that Health Boards and health researchers in Scotland have been relatively slow to respond to the issues presented by a minority ethnic population. Whilst in England, debate in many areas of healthcare has been extensive (e.g. Ahmad 1993), in Scotland there has been very little work. Similarly in England, many health initiatives have been directed at minority ethnic communities, while in Scotland the record is sparse. The Royal Edinburgh Hospital has an Ethnic Minority Unit which facilitates access to mental health services, the Glasgow Healthy Cities Project has an ethnic minority health initiative, CSV Glasgow has a Health Action Project developing linkworker schemes, and there are smaller, more locally-based projects which offer, for example, mobile cervical screening sessions.

Greater Glasgow Health Board adopted a policy for race equality in health and health care in May 1996, following recommendations from a health gain commissioning team. Three subgroups are currently (November 1996) examining issues in communication, training and primary care. The same Board has also set up an ethnic minority health team which visits community groups offering services, especially mental health services. These services are few and far between and there is considerable scope for further initiatives.

In terms of research on the health of minority ethnic groups, there has been a strong tendency to attribute health problems to minority cultures (Ahmad 1993b).

In Scotland, this was especially clear in Goel's (1981) early work on 'Asian rickets', in which the focus was on aspects of Asian culture, especially diet, as causative factors. Generally, rather less attention has been given to the influence of socio-economic disadvantage on health, or of the exclusionary aspects of health services. All the contributors to this book who look at health are critical of the victim blaming which can be engendered by an emphasis on culture.

Contributions to the book also reflect issues of inequality in health care and problems of access. Bowes and Domokos's work shows clearly the problems of communication between Pakistani women and health professionals, while Paul's paper demonstrates difficulties of access by South Asian women to cervical screening. Donaghy suggests that we have insufficient understanding of the causes of depression in Asian women and that 'culture conflict' is an inappropriate explanation.

Issues addressed within the book

Against the background of the policy changes of recent years, researchers contributing to this volume address a series of key themes. The most important of these is an emphasis on service users' own views, reflecting their particular concerns, and this is a perspective which has tended to be absent from much previous work. Many of the papers are concerned with the use made of services and utilise detailed interviews with members of minority ethnic groups in order to establish the appropriateness of the service concerned. At a time of major policy and service upheaval, such an approach is essential.

A second theme which runs through the book relates to the issue of service delivery. Many services are shown to be poorly advertised to minority groups, difficult to access or are felt to be inappropriate or insensitive to minority ethnic needs. This is particularly the case in relation to minority ethnic elderly people who suffer from a dual disadvantage. They are vulnerable because of their age and also tend to have poor knowledge of English which makes access to services difficult; the situation seems equally poor in relation to both housing and social work.

Thirdly, issues of racism are explored in a number of papers. Many minority individuals complain about racism, some of which, like harassment in housing estates is particularly explicit. In other cases, insensitivity within services provided may be construed as a form of implicit racism. The former may need to be tackled through direct legal action or through firm application of tenancy agreements; the latter may be tackled through better staff training, and a more thoughtful approach to service provision.

Another theme which runs through several of the papers is the role played by different agencies. Housing, social work and health are all statutory services, but all have a significant voluntary component. Minority ethnic groups may sometimes feel more comfortable accessing advice and services through voluntary agencies, particularly those run or controlled by minority groups themselves. Staff in such agencies may be felt to be more sensitive to minority needs and have the necessary language skills to communicate effectively. The links between statutory and voluntary agencies and the contribution which each can make is a significant element in research in this area.

There are also important methodological issues addressed within the book. In order to establish the views of minority ethnic service users, researchers have used a variety of techniques, including qualitative semi-structured interviews, structured questionnaires and work with groups. There are also quantitative surveys of service providers referred to in the papers. This helps to demonstrate that no one research technique is appropriate but that, through a variety of different approaches, the fullest picture of service use can be generated.

Papers on each service sector are grouped together within the book, although clearly services in housing, health and social work all overlap, particularly in relation to community care. The conclusion therefore attempts to bring together the various substantive, theoretical, methodological and policy issues addressed in the separate papers. It is hoped that this volume, comprising these individual papers, together with the introductory and concluding chapters, represents a useful step forward in disseminating research to a wider audience, in identifying areas for further work, and ultimately in promoting a greater awareness of the issues affecting minority ethnic groups in Scotland.

2. The demography of minority ethnic groups in Scotland

Nick Bailey, Alison Bowes and Duncan Sim

Introduction

Before the 1991 Census, there was no accurate count of the minority ethnic population of Scotland. Census data were limited to details of the country of birth of persons enumerated and the size of the minority ethnic population was estimated from counts of the numbers of persons born in the New Commonwealth or Pakistan (NCWP). This measure was problematic, firstly because it included white ex-colonials and children of service personnel, born in the NCWP but who did not belong to the relevant ethnic groups. Secondly, and more importantly, it excluded children born in Scotland of immigrant parents and this limitation became more serious with the passage of time from earlier periods of immigration in the 1950s and 1960s. There was therefore an increasingly significant underestimate of the minority ethnic population.

Some local studies attempted to estimate the minority ethnic population for particular settlements. In Dundee, Jones and Davenport (1972) estimated the city's Pakistani community to be 500-600 in number, relying in part on Employment Exchange information. A second study, in Glasgow, by Kearsley and Srivastava (1974) estimated the city's Asian population to be around 12,000 at 1971, representing 1.3 per cent of the total Glasgow population; this was an increase from an estimated 3,000 in 1961. In this case, the annual Register of Electors was used as the major source of information, with minority ethnic names being identified.

Following the 1981 Census, the Scottish Office attempted to provide estimates of the size and distribution of the minority ethnic population in Scotland (Scottish Office 1983). This was achieved primarily through the identification of minority ethnic names on Electoral Registers but also it used adjusted Census figures and detailed information on particular groups, such as Vietnamese refugees. The total size of the minority ethnic population of Scotland was estimated at 38,000 or 0.8 per cent of the total. The majority (25,000) was thought to be South Asian and a further 6,000 were thought to be of Chinese extraction. Of these two groups, totalling 31,000, it was estimated that 18,500 (approximately 60 per cent) lived in Strathclyde, with a particular concentration in Glasgow. A further 4,000 (13 per cent) lived in Lothian, primarily in Edinburgh. There was also a small concentration in Dundee.

Within the cities, there were known to be important concentrations within particular electoral wards, mainly in the inner city. There were also significant numbers of Asians in suburban areas around Glasgow, notably in the Districts of Bearsden and Milngavie, Strathkelvin and Eastwood, although the exact size of these communities was not known.

The 1991 Census

The inclusion, for the first time, of a question in the 1991 Census on ethnic grouping allows us to establish a much clearer picture of the demography of the minority ethnic communities in Scotland. It allows us also to examine this picture in relation to previous studies and to attempt to assess what changes, if any, have occurred in the characteristics of the communities. There are, of course, problems with using the Census as the question on ethnic group, although heavily tested in advance, was nevertheless controversial and this may have affected response rates. Despite this, it remains the best recent information which we have.

According to the 1991 Census, the number of persons describing themselves as being members of a minority ethnic group was 62,634, representing 1.25 per cent of the total Scottish population. The position is summarised in Table 2.1, which shows that the largest grouping was the Pakistanis with a population of 21,192 (34 per cent of the minority ethnic population), while the other main groupings were the Chinese (10,476, or 17 per cent) and the Indians (10,050, or 16 per cent). There were also substantial numbers in the 'Other-other' category, which included people of mixed ethnic origin (8,825, or 14 per cent of the minority ethnic population). This paper focuses on the three main groupings - the Pakistanis, Chinese and Indians - as the 'Other-other' category is perhaps too diverse to allow for meaningful analysis and the other categories are too small.

Table 2.2 lists the twelve local authorities with the largest proportions of minority ethnic persons enumerated, and where that proportion is greater than 0.8 per cent. The table also shows the largest minority ethnic group in each case and in seven local authority Districts, the Pakistanis are the largest group. The Indians are the largest group only in the two Glasgow suburban Districts of Bearsden and Milngavie and Strathkelvin, while 'Other' categories are the most significant in Argyll and Bute and Stirling. In the case of Argyll and Bute, 'Black-other' probably refers to the large presence of black American ex-service personnel around the Dunoon and Holy Loch area; in the case of Stirling, the 'Other-other' category may arise from the presence of overseas students at the local University, which will have a disproportionately large impact on a small town. The city of Aberdeen stands apart from the other major urban authorities as having the Chinese as its largest minority ethnic presence. This may be due to the longer existence of a South Asian community in the west of Scotland; the Chinese, being more recent arrivals, may have found it hard to obtain housing there and it was therefore easier to move into the east.

The final column of Table 2.2 shows the relative preponderance of the largest minority group in each District. In the west of Scotland, there are Districts where there is a clear dominance by Indians or Pakistanis. The situation is less clear-cut in the east and, although Pakistanis and Chinese may be the largest groups within Edinburgh and Aberdeen respectively, it is clear that there is actually a much more even distribution of different minority groups than is the case, for example, in Glasgow.

Table 2.1
Minority ethnic population of Scotland

Minority Group	Total No	% of total population	% of minority ethnic population
Black Caribbean	934	0.02	1.49
Black African	2,773	0.05	4.43
Black Other	2,646	0.05	4.22
Indian	10,050	0.20	16.04
Pakistani	21,192	0.42	33.83
Bangladeshi	1,134	0.02	1.81
Chinese	10,476	0.21	16.73
Other Asian	4,604	0.09	7.35
Other other	8,825	0.18	14.09
Total	62,634	1.25	100.00

Table 2.2

Local authorities with largest proportions of minority ethnic groups

District	Total Pop.	Minority Ethnic Pop.		Largest Minority Group	Largest group as % of all minority ethnic groups
		Total	%		
Glasgow	662,853	21,517	3.25	Pakistani	50.9
Eastwood	59,959	1,918	3.20	Pakistani	47.9
Bearsden & Milngavie	40,612	1,292	3.18	Indian	52.2
Edinburgh	418,914	9,870	2.36	Pakistani	26.6
Dundee	165,873	3,243	1.96	Pakistani	35.7
Strathkelvin	85,191	1,348	1.58	Indian	48.1
Aberdeen	204,885	2,999	1.46	Chinese	23.6
Cumbernauld & Kilsyth	62,412	768	1.23	Pakistani	27.5
Argyll & Bute	65,140	664	1.02	Black-Other	32.1
West Lothian	144,137	1,350	0.94	Pakistani	33.9
Stirling	78,833	693	0.88	Other-Other	19.0
Kirkcaldy	147,053	1,247	0.85	Pakistani	40.5

As might perhaps be expected, the minority ethnic population in Scotland is predominantly urban. The relatively high scores by the Glasgow suburban Districts also suggests that the minority ethnic population is becoming suburbanised. This movement of minorities into comparatively prosperous areas such as Eastwood mirrors an earlier migration by Glasgow's Jewish community (Benski 1976, 1980, 1981). On the other hand, individual minority ethnic households are also widely dispersed across Scotland, with the Chinese community in particular being quite dispersed. Every single local authority in Scotland recorded a Chinese presence in 1991, even the more geographically remote parts of the Highlands and Islands.

Comparisons with previous estimates suggest that the minority ethnic population may have been underestimated in the past. If the Scottish Office's estimate of the minority ethnic population as being 38,000 in 1981 were accurate, then the increase in population to 1991 would have been 24,600. This would suggest a rate of increase of 65 per cent, which is very high. It is more likely that the previous methods of counting, using birthplace in the NCWP and the Electoral Register, have somewhat underestimated the minority ethnic population, largely through the exclusion of those born in Britain, principally dependents.

Although there has been a South Asian community in Scotland since the mid-nineteenth century, it did not grow substantially until after the Second World War. Members of minority ethnic groups who are UK-born therefore, will generally have been born from the 1950s onwards. There are some differences between groups, however, and Table 2.3 shows the proportion of different ethnic groups born in the UK or Scotland. The table reveals that only a little over a quarter of all Chinese residents are Scots-born and less than one third are UK-born. The comparison with the Pakistanis, over half of whom are UK-born is particularly striking. When heads of household are considered, the number of UK- or Scots-born amongst the three main minority ethnic groups is relatively small but even so, the Chinese stand out as having a particularly small number. It is likely that the figures for Scots-born household heads within the minority ethnic communities will inevitably increase with continuing or new household formation in the next decade.

Table 2.3
Proportion of different ethnic groups living in Scotland, born in UK or Scotland: all persons and household heads (%)

	All Persons		Heads of Household	
	% Born in UK	% Born in Scotland	% Born in UK	% Born in Scotland
All	97.09	89.20	96.88	87.97
White	97.73	89.88	97.55	88.61
All Ethnic Minorities	45.98	35.45	15.83	10.34
Black Caribbean	55.59	36.99	44.44	24.81
Black African	27.78	20.68	13.17	7.60
Black Other	69.82	54.78	60.63	43.87
Indian	46.23	33.50	12.23	8.18
Pakistani	54.30	41.07	11.31	7.02
Bangladeshi	37.13	29.51	6.90	3.45
Chinese	32.00	28.14	4.02	2.77
Other Asian	19.27	14.70	5.92	3.12
Other Other	53.71	42.23	32.37	21.69

This hypothesis is supported by Table 2.4, which shows the age structure of the different communities. The white community has a relatively flat age distribution, but those for the ethnic minority groups show a much higher proportion in the younger age groups and very few people aged over 60. The differences between the age groups are particularly pronounced for the Chinese, who have the greatest percentage in the 16-39 age group, precisely the main group responsible for household formation.

Table 2.4
Age distribution and household size (Scotland) (%)

	Age Group				Average Household Size
	0-15	16-39	40-59	60+	
Total	20.2	35.0	24.1	20.6	2.44
White	20.0	34.8	24.3	20.9	2.43
All Ethnic Minorities	34.1	46.0	16.1	3.8	3.63
Chinese	26.0	51.6	17.7	4.6	3.37
Pakistani	39.2	43.1	14.9	2.8	4.75
Indian	29.9	43.3	21.2	5.6	3.66

Household size and composition

The average size of minority ethnic households is bigger than that for whites, although the position varies between the different ethnic groups. Pakistani households are clearly the largest. While the average Chinese household is slightly smaller than the minority ethnic average, it is still higher than that for whites. This is illustrated in Table 2.4 and the figures would seem to accord broadly with previous research in Glasgow and Edinburgh (Bowes, McCluskey and Sim 1989, 1990a; SEMRU 1987).

The composition of households by ethnic group is shown in Table 2.5, and there are several conclusions which can be drawn. Firstly, as demonstrated in Table 2.4, there are relatively few pensioner households in any of the minority ethnic communities, compared to the population as a whole. Secondly, there are slightly more single person, non-pensioner households in the Chinese community than in the other main minority ethnic groups or, indeed, the population at large.

As far as households with two or more adults are concerned, there are major differences between the minority ethnic communities and the population as a whole. Minorities are generally much more likely to have children, although the Chinese are slightly less likely to do so than the Indians or Pakistanis. Coupled with the slightly greater number of single person households, this reinforces the statistics in Table 2.3 which showed the smaller Chinese household size.

21

Table 2.5 also shows the occurrence of larger households, possibly extended families with three or more adults with one or more children and, once again, the minority ethnic communities present a quite different picture from the population as a whole. The Chinese, however, have fewer extended families than the Indians or, in particular, the Pakistanis. The Chinese, indeed, emerge as having a pattern of household composition rather different from the other main ethnic groups although closer in household type to the Indians than to the Pakistanis.

Table 2.5
Household composition and ethnic group (Scotland)

Household type	Total Population	All Ethnic Minorities	Chinese	Pakistani	Indian
	%	%	%	%	%
1 adult pensionable age	15.7	1.9	1.7	0.7	1.9
1 adult under pensionable age	12.9	14.6	13.9	7.7	11.3
1 adult plus 1 or more dependent child(ren)	4.9	4.5	3.3	4.2	3.6
2 or more adults no children	41.2	24.5	28.6	17.0	27.2
2 adults with dependent child(ren)	19.9	38.0	36.5	42.1	37.3
3 or more adults with dependent child(ren)	5.4	16.4	15.6	28.2	18.5
Number	2,020,050	16,430	3,033	4,546	2,885

Thus, minority ethnic households are, in general, larger than those of the white population, although there are variations between different minority groups. Few household heads are UK-born and the largest age group is that between 16 and 39, representing almost half of the minority ethnic population. The population is generally urban, although minorities, particularly the Chinese, are represented in every Scottish local authority area.

The economic position of minority ethnic groups

For many years now minority ethnic groups have been associated with the retailing and restaurant trades and, for example, Asian-owned shops, restaurants and 'take-aways' have become commonplace in Scottish towns and cities. Large numbers of Pakistanis had also been recruited by local authority transport departments in the 1950s and early 1960s as bus and tram drivers or conductors. The exception to this pattern was Dundee where a number of Pakistani workers found employment in the city's jute mills. There were also Indian and Pakistani doctors and nurses, recruited to alleviate understaffing in lower status areas of the National Health Service (Ward 1993).

During the last twenty years, there have been significant increases in the numbers of Asian-owned businesses and Maan (1992) estimates that, by 1990, around 65 per cent of Asian families owned a business, usually in the retail or wholesale trades. More recently, it would appear that younger Pakistanis are entering other areas of economic activity, including the motor trade, estate agencies, property development and the leisure industry. For example, two of the larger video-leasing firms, Azad and Global, are Pakistani-owned.

The overall economic position of the Scottish minority ethnic communities is shown in Table 2.6. All minority ethnic groups have significant numbers who are self-employed and fewer employees than the population as a whole, a reflection of the number of small family businesses, including restaurants and shops. In the past, these businesses have provided a source of employment for younger members of the minority ethnic communities but this seems no longer entirely to be the case and the unemployment rate, particularly among Pakistanis but also among Indians, is now higher than the Scottish average. The Chinese rate is still relatively low, however, suggesting that family businesses in the 'Chinese economy' can still absorb its younger adults. The smaller family size amongst the Chinese will also help to reduce pressures. Writers such as Ram (1992) and Cashmore (1992) have suggested that minority-owned enterprises will continue to face particular difficulties due to racism and that businesses which do well may succeed by employing more white workers in senior positions, as they may be more 'acceptable' in the external, racist, environment; this Cashmore calls 'racism by proxy'. Both writers suggest that the minority ethnic business sector may therefore be unlikely to be of widespread benefit to members of minority groups.

Of those who are economically inactive and under 25, all minority ethnic groups have large numbers involved in education. In the case of the Chinese, over half are accounted for in this way, the largest proportion of the three main minority groups. For all three groups, the figures are much higher than for the population as a whole, although this will be due, in part at least, to the younger age structure within minority ethnic groups; it may not necessarily indicate a stronger attachment to education.

Table 2.6
Economic position of minorities and total population: Scotland (%)

Category	Total Population	Chinese	Pakistani	Indian
Total 16+	3,988,247	7,750	12,882	7,043
Economically Active	60.4	57.4	52.9	62.8
Economically Inactive	39.6	42.6	47.1	37.2
Economically Active and Under 25	11.8	8.8	14.2	10.2
As % of economically active				
Employees (full-time)	63.6	50.5	31.9	47.0
Employees (part-time)	15.4	11.8	8.9	10.2
Self-employed with employees	3.8	20.7	22.1	16.6
Self-employed without employees	5.1	7.3	16.1	12.1
Unemployed	10.3	8.0	19.5	11.9
As % of economically inactive				
Students	9.1	52.1	26.5	31.2
Permanently sick	14.1	3.1	9.8	11.0
Retired	45.7	9.2	5.1	12.1
Other	30.8	35.7	58.8	45.7

The spread of occupations within the minority ethnic communities is illustrated in Table 2.7 and suggests a more limited spread than is the case with the population as a whole. There seem to be large numbers of junior non-manual and skilled workers (socio-economic groups 6, 8, 9, 12) and, in the case of the Chinese, substantial numbers in socio-economic groups 7 and 10 (service workers and semi-skilled, including restaurant workers). This might suggest that the Chinese have been unable or unwilling to expand into other areas of work. There is also a large proportion of minority ethnic workers in groups 1 and 2 (managerial), reflecting the number of individuals with their own businesses. It should be remembered, however, in interpreting this Table that the figures are based on only a 10 per cent sample and will be subject to sampling errors.

Table 2.7
SEG and ethnic group (10% Sample): Scotland (%)

Socio-Economic Group	Total Population	Chinese	Pakistani	Indian
1, 2 (Employers/Managers)	12.6	25.0	36.1	20.9
3,4 (Professional)	4.7	12.2	4.7	17.2
5 (Intermediate non-manual)	14.5	4.1	4.5	8.8
6 (Junior non-manual)	21.0	5.8	20.8	17.2
8, 9, 12 (Skilled)	20.6	10.5	20.8	18.8
7, 10 (Service Workers; semi-skilled)	15.5	35.8	9.8	12.3
11 (Unskilled)	7.0	4.4	0.4	1.3
13-17 (Other)	3.9	2.3	2.7	3.5
Total	207,378	344	509	373

The housing position of minority ethnic groups

The housing position of minority ethnic groups is a particularly important area of study if current patterns of settlement are to be understood. Table 2.8, derived from the Census, shows the basic patterns of tenure, overcrowding and standard of amenities. While this depicts the general situation, it is also important to look at the pattern in more detail.

As far as tenure is concerned, 63.9 per cent of all minority ethnic households are owner-occupiers, and the figure is even greater for the two main South Asian groups. It is clear therefore, that there is a far greater propensity, amongst all ethnic minority groups, to buy rather than to rent, although the Chinese have the lowest rates of ownership of the three main minorities. Dalton and Daghlian (1989) suggested in their survey of Glasgow that the Chinese tended to be outright owners, rarely using the services of estate agencies and building societies. The Census, however, does not bear this out, indicating that only 19.5 per cent of Chinese owner-occupiers own outright rather than the two-thirds identified by Dalton and Daghlian. In the case of Pakistani and Indian households, the figures are 20.7 per cent and 17.3 per cent respectively.

As far as the rented sectors are concerned, there is a larger proportion of minorities who rent privately, than is the case in the population as a whole, and the Chinese have the largest representation in privately rented property. In some instances, this is likely to be tied housing, owned and controlled by employers. There is a certain logic in this system in that restaurant workers are employed for long hours and require housing which is close to their work and to which they can easily return late at night (Watson 1977). But tied housing, linked to a system of economic patronage, can pose problems in the long term, making it difficult for workers to seek alternative employment, and making them vulnerable to the dictates of their employer. In the social rented sector, the position is quite different, with fewer households in the three main minority groups renting than in the population as a whole. There are some groups who rent from social landlords, however; in the Black Caribbean group (not shown in the table), the proportion of households which rents rises to 29.4 per cent, closer to the Scottish average, although the absolute numbers are small.

It is likely that the high proportion of minority ethnic households in the private rented sector helps to account for the similarly higher proportion of minorities lacking or sharing facilities and lacking self-contained accommodation. The presence of such large numbers in housing which is clearly of a poor quality would tend to confirm that minority ethnic households have limited choice, particularly in regard to access to rented accommodation.

The Census suggests that, as well as the problems of shared facilities, there is significant overcrowding, particularly affecting the Pakistanis with their larger household size. The percentage of households living with over one person per room is 4 per cent for the population in Scotland as a whole and 3 per cent for white households; for Pakistanis the figure is 34 per cent, the highest of all the minority ethnic groups and indicative of the lack of sufficiently large houses in Scotland.

In terms of house type, minorities are over-represented in flatted property with 49.1 per cent of non-white households living in purpose-built flats (likely to be tenements) compared with 36.2 per cent of the Scottish population as a whole. Minorities are under-represented in semi-detached housing (15.4 per cent to 20.2 per cent), and terraced housing (12.6 per cent to 24.1 per cent). This reflects the concentration of minority ethnic households in inner city areas. Interestingly, however, 18.5 per cent of minorities live in detached housing, compared with 17.0 per cent of whites; this suggests it is a house type to aspire to and may reflect the suburbanisation of the minority ethnic population - particularly the Indians, 28.4 per cent of whom are in detached houses - in recent years.

In summary, the most unsatisfactory living conditions seem to be experienced by the Pakistanis, who emerge as the most overcrowded and the most likely to lack central heating. The Chinese are most likely to lack self-contained accommodation and share basic amenities.

Table 2.8
Housing by ethnic group: Scotland (%)

	Total Population	Chinese	Pakistani	Indian
Overcrowded (> 1.5 persons per room)	0.56	3.40	11.02	3.36
Tenure:				
Owner-occupied	52.11	68.91	75.58	77.64
Privately rented	4.85	13.68	10.51	8.84
Housing Association	3.06	1.38	2.07	1.94
Local Authority	34.11	12.46	10.01	7.56
New Town/Scottish Homes	3.81	1.22	0.88	1.11
Lacking or sharing bath, shower and/or inside wc	0.59	2.87	1.61	1.42
Not in self-contained accommodation	0.35	1.88	0.86	0.83
Lacking central heating	22.26	20.31	31.30	18.72

Table 2.9

Housing situation of minority ethnic groups: comparison between Scottish cities (%)

	Aberdeen			Dundee			Edinburgh			Glasgow		
	Ch.	Ind.	Pak.	Ch.	Ind.	Pak.	Ch.	Ind.	Pak.	Ch.	Ind.	Pak.
Overcrowded (> 1.5 persons per room)	1.8	2.5	3.4	2.4	3.2	14.5	3.2	3.2	9.3	4.0	6.5	15.0
Tenure:												
Owner-occupied	49.3	49.6	50.0	63.4	66.3	58.6	69.4	74.2	78.6	65.0	76.1	76.3
Private rented	12.2	17.6	20.7	24.4	16.0	12.4	19.6	15.4	13.3	18.0	10.0	12.3
Housing association	0.9	0.0	1.7	1.6	2.1	2.6	1.5	2.2	1.0	2.5	4.1	3.1
Local authority	31.7	19.3	24.1	13.8	13.4	23.5	8.7	6.0	6.2	13.4	7.7	7.5
Scottish Homes	0.0	0.8	0.0	0.8	0.0	2.1	0.0	0.5	0.4	0.6	1.1	0.5
Lacking or sharing bath, shower and/or inside w.c.	3.2	1.7	0.0	0.8	0.0	2.1	4.1	0.8	1.7	3.8	2.6	1.7
Not in self-contained accommodation	1.8	2.5	0.0	0.0	1.1	0.4	2.4	0.8	1.4	3.2	1.4	1.0
Lacking central heating	20.8	16.0	12.1	25.2	19.8	35.9	22.3	21.4	25.1	29.1	35.7	45.7

Ch: Chinese Ind: Indian Pak: Pakistani

As far as city comparisons are concerned, Table 2.9 shows that there are a number of differences between the Scottish cities. In terms of housing tenure, Aberdeen has a significantly different pattern from the other cities with all three of the principal minority ethnic groups recording their lowest levels of owner-occupation and their highest levels of local authority renting. It may be that, for some, the pressures on the Aberdeen housing market caused by the oil industry have affected the ability of minorities to purchase appropriate accommodation. There may also be some minority ethnic students who have been allocated formerly 'difficult-to-let' local authority housing.

Dundee also stands out as having a relatively high proportion of Pakistanis in council housing and also in Scottish Homes housing. This may be related to the industrial base of the city's Pakistani population; it may be that, like their white counterparts, Dundee Pakistanis lack the income levels to allow entry into owner-occupation on a scale comparable to those in Edinburgh or Glasgow.

These findings from Dundee are not dissimilar from those of Robinson (1986) in Blackburn. There too, the Pakistani population was employed in traditional industries and was not particularly well paid. Prior to 1973/4, there were few Asians in council housing, a fact which Robinson ascribes (in part) to the prohibitive cost of council renting. A combination of clearance of older properties, and the introduction of more generous rent and rebate schemes, however, led to important increases in the number of Asian families applying to the local authority sector.

The small proportion of minority ethnic households in the expanding housing association sector in Scotland is interesting, suggesting that difficulties of access and information may exist here. A recent formal investigation by the Commission for Racial Equality into Scottish housing associations (CRE 1993) would confirm this. They found little evidence that associations were complying fully with the recommendations by Scottish Homes that anyone in housing need should be able to apply for it. Some associations had closed their waiting lists and even those with open lists rarely advertised the fact. They expected people to approach them for housing, learning of vacancies 'on the grapevine' but as there were few minority ethnic tenants in housing association properties, this is unlikely to have made associations more accessible to them. Only in one or two areas of inner Glasgow were there significant numbers of minority ethnic housing association tenants. It should be added, however, that an important supply-side reason for uneven tenure patterns may be the lack of housing of adequate size, particularly for Pakistani families; housing association properties, often in rehabilitated tenements, are generally small.

The numbers of Chinese in housing association properties are small and, only in Glasgow, does the proportion begin to approach the Scottish average of 3.06 per cent. Dalton and Daghlian's (1989) research showed that restrictions on access to associations existed through limited advertising of housing opportunities and closed waiting lists. Chan (1991) demonstrated a lack of awareness of housing association opportunities, among Chinese within Central Region.

There have been, however, significant developments within this tenure sector, in both Dundee and Edinburgh, where locally-based housing associations (Cleghorn and Fountainbridge respectively) have built sheltered housing complexes specifically for the cities' Chinese communities. A third, similar, development is being planned in Glasgow by Charing Cross Housing Association.

Finally, it is perhaps useful to refer to the clustering which has taken place within Scottish cities and which has resulted in the development of distinct minority ethnic community areas, often grouped around facilities such as mosques and temples. Within Glasgow, the Chinese are particularly concentrated in Garnethill and the area to the north-west of the city centre. This focus has recently been strengthened through the conversion of a former warehouse to a community centre/market/shopping area and by the construction of a Chinese arch beside it. While this is small in scale compared, say, with the arches at the entrance to Manchester's 'Chinatown', it is indicative of a growing Chinese presence and a physical symbol of the community's importance. There is also a significant Chinese presence in peripheral private housing estates, notably Crookston, Summerston and Hogganfield. This is consistent with the trends identified by Bowes, McCluskey and Sim (1989, 1990) in their previous research in Glasgow.

In Edinburgh, most Chinese live on the south side of the city centre, particularly in the Tollcross area, a position identified by SEMRU (1987). Once again, there are significant numbers in private housing areas such as Liberton/Gracemount, Kingsknowe, Craigleith and Corstorphine. The availability of private housing in these areas, often in the form of new estates, coupled with rehabilitation and gentrification of traditional inner city housing areas, is all leading to the suburbanisation of the Chinese community in Scottish cities.

Pakistani settlement in Glasgow is focused in three areas, namely Woodlands (north west of the city centre, just beyond Garnethill) and Pollokshields and Govanhill, south of the Clyde. As noted above, there appears to be a connection between Pakistani settlement and areas of inner city tenemental property but there are large areas of such housing in the east end of the city where very few Pakistanis have settled. Bowes, McCluskey and Sim (1990a) also identified a process of suburbanisation, with Pakistani households moving to areas of new private housing, outwith traditional areas of settlement. This process seems to be continuing with a significant Pakistani presence in Newlands, in the south of the City and also in

Robroyston and Mount Vernon to the north east and east. The development of new private housing may also account for a Pakistani presence at Glasgow Green, immediately east of the City Centre.

The two main areas of Pakistani settlement in Edinburgh are again in parts of the city characterised by tenemental property, namely the Southside, extending westwards into Gorgie, and Leith/Broughton, north east of the City Centre. There is, however, a significant Pakistani presence in the wealthier suburbs south of the City, in Morningside/Comiston.

The Dundee situation is slightly different, probably reflecting the different tenure pattern of the City's Pakistani community, and a greater presence in council housing. The main area of Pakistani settlement is in Hilltown, an area of mixed public and private housing, including several multi-storey blocks, immediately north of the City Centre. There is also a significant presence in a ring around the centre to west and east. The Perth Road area, to the west is relatively better off but otherwise there seems little evidence of a move to wealthier private suburbs.

Finally, the Indian community appears much less concentrated within Glasgow and is much more suburbanised. Thus, there are large Indian communities in both Bearsden and Bishopbriggs, two middle class suburbs north of Glasgow.

Conclusions and issues for further research

The 1991 Census has provided us with invaluable quantitative information on the minority ethnic population, as a result of the inclusion, for the first time, of a question on ethnic group. As indicated earlier, this has allowed us to update much of the earlier research carried out in this area and correct some of the earlier population estimates. That said, the Census is in no way a substitute for good qualitative data and our understanding of the minority ethnic population needs to be informed by other, related work. This section therefore seeks to identify some of the issues raised by the Census data and where further research may be required.

It is important to recognise that the various minority ethnic communities are not necessarily homogeneous and there may be differentiation within the ethnic categories used. It is, of course, convenient to use the categories in the Census but, as Khan (1976) has pointed out in relation to the Pakistani population, they may share a common nationality and religion but remain differentiated on ethnic/regional origin and class lines. She suggests, however, that minorities such as the Pakistanis have become aware over time of how outsiders see them and this external definition may catalyse the population into becoming more of a 'community' over time. As a process, this is under-researched.

Although the Census helps us to identify patterns of settlement and housing tenure, for example, it cannot explain how those patterns evolved. In housing, it is often stated that minorities 'prefer' to become owner-occupiers but it is never clear whether the dominance of home ownership is due to cultural preferences, to difficulties in accessing the alternatives, to supply constraints, or to a combination of these. Such generalisations also fail to take account of different home ownership rates between different minority ethnic groups. There is an increasing body of literature (Henderson and Karn 1987; Bowes, McCluskey and Sim 1989) which has demonstrated the difficulties faced by all minorities in gaining access to public sector housing. Yet access to mortgage finance has also been problematic and Karn (1978) suggests that the dependence of minority ethnic home owners on less conventional forms of loans and mortgages has sustained their concentration in the inner cities. Research has so far tended to focus on issues of access and the nature of lending institutions and little work has so far been carried out on the wider question of minority housing preferences and housing careers; such work is now in progress at Stirling.

Problems of access are not, of course, confined to housing and exist in relation to all welfare services, which are also dealt with in this book; it is nevertheless true that most of the research which has been conducted has focused on the housing problem. Minorities may have special needs in relation to education, for example, but may only be able to satisfy them in particular schools. There has been some research by SEMRU (1987) into the use made of the education service but this has been limited to Lothian Region. Brown and Riddell (1992) make it clear that there is no public domain research record on minority ethnic education in Scotland. Similarly, the problems of health care faced by minorities are only beginning to be understood and some research has now taken place in Glasgow and Edinburgh, involving Asian women. Some of this work, by Bowes and Domokos, by Paul and by Donaghy is summarised later in this book.

It may be that, in the health field, there is a need for proactive, outreach work with certain minority ethnic groups, sensitive to their particular needs. A good example of this is the London Chinese Health Resource Centre, established in 1988, and which provides Sunday surgeries with bilingual doctors, Sunday being the only day off for most of the Chinese community. Doctors can refer cases on to the patient's own GP but, in many cases, can deal with problems there and then. The Centre also has an important training role which ultimately contributes to the development of community care for the Chinese (Li, 1992). Such developments would certainly be appropriate in Glasgow and in Edinburgh.

The low take-up of services, even in areas of minority ethnic settlement, highlights the need for such services to be carefully targeted. In other areas, however, where numbers are small, such targeted services may be difficult or impossible to offer. The Census shows the increasing numbers of minority households located in outer suburban areas either through choice in the private housing market or through the allocation of a public sector house. It also shows that all Scottish District Council areas recorded a minority ethnic presence, and therefore that there are minority households located across Scotland, often remote from specific services. This issue of service delivery is one which will require to be addressed in order that minorities do not become isolated and lacking in support. There is also some research evidence that ethnic minorities living in areas of dense and dispersed settlement have significantly different characteristics (Ecob and Williams, 1991).

Previous research (McCluskey, 1991; Wardhaugh, 1991) suggests that experience of and usage of the various social services will differ according to gender. Wardhaugh, in particular, has recorded the work of the Asian Womens Action Group in Glasgow and its work in helping to break down the isolation which it believed many Asian women experienced and suffered. The Census, however, does not suggest any significant *demographic* differences between minority men and women, and further study of this area would require to be aimed at social attitudes and beliefs rather than Asian women's population profile.

For many women, isolation may be compounded by a lack of proficiency in English and can be quite serious. For the Pakistani and Indian communities, the work of organisations such as the Asian Women's Action Group in Glasgow (Wardhaugh, 1991) demonstrates how such self-help groups can go some way towards breaking down such barriers. The further development of such groups in relation to English language teaching, perhaps using local schools, may be a useful way forward, and there needs to be a better evaluation of interpreting and linkworking in this area.

One area in which gender differences have been significant in the past is in relation to migration history since women tended to follow men to the UK from countries such as India and Pakistan. The Census would tend to suggest that such gender differences do not now affect the population structure, although there is still some evidence of minorities being relatively mobile in comparison with whites. In Scotland in 1991, 10.4 per cent of the white population had a different address a year previously whereas for the Pakistanis the figure was 13.4 per cent. The most mobile of the major ethnic minority groups was in fact the Chinese, 22.7 per cent of whom had moved in the last year. Minority ethnic migration may therefore be a possible subject for further research.

One final issue may be the contextual effects of different cities. It has already been shown from the Census data that the socio-economic situation of minority ethnic groups is significantly different in Dundee, as compared to Glasgow, because of a different employment history. This appears to have affected housing tenure with a relatively high proportion of minorities in council housing in Dundee, and there is also a large number of minorities who rent in Aberdeen. There are therefore significant social and economic variations within the minority communities, depending on the economic history of their place of residence and this may also be deserving of further study.

3. Pakistanis and social rented housing: a study in Glasgow

Alison Bowes, Naira Dar and Duncan Sim

Introduction

The question of housing preference and the strategies adopted by households to try and achieve their preferences have become issues of considerable interest to policy makers at both national and local level, not least because of the way in which the promotion of choice has dominated central government policy-making. Within the UK., recent housing legislation has sought to promote a range of tenure choices, by continuing to encourage owner-occupation, by seeking to revitalise the private rented sector, and by encouraging tenants to transfer from the public sector to other alternative landlords. In the event, however, the numbers of tenants who have changed landlord remain small and the growth of owner-occupation has been hampered by the relative stagnation of the housing market.

Research suggests that such policy changes may be largely irrelevant for disadvantaged groups in society who have little opportunity to exercise choice in the housing market, or whose housing is determined by forces largely outwith their control. In relation to the social rented sector, the primary focus of this paper, British South Asians, for example, have long suffered from discrimination in the allocation process (Henderson and Karn 1987; Bowes, McCluskey and Sim 1989), while housing association policies have been shown to pay insufficient regard to the needs of minority ethnic communities (Dalton and Daghlian 1989).

In part, this may be due to the widespread belief that South Asians prefer owner-occupation and little attention has therefore been paid to those South Asians who are, and may prefer to be, council tenants. Robinson (1980), for example, showed the extensive use made of the local authority housing sector by those East African Asians who had entered Britain as refugees, while many younger Asians, born in the UK. are showing an increased willingness to consider renting as a tenure. Bowes, McCluskey and Sim (1989) identified a similar trend in Glasgow, a reflection perhaps of the greater availability of council housing in certain parts of Scotland.

Indeed, the differences in housing policy and housing structure in different parts of Britain have often been ignored and some previous research (e.g. Brown 1984) has simply generalised findings from England and Wales to cover the whole of the United Kingdom. In fact, Scotland has a different institutional and legal structure, a different migration history and ideology about migrants and a different set of minority ethnic groups (Miles and Muirhead 1986). In housing terms there are important differences in tenure structure between Scotland and the rest of the UK., with a traditional dominant local authority housing sector north of the border. Housing associations in Scotland on the other hand, tend to be smaller and more locally-based; unlike England, there are no black or minority ethnic associations.

The South Asian housing experience in Scotland is thus likely to be different from that in England, and the present paper examines the experiences of Pakistani households within the social rented sector. Previous research in Glasgow (Bowes, McCluskey and Sim 1989) focused on the constraints within council housing affecting the minority ethnic population. The present paper, using findings from a research study conducted in Glasgow in 1994, specifically follows up previously identified issues and findings but the approach is a qualitative one, exploring the strategies adopted by households in overcoming those constraints in order to satisfy their housing needs. Difficulties of access to social rented housing will have affected the perception of social housing by Pakistanis and attitudes to council housing are explored in some detail; knowledge of and usage of housing associations is similarly examined. Finally the study considers in more general terms, the housing likes and dislikes of Pakistani families. Thus, the research helps to illustrate the degree to which Pakistanis are able to make genuine choices in social housing and the extent to which those choices are constrained.

The study

The study developed a life history interviewing technique and used it to investigate the housing strategies and experiences of Pakistanis in Glasgow. According to the 1991 Census, the number of persons in Glasgow describing themselves as being of Pakistani origin is 10,945; this represents 1.65 per cent of the total population, making the Pakistanis the largest minority ethnic group in the city (Bailey, Bowes and Sim 1995). The average household size of Pakistani households was 4.75 persons, almost twice the Scottish average, and 39.2 per cent of Pakistanis were aged under 16. Three quarters lived in owner-occupied housing, mainly in the inner city, although there were growing numbers in the outer suburban areas. For this particular study we focused on the south side of Glasgow, in both inner city and suburbs.

Our study was intended to be exploratory, and aimed to identify as wide a range of strategies as possible. To ensure that respondents had a reasonably long housing history, we identified interviewees who were aged at least around 40; they were likely to have grown up children and this would therefore allow the collection of data on the possible dispersal of households. In the event, the ages of those interviewed ranged from 40 to mid-60s. Nineteen successful interviews were achieved.

The interviews were carried out by Dar in the language of the respondents' choice, with 11 being interviewed in Punjabi, 3 in English and 5 in a mixture of the two languages. Most were tape-recorded, then translated if necessary, by Dar, for transcription. Generally the interviewees were the female heads of household, as they tended to be more often available for interview; two male heads, however, were interviewed. On seven occasions more than one household member was present and added their comments to the interview.

In order to explore people's strategies in an environment where access to housing is constrained, a semi-structured schedule was used, focusing on housing preferences, housing moves and experiences. Interviews began by focusing on the present home, its characteristics and its positive and negative aspects from the interviewee's point of view. Respondents were also asked about the household composition and about any other relatives who might live locally. The next topic was the move from the previous house, with particular reference to the exercise of choice, the identification of any difficulties in achieving that choice and the levels of awareness of any alternatives. The interview then explored the same factors in relation to the previous home. This initial focus on recent housing experiences was important, as it has been argued by Dex (1991) that life history interviews should begin by discussing issues and events which are easily recalled by the interviewee.

Respondents were then asked to look back to their first marital home, a standard starting point of household formation. Several preferred to refer back to their first home in Britain, following migration from Pakistan; the flexible structure of the interview schedule allowed for this sequence of discussion. From the first marital home, interviewees were asked to talk about the sequence of homes, the same factors being covered in each case. The final part of the interview concerned aspirations for the future.

After transcription, the interviews were used to construct a chart of each household's history. Given the small number of interviews (19), the charts could be compared visually. The transcripts were also indexed and coded, then sorted, using a word processing facility, to produce collated lists of comments on the items in the index. The research findings are presented below, focusing specifically on those households with experience of the social rented sector. In presenting these findings, we use illustrative quotations from the interviews.

Current housing and household size

Of the nineteen households interviewed, twelve were currently owner-occupiers, two were council tenants, four were private tenants, and one was a housing association tenant. At first sight, this would seem a disappointingly low number of social renters but, in fact, four of the interviewees currently in the private sector had previous experience of social renting, three from the local authority (all now in the private rented sector) and one from the former Scottish Special Housing Association. The number of respondents with experience of social renting therefore totalled seven, and the views of the other twelve respondents, in relation to social housing, were also sought.

All nineteen households interviewed contained children. At the time of interview the average household size was 5.2 but, at its maximum, average household size had been 5.7; there were some instances where older children had moved out. Thirteen of the nineteen households had, at some time, had other members of the family staying there. In seven instances it was a brother or sister, while in four cases older sons had married and a daughter-in-law had joined the household. Only one household had grandparents living in the house, while in three cases friends had lodged with the household. Children were seen as having an important role to play in decisions about the household's future.

As well as being part of individual households, relatives were extremely important as part of the wider social network and helped to influence some locational decisions. Ten of the nineteen interviewees had relatives living locally, while a further two had relatives living just outside Glasgow. This is consistent with the findings of Sarre, Phillips and Skellington (1989: 173) in Bedford, where the locational preferences of Pakistanis owed a great deal to 'proximity to kith and kin'.

Our life history interviewing seemed particularly effective in identifying the way in which the composition of Pakistani households changed over time, with relatives moving in and out, sons marrying and bringing daughters-in-law to stay and then ultimately moving out into a separate household. The long term aspirations of the household could also be explored, with the role of sons in helping to shape the future housing careers of families being perhaps an area which is incompletely understood. Changing household size and household patterns clearly had an important impact on the frequency of moves and on Pakistani housing strategy. Family relationships were an important consideration when housing plans and decisions were made.

Applying for council housing

In our sample only two households were currently council tenants but three others had previously been tenants, including one family who had been housed by the District Council as homeless. We found considerable ignorance, however, concerning the allocation system and even those who had been successful in obtaining a council house had needed to have the system explained to them, sometimes by housing staff, sometimes by social workers or staff in voluntary agencies. Some interviewees had virtually no knowledge at all of the process, although others knew that houses were allocated on the basis of a points system. When asked to explain the allocation system, some individuals were able to relate this directly to their own experiences. For example:

> No. I know a little about it, someone told me. A lady came to visit and.....she told me there was an office and, if you go to this office, you fill in some forms. We handed in the forms and we got a letter two months later that you have very little points and therefore are not eligible for a house.

> Yes, if you get enough points, you get a house. I have enough points but I didn't get the house I want.

> Yes. He said I didn't have enough points and he checked on the computer and they said you need more points. He said you need about 200 or something points.

> Yes, if you have sick children or elderly parents, like my mother-in-law, and if you have 400 or 500 points, then you get [a house]. I had only around 300. My number was O.K. in places but they still weren't enough. So we got the doctor to

write a letter for us.

This last quotation is interesting because a number of households stated that they had applied to the local authority for a council house on health grounds. It suggests that the public sector is seen more as a safety net, rather than as a form of tenure to be sought in its own right.

Older people recognised that younger members of the household might make greater use of the Council sector in future but there were clearly some rather ambivalent feelings about this. Asked if an application for a council house had ever been made, one respondent answered:

> No, but I think the children will in the future, because they won't be able to get a house, because houses have become so expensive. They will have to get a job and work but that's if they manage to get a job. If the children are unsuccessful, then they will have to apply for council houses. But if it's ever mentioned they feel ashamed, that why should we have to live in a council house? But, it's their right, isn't it?

Several households who had made applications for council housing were unimpressed with the way in which their application had been handled. In particular, the Council was felt to be very slow in processing it:

> I have already applied on medical grounds. I applied three, four years and request them to please give me the house because of living three up. I am a patient from arthritis and got trouble, you know, but I haven't got any successful reply so far. I want to move.....because of the arthritis.....I am looking for some ground floor flat this time.

> It's been about two or three years.....and they still have our card, City of Glasgow.

> Since 1986, so it has been eight or nine years.

> We've applied for another [house] and it's been three years, they're taking their time.

These expressions of dissatisfaction are echoed in work previously carried out by the Council itself. In 1992 the Council undertook a survey of residents' satisfaction with Council services and it is clear that, in housing, minority ethnic groups were unhappy with the service offered. Of those who had been offered a house, most had refused it because of the area in which it was located. Satisfaction rates were low and 45 per cent of the 59 respondents were very dissatisfied with the work of the city's Housing Department (Glasgow City Council 1993a).

The size of houses on offer

Although five interviewees had at different times accepted the offer of council housing, there was concern at the size of the accommodation on offer, particularly in view of the generally larger size of Pakistani families. It was felt that the Council simply did not have a sufficient number of large houses:

> We always went to the District Council but there's no house anywhere you know. They don't have three bedrooms or four bedrooms.

> I asked them but the Council said they are all small houses here, and they said for us, you need one room each for your children and you should have a separate room for the husband and wife. We don't have a house like that for you, so you have to look for one for yourself privately. Then I found this house, my children are happy....

> When [he] came here for the first time in Glasgow, after ten days he applied in the Eastwood areas [in the suburbs] and Govanhill [in the inner city] but no house. They said, you want a big house, you can find it yourself. There are no three bedrooms or four bedrooms that we have, only two bedrooms.

In such cases, families had been forced to look elsewhere for accommodation and, in at least three cases, had moved from the public to the private rented sector, in order to get an appropriately-sized house. In the case of a family housed by the Homeless Persons Unit, the Council appear to have been unable to offer appropriately-sized follow-on accommodation:

> I asked them to give me a bigger house and, after staying with the Homeless Unit, they told me to take a house in Pollok [an outer estate]. But people told me it wasn't a good area for the children, so I started looking for a house....

The interviewee eventually found one in inner city Pollokshields, an area with a large local Pakistani community.

In another case:

> ...they gave us another house with even smaller rooms, where
> you could only get single beds in. They told me if the house
> was not suitable, that I could move, so I told them that the
> house was too small and could we go back to the other house
> that we had. And they said, 'No. It's too late now.' And so I
> had to leave that council house and move into a private rented
> house.

> Well, first I stayed in a council house and that was really small
> and a family our size could not stay there and there was a lot
> of damp in the house, and I have waited for a long time to get
> a suitable house - at least five or six years. My story was even
> on television but the Council have done nothing and,
> eventually, when I heard that my friend was moving house, I
> asked her to give me the house on rent and she said O.K.

The problem of a lack of suitably sized accommodation is not peculiar to
Glasgow, although the city did concentrate on building two- and three-
bedroomed flats in the immediate postwar period. Bowes, McCluskey and
Sim (1989) calculated that only 3.2 per cent of council housing in Glasgow
had four or more bedrooms and, as a result, there was evidence that Asian
families were being forced to under-estimate their needs in order to obtain a
house. The situation had become even more serious by 1993, with the
proportion of council stock which was of 5 apartments (four bedrooms) or
more falling to 2.6 per cent (Glasgow City Council, 1994). The Council has
recognised the problem but seems not to be tackling it; indeed, it seems to
suggest that, over time, the issue will become less significant, perhaps
justifying present inactivity:

> The shortage of large family housing which can be adapted
> poses a particular difficulty in meeting special needs arising in
> the ethnic minority communities, as many families would wish
> to be rehoused as a single household. However, though large
> properties are needed by many households now, it is unclear
> whether or not this pattern will continue over the next
> generation (Glasgow City Council 1994,:11).

The absence of any clear programme of action for tackling this issue does
seem surprising. The City Council accepts (Glasgow City Council 1994:12)
that the unemployment rate among minority ethnic communities is 50 per
cent higher than the city average; that there is a high proportion in part-time

and low-paid jobs; and that among minority ethnic households, the ratio of dependents to those who bring in an income is far higher than among the white population. Such statistics would suggest that minority ethnic households are far from wealthy and might, as a result, look increasingly to the local authority for housing, but the data are not used by the Council to develop appropriate policies for action.

Because this shortage of large houses has a disproportionate impact on the Asian communities, the Association of Metropolitan Authorities (1988) has suggested that this constitutes indirect discrimination under the race relations legislation. Certainly, the decline in the proportion of large dwellings in Glasgow (probably due to tenants exercising the right-to-buy) indicates that the problem is getting more serious with the local authority seemingly unable (or unwilling) to stem the process.

The experience of harassment

It would appear that the somewhat ambivalent attitude towards council housing displayed by Pakistani families is related to a concern that the allocation system is not geared towards their specific needs. The constrained choices with which Pakistani households were faced, were illustrated by the widely held belief that Pakistanis might be allocated a house in an area where they might be vulnerable to harassment:

> I was not in Glasgow long enough, you know, to get certain points. Also, I don't know which area they're going to give me the house and that's worrying. So I prefer to live in smaller accommodation, you know, with less facilities, than going to a place where I can face harassment and other things, you know.

> That's what most people in our Asian community view, you know, it's not worth applying and you apply after years and, you know, you never manage to get a house of your own choice. You always get offered where you can't survive - Castlemilk [a peripheral estate], Gorbals and things [both areas with small Pakistani populations]. If you don't have transport, if you can't speak the language, if you don't have any extended family to give you some kind of help, then obviously you prefer to stay within the community, so you can make friends, you can get help from them, instead of, you know, staying on your own. You know, if you took ill and you have two children, who is going to phone the doctor or do things for you?

One of the greatest problems faced by Pakistani people is racial harassment and this has been shown to be particularly prevalent on local authority housing estates (CRE, 1987; Bonnerjea and Lawton 1988; Bowes, McCluskey and Sim 1990b). This is an issue which is tied closely to that of house allocation, because an allocation policy which is 'colour blind' may result in black families being offered houses on predominantly white estates. It is important therefore that policies take into account the particular needs of black families, and the need to protect them from various forms of harassment. The evidence from our sample suggests that the allocation policy in Glasgow has not been particularly sensitive:

> The problem was, there was a white lady who didn't like us. She said your children make too much noise upstairs, because she was an elderly lady. She said, if you don't stop it, I'll call the police. If my children make a noise at night, she can call the police but during the day, they're going to walk about the house. She just complained......The children couldn't go out because there was a pub nearby and, in the evening, they would throw stones at the children and call them names. They were all white people that lived in this area and I had to take this house because that's all there was.

Another, particularly serious, case involved an allocation in the North Govanhill area [an inner city Council estate]:

> The day we put our things in the house, they got stolen. They made a mess, they spread flour all over the flat, they didn't leave anything, they broke everything. My children were young as well, so I got really scared and I left the house that day and rented a place [privately]. I asked them to give me another place - I still ask them -but they haven't yet. They said your points have been greatly reduced because you left that house and that was our only setback, but we're O.K. just now. You know, they give you houses in areas that aren't very safe and I get scared. They're all white areas.

The experiences of harassment identified above are of particular concern and accord with the findings of Bowes, McCluskey and Sim (1989) in Glasgow. At that time, we drew attention to the difficulties faced by Asian families who were allocated properties in areas where they were distant from family, friends and Asian shops and community facilities. Although the findings of the report were accepted by the City Council, it is not clear that the allocation system has become any more sensitive to Asian needs.

Pakistani families found themselves particularly constrained in relation to council housing and there seemed to be a general consensus that the allocation system did not pay sufficient attention to their needs. There were, for example, concerns that families might be allocated houses in areas at some distance from friends and relatives and where they might be vulnerable to racial harassment. In such cases, where it became clear that the local authority was unable to meet particular needs, the strategy of Pakistani households seemed to be to move to a safer area, even if this resulted in overcrowding, a change of tenure and the potential loss of a place on the Council waiting list. Pakistani families seemed willing to move from the public to the private rented sector, a step which is probably less common with white families.

The sense of isolation is undoubtedly heightened if heads of household are unable to speak fluently in English or if the local authority has no Urdu or Punjabi speakers in its local housing offices. In relation to the points system, one interviewee stated that she had sought help in understanding the system from a social worker, another from a locally-based Asian Women's Action Group. There was some anger at a local authority which was prepared to offer accommodation but seemed unable to offer follow-up support and advice:

> What happened was.....my in-laws got a house, a council house, it's only been one or two weeks since they got the house......It was very difficult for them because they couldn't speak English. Then they were told that they could get a council house and they got angry. They said,'We can't speak English, so what are we going to do with a council house; what we need is help'.

These problems of communication, particularly in terms of language, were highlighted by Bowes, McCluskey and Sim (1989) but it would appear that they have not yet been resolved.

Housing associations

The relationship between ethnic minorities and housing associations in Glasgow is not an entirely satisfactory one. Although most of the city's associations operate in the inner city, precisely the areas where ethnic minorities would apparently prefer to live, their record in housing minority families is not impressive. Partly, this reflects the background to the establishment of housing associations in Glasgow, which were set up primarily to rehabilitate tenemental housing within Housing Action Areas for Improvement. The houses they acquired were therefore already tenanted and the turnover of tenancies was too slow to make much impact on their waiting lists. It was only as the rehabilitation programme approached its end that associations undertook a larger proportion of new build, thereby offering greater opportunities for rehousing for, amongst others, minority families on the waiting lists.

The slow progress made by associations in this area became a matter of concern for the Commission for Racial Equality, who funded a major study of four case study associations in 1989 (Dalton and Daghlian 1989). More recently, the CRE launched a formal investigation of housing associations and racial equality and the Scottish associations fared poorly. The only three associations without a racial equality policy were all Scottish; the only two which did no ethnic monitoring were both Scottish; and there were few representatives of the minority ethnic communities on Scotland's housing association committees (CRE 1993).

Unsurprisingly then, housing associations did not emerge very positively from our study. Indeed, the only housing association tenant in our sample was actually under the impression that the house was rented from the local authority, although we were able to establish later that this was not in fact the case. Two other households had applied for housing association properties but had not been offered a house, mainly because of an insufficient number of points. Indeed, one complained that she had been rudely treated by the Allocations Officer at the association in question and as a result had felt threatened.

It is difficult to draw too many conclusions about housing associations because of the small number of people interviewed who had knowledge or experience of this form of tenure. It would appear, however, that associations, like local authorities, are part of the constraining environment and need to do more to improve their sensitivity to minority ethnic needs.

Housing likes and dislikes

Not surprisingly, a proximity to Asian facilities was seen as being particularly important in housing search strategies, although it was not the only factor. Generally, the presence of good neighbours, of whatever ethnic origin, was essential:

> Great neighbours - they're really, really nice, and also we've got a lot of Asian people living within the community, which is good for my mum, so she doesn't feel so lonely. Even the white neighbours that we have are very, very understanding, very, very nice.

A great deal of importance was attached to the existence of a local school with a good reputation and this was mentioned by several interviewees. Transport was also important, to enable those interviewees without access to a car, to travel to visit family and friends and to reach shops. Proximity to Asian shops, to doctors and to the Mosque were all positive attributes of interviewees' housing.

In terms of individual houses, a number of households had actively sought a property on the ground or first floor because of the presence of an elderly relative in the family. Four households liked the house they were in because of its size, while the presence of a garden was beneficial to those households with children. One important advantage of a larger house, for some, was that it allowed families to have separate facilities for men and women:

> I like two rooms downstairs, and sitting and dining separate. I like, because in our families, we like men separate and ladies sit separate... I feel I don't like only one room. Sometimes two families come and they have to sit together, and I don't enjoy it... with men.

No matter how accessible facilities might be and how appropriate the housing was, the key issue for many respondents was the safety of their family within the area. Freedom from fear and harassment therefore transcended other factors influencing a choice of house:

> First, you know, the area. I always look for the area, if it's a nice area, there's no harassment and the kind of people that live in the area.

Another respondent, asked what the first thing was, that they would look for, confirmed: 'The area - it has to be good'. Families therefore distinguished quite carefully between the characteristics of the house and those of its surroundings: 'The house was on Hollybrook Street [in North Govanhill]. The house was O.K. but the area wasn't'.

Our interviews suggested clearly the strategy of Pakistani households in assessing the quality of an area in terms of its access to facilities and its safety. Indeed, many households indulged in trade-offs between a particular area and a particular house, or in some cases, between different tenures. These findings are consistent with those by other researchers in this area. Sarre, Phillips and Skellington (1989), for example, found a general reluctance by minority ethnic groups to move to particular suburban areas, even though the housing was of high quality, because of an increasing incidence of racial harassment in those areas. Shaw (1988) similarly referred to Pakistani housing decisions, suggesting that the characteristics of the house, particularly its size, were important factors, but perhaps more important was the fear of racism and harassment if the family moved from a familiar locale. Racist incidents, Shaw found, led to the household opting for a safe area in preference to more appropriately sized housing.

Conclusions

Our study clearly indicates that Pakistani families operate within conditions of considerable difficulty, particularly in relation to the social rented sector. The first of these is the continuing problems faced by Pakistani families in applying for local authority housing. There is a frequent lack of understanding of the allocation system and many families have had to have it explained to them - not always by housing staff. There also appeared to be a belief that the City Council was very slow in processing applications and making appropriate offers of accommodation.

A second problem relates to the continuing failure by the local authority to meet the housing needs of the Pakistani community, in terms of the size and type of property offered. As demonstrated earlier, Pakistanis have often been allocated housing in inappropriate areas and of inappropriate sizes and indeed, the provision of suitably-sized local authority accommodation is actually worsening. For some of the households whom we interviewed, the private rented sector had proved an acceptable alternative, but, given that this sector is in decline, the option of rented accommodation is one which may become less available to Pakistani families in the future.

Thirdly, racial harassment continues to be an extremely serious problem and it is clear that in certain parts of Glasgow, notably the peripheral local authority housing estates but also inner city estates such as North Govanhill, Pakistani families are treated in a hostile fashion. This is still an issue which, despite official expressions of concern, is waiting to be tackled thoroughly and effectively. For many families, the characteristics of an area (particularly its safety) were more important than the house itself. Proximity to Asian shops, facilities such as the Mosque, good schools and transport and, above all, good friends and neighbours, were seen as the key factors in finding a suitable house to live in.

At a time when local authority housing is being depleted through stock transfer and the right-to-buy, it might be expected that housing associations might become more significant providers of housing for Pakistani - and other minority ethnic - households. Indeed, the fact that associations often operate within the inner city, sometimes in areas of Pakistani settlement, led us to believe that Pakistanis themselves might see them as increasingly important. This turned out not to be the case and our (rather limited) findings regarding associations would seem to confirm the findings of the

1993 CRE report on their failings.

This is not, of course, to imply that housing agencies are necessarily complacent. Glasgow City Council has taken considerable steps over recent years to address the needs of minority ethnic groups. Its Action Plan for Racial Equality addresses housing issues, greater priority is now given to resolving cases of racial harassment in Council estates and some new letting initiatives have been introduced, albeit in relation to minority ethnic elderly people (Glasgow City Council 1993b). Nevertheless, the lack of suitably-sized accommodation has not been addressed and there must also be some concern that seven years after a major study of ethnic minority housing needs in Glasgow (Bowes, McCluskey and Sim, 1989), Pakistani attitudes towards the local authority are still so ambivalent.

It was clear that Pakistani households have pursued a number of housing strategies. The life history interviewing technique which we used provided us with good quality information on the frequency with which households had moved and the factors which were important to them in their move. We have already referred to the importance of area characteristics in choice of accommodation; the interviews allowed us to assess the extent to which households indulged in 'trade-offs' between a particular area and a particular house, or indeed between different tenures. The private rented sector, for example, has tended to be seen by many white households merely as a stepping-stone on the way to the majority tenures and not as a long term destination (Crook 1992). Pakistanis in our sample, however, were quite willing to move from what was presumably a secure tenancy in the local authority sector, into private rented accommodation in order to get a house of the right size in the right place.

The life history interviews also enabled us to assess the cumulative nature of choices; thus, the choice made by a household at a particular point could in time constrain further choices. In the council sector, Pakistani families had frequently discovered that they had insufficient points to obtain a house of their choice but had lacked the knowledge of the points system to apply earlier, a decision which might have earned them some points for waiting time. Thus choice may increase or reinforce constraint and it is only through studying a household's life history that the longer term impacts of decisions can be appreciated.

One of the most important gains from our life history technique is in the avoidance of stereotyping. There has often been a tendency, on the part of housing officers, to homogenise Pakistanis - and indeed sometimes all minority ethnic groups - and to make assumptions regarding Pakistani housing needs. While it may be true that the majority of Pakistanis are owner-occupiers and the majority live in the inner city, it is essential that those households with needs and aspirations which depart from this 'norm' are not ignored. The interviews demonstrated clearly that Pakistanis, like white people, have widely varying attitudes and aspirations and these change as housing policies change and as levels of knowledge change. These issues of Pakistani housing aspirations, attitudes and knowledge are now being addressed in further research at Stirling.

Acknowledgements

The research reported in this paper was funded by the University of Stirling's Internal Research Fund.

4. The housing experience of minority ethnic groups in Scotland

Hilary Third with Martin MacEwen

Introduction

Prior to 1993, the housing situation of Scotland's minority ethnic groups was a relatively neglected issue at a national level. Since then, Scottish Homes has funded a series of major research projects on minority ethnic groups and housing. This chapter is based on three of those studies, all carried out within the Scottish Ethnic Minorities Research Unit (SEMRU) at the School of Planning and Housing, Heriot-Watt University, Edinburgh. Separately, the studies examine the housing situations and aspirations of minority ethnic groups in Scotland from a range of perspectives. Collectively, they provide a comprehensive range of evidence about their housing experiences. This chapter begins by setting out the context for the research. It then introduces the three studies and explains their different but complementary objectives and research methods. The body of the chapter reports key findings of each of the three studies. Finally, the chapter draws together the strands of the different studies, presents some overall conclusions and discusses the implications for policy development.

Context for the research

A substantial amount of research on 'race' and housing in Scotland has now been carried out, and research in England contributes to the evidence that

Britain's visible minority ethnic communities have suffered significant restrictions on their housing choices as a result of direct and indirect discrimination.

Research on 'race' is particularly important in Scotland because the minority ethnic population is so small that it is unlikely to be properly represented in large-scale surveys of the general population. While English research provides a useful context for a Scottish study, it would be dangerous to assume that the housing experiences, needs and preferences of minority ethnic groups living in Scotland will mirror those south of the border, given that the regulation, administration and history of housing provision in Scotland is different from that in England and Wales.

It should also be noted that the composition of Scotland's minority ethnic population differs from that of England and Wales. In particular, there is a lower proportion of African Caribbeans and a higher proportion of Chinese. To the extent that housing experiences and aspirations may reflect the particular cultural norms of individual groups, then this too may also indicate that the situation in Scotland is likely to differ from that in England and Wales.

The development of Scottish Homes policy on minority ethnic groups

In December 1993, Scottish Homes issued a Consultation Paper on Ethnic Minority Housing (Scottish Homes, 1993c). The paper referred to an inter-directorate project team which had been established in May 1992 to consider how successful existing policies on race equality had been. The team recognised the benefits of previous initiatives, including the development of performance standards in monitoring the performance of registered housing associations and checking compliance with the CRE Code of Practice in Rented Housing, as well as the provision of training for their staff and some other promotional activities. It concluded, however, that Scottish Homes did not know enough about the minority ethnic communities in which it operated or the impact of its policies upon such groups. The Consultation Paper intimated that Scottish Homes was now committed to:

a)   improving its information base;
b)   providing systematic training on how to deal with racial harassment both for tenants and Scottish Homes staff;
c)   producing further translated material; and
d)   improving employment opportunities for people from minority ethnic groups.

That document took stock of recent research including, firstly, that undertaken in Glasgow by Dalton and Daghlian (1989) in respect of housing associations; secondly Bowes, McCluskey and Sim (1989) in respect of the local authority sector; thirdly, analysis by Scottish Homes of the 1991 Census; and fourthly, SEMRU's own qualitative research. Scottish Homes concluded that action was required to ensure that access to a diverse rented sector became a reality, and that the housing needs and aspirations of the minority ethnic community needed to be more firmly embedded in policy development. The options for future action were threefold, namely:

a)   to encourage the establishment of new black housing associations;
b)   to earmark an element of the budget for the provision of housing for minority ethnic groups; and
c)   to adopt a flexible approach.

The third option - adopting a flexible approach - was the preferred one, and was to include the following elements:

a)   ensuring that all housing associations gave appropriate attention to race equality issues;
b)   the production of appropriate guidance;
c)   integrating the assessment of housing needs into a new district planning process to promote the development of locally-based strategies;
d)   monitoring of resource allocation at a local level to ensure equitable access to housing opportunities; and
e)   agreeing a set of out-turn indicators to gauge performance on race equality issues.

In October 1994, following a period of consultation, Scottish Homes issued its policy statement 'Action for Race Equality' (Scottish Homes, 1994). The statement confirmed the preference for the flexible approach, while acknowledging that the terms 'flexible' and 'locally responsive' had the danger of being indistinguishable from doing nothing, and maintaining the status quo. To safeguard against such potential complacency, Scottish Homes agreed to set targets for improved access to housing by minority ethnic households and to set aside at least 1.25 per cent of its new and existing resources to be of direct benefit to them.

Introducing the three research studies

In 1993, as part of its review of housing for minority ethnic groups, Scottish Homes commissioned its first research project on 'race' and housing in

Scotland. The aims of the project were to provide a greater understanding of the housing careers and circumstances of Scotland's minority ethnic groups, to assess feelings about current housing arrangements, and to describe expectations and aspirations for housing provision and housing service.

The research brief was met by two main methods; a comprehensive review of relevant research to date principally relating to Scotland (MacEwen, 1993) and an in-depth qualitative study, which explored the experience of households from minority ethnic groups in the Scottish housing system (Wainwright, Murie and MacEwen, 1994). These two elements of the research study - together with other complementary sources of information - were intended to inform the work of the Scottish Homes Ethnic Minorities Policy Working Group by establishing a 'baseline' position on which research could be built, and by identifying the key issues and areas for policy attention.

In 1995, Scottish Homes (Lothian and Borders District) in partnership with the City of Edinburgh District Council and Port of Leith Housing Association commissioned a second study, which focused in some detail on the housing situation and attitudes of minority ethnic households living in the Leith area of Edinburgh. The research objectives of the Leith study followed closely from some of the findings of the first study, and part of the rationale was to address some of the key issues which had been raised by that earlier study at a local level, employing a more quantitative approach.

Specifically, the research was designed to provide information on the social, economic and housing circumstances of minority ethnic households in Leith, to assess their housing needs and circumstances, and to compare these characteristics with those of the white community living in the same area. This research was intended to inform local needs assessment and planning processes, and to feed into a discussion about different options for meeting housing need, in the light of preferences and currently available opportunities in the area.

Shortly after the local study in Leith was carried out, a third study entitled *Constraint and Choice for Minority Ethnic Households in the Home Ownership Market in Scotland* (Third, Wainwright and Pawson, 1997) was commissioned by Scottish Homes. The main aim of the research was to improve understanding of the housing preferences and choices of minority ethnic owner occupiers. The focus on owner occupation was important, as the earlier two studies and other data (not least the 1991 Census) showed that minority ethnic households in Scotland were much more likely to be owner occupiers than white households. The central questions for this research were concerned with exploring the extent to which housing choices may be limited. It was also designed to assess the differences between the housing conditions which minority ethnic owners actually experience and those which they would reasonably prefer and might, on the basis of prevailing norms in the indigenous community, reasonably expect.

Specifically, the overall requirements of this third piece of research were to provide information on the housing aspirations and constraints - or perception of constraints - of minority ethnic households in housing markets, and to record some of the physical characteristics and perceived suitability of the properties in which they lived. The study was also charged with exploring the nature of access difficulties encountered by minority ethnic households in respect of identifying and securing suitable accommodation, and making recommendations on ways which any difficulties may be most effectively overcome.

Ultimately, the aim of this series of research studies into the housing situations of minority ethnic groups in Scotland was - and is - to assist in policy development by Scottish Homes, in its capacities as enabler, influencer, provider and employer. Shortly after the first study was completed, Scottish Homes published its policy statement entitled *Action for Race Equality* (mentioned above), which included a recommendation to fund further research through which strategies for achieving greater equality in housing might be better informed (Scottish Homes, 1994). Since then, Scottish Homes has continued to consider its position on meeting the needs of minority ethnic groups, and some of these issues, such as the funding and provision of housing, and improving the access to and management of public sector housing, are discussed later in the chapter. First, the key findings of each of the three Scottish Homes studies are presented.

The experience of households from minority ethnic groups in the Scottish housing system

This first piece of research (Wainwright, Murie and MacEwen, 1994) was an in-depth, qualitative study, carried out amongst households from a wide range of tenures, ages and ethnic origins throughout Scotland. Respondents were asked about their own personal housing experiences rather than the general problems of minority ethnic groups. The research involved 40 in-depth household interviews and nine group discussions in both urban and rural areas. Such methods have particular advantages in gaining a full account of households' experiences, attitudes and aspirations. The aim of this work was not to develop quantified representative data, but to illustrate a wide range of household experiences and to gain a fuller understanding of aspects of housing experience than is possible from other sources.

The research identified a clear link between the experience of housing and employment, and emphasised both the importance and the limitations of economic and employment factors in determining housing situations and choices. In particular, the circumstances of households without a wage earner were marked by lack of choice and a dependency on rented housing. It was also evident that self-employed households - very much more common amongst minority ethnic than white households - were often far from affluent; many had invested all of their available resources and profits, including the proceeds from the sale of a previous house, in their businesses leaving them with very little net disposable income, and this often limited their housing choices. A high proportion of the minority ethnic respondents had insufficient incomes to gain access to home ownership, and many others gave examples of their inability to sustain home ownership once they had bought, because of limited incomes.

Minority ethnic households in this study were under represented in the public rented sector, and indeed this reflects national trends (1991 Census). The research reported widely held views that social landlords did not fully understand the minority ethnic communities' cultures and experiences, especially in respect of the traditional Asian extended family. Many of the minority ethnic respondents felt that social landlords did not attempt to cater for them in terms of the size, type or location of housing provided and offered, and it was often felt that they had done little to overcome language and other barriers. In short, it was felt that there was little commitment to meeting the particular needs of minority ethnic groups. However, social housing was not necessarily unattractive to minority ethnic households; for example, while there was a widespread ignorance of housing associations, those who were familiar with this form of tenure often regarded it as desirable, but unobtainable.

In general, accounts of experiences of housing organisations - including landlords in the public sector - were of unhelpful and unresponsive agencies. Consequently, confidence in these organisations, and expectations of a positive response were limited. In particular, there was some mistrust of the processes of application, allocation and transfer of housing. In a number of cases, minority ethnic households regarded the processes and those involved in them with suspicion and as racist.

Few of the minority ethnic respondents in this study were renting privately at the time of the research, but nearly all had done so at some time. There was general dissatisfaction regarding rents, the condition of properties, and the attitudes of landlords in the private rented sector. Rents were perceived to be unaffordable, even by those on housing benefit, and were anticipated as being too high for the wages respondents expected to earn if they did get a job.

A key element in the housing experiences of minority ethnic groups involved racial harassment and attacks, and there was a dominant concern with safe neighbourhoods. Harassment was seen to be directly linked to the neighbourhood and was not confined to those who rented. Again, this influenced housing aspirations and preferences, and perceptions of landlords who appeared unresponsive to problems of harassment. Incidents of harassment were of varying nature, but the general view was that neither the police nor landlords had taken sufficient action. Victims of harassment did not always want to move because there was no guarantee of peace elsewhere. Even when harassment was not experienced, there was a general feeling that members of minority ethnic groups had to make a special effort to fit in, wherever they stayed.

Housing aspirations were generally associated with immediate household needs, particularly in relation to dwelling size and condition. Respondents, generally, wanted housing which was safe from racial harassment, in good condition, with a reasonable rent, good storage space, relatively free from crime, in a quiet, clean, peaceful environment and with good general services and facilities. There was no demand for special services for members of minority ethnic groups, apart from adequate policies on harassment and more space for extended families.

Although home ownership tended to be identified as the preferred tenure, this was closely related to assumptions about the types of dwellings and neighbourhoods in that sector. Furthermore, the research identified a number of 'reluctant home owners' who said they felt forced into owner occupation in desperation at not finding anywhere to rent which was suitable and free from harassment. Whether this was because of the inadequate and unsympathetic allocation policies of social landlords or simply a lack of housing for rent, the result was the same - a restriction of options. However, owner occupation did not necessarily give people a wider choice, or provide an adequate solution to their housing problems. Harassment was still as prevalent in private housing and overcrowding was often a problem.

Housing needs and preferences of minority ethnic households in Leith

This second study (Wainwright, Pawson and Third, 1997, forthcoming) was a household interview survey, carried out amongst a sample of 88 minority ethnic households in the Leith area of Edinburgh. A small 'control group' of 46 white households was also interviewed to provide comparative information and to test the specific effect of ethnicity on housing experiences and preferences.

Like the first study, this second study found owner occupation to be the preferred tenure across all ethnic groups. The principal attraction of home ownership appeared to be a perception that it was the tenure which offers the best value for money and/or an investment opportunity, and this was a particularly widespread view among white households. However, it was also noted that there was some demand for rented property - either in the public or private sector - from owners. Furthermore, a considerable proportion of renters said they *preferred* to rent, and expected to continue to rent in the future. Amongst those owner occupiers involved in the study, the research found some evidence to suggest that there was a 'housing sub-market' in Leith amongst the minority ethnic communities, such that minority ethnic home owners were likely to have bought houses from vendors belonging to their own ethnic group, and to have gained their information about the range of houses for sale via informal networks. The Leith study recommended that future research attempt to quantify the extent to which this might be true.

Consistent with national trends (and the findings from earlier studies), minority ethnic respondents were very much less likely than white respondents to be living in social rented housing, or to expect to do so in the future. This may have been associated with *perceptions* of social housing, or to *lack of knowledge* about housing in the social rented sector amongst Leith's minority ethnic communities. It may be significant that twice as many minority ethnic as white respondents said they were unaware of housing associations. Unexpectedly however, a higher percentage of minority ethnic than white respondents actually named a housing association correctly.

The much larger size of minority ethnic households in this study and nationally pointed to a particular need for the provision of larger houses; that all of the respondents who were living in 'very overcrowded' conditions were from minority ethnic groups provides clear evidence of this need. In areas such as Leith, where there are relatively large concentrations of minority ethnic households, the provision of larger homes is especially important.

Financial considerations were a key issue, not only for influencing tenure choice but also in relation to the range of accommodation itself, particularly for owner occupiers. Of those owners who experienced difficulties in finding accommodation, or who at the time of the interview considered their present house unsuitable for their needs, approximately half said they were unable to move to suitable accommodation because of financial limitations.

South Asians were significantly more satisfied with Leith as a place to live than other groups. The main reason seemed to be related to the proximity of cultural and religious facilities (such as the mosque, family and friends), access to work and local people. Although some respondents were concerned for their personal safety, or about the possibility of racial attacks, a majority considered it to be a safe place to live.

The picture provided by this second study was a moderately encouraging one. It did not reveal a large backlog of unmet need, or a serious concentration of social or physical housing problems, and most households (whether minority ethnic or white) appeared reasonably satisfied. The conclusion of the research was that Leith appeared to be playing a valuable role in the wider Edinburgh housing market, by offering relatively cheap opportunities for home ownership in stable communities with good access to jobs and services. The system did not appear to be generating gross inequalities in the outcomes and experiences of the minority ethnic and white households involved in the study in that particular local area.

Overall, it was clear that the size of the minority ethnic community in Leith - although still less than two per cent of all households - was important in making the area attractive to minority ethnic respondents - South Asians in particular seemed to be strongly attached to the immediate locality. Housing intended for minority ethnic groups should therefore generally be provided in areas where they will be close to other members of the same ethnic group, and where some cultural facilities already exist.

Constraint and choice for minority ethnic households in the home ownership market in Scotland

This was the largest of the three studies (Third, Wainwright and Pawson, 1997), involving a national survey of more than two hundred minority ethnic home owners, and a matched control group of a hundred white home owners. Research methodologies piloted in the Leith research, as well as other studies - such as analysis of the Census to distinguish areas with a higher than average proportion of minority ethnic households, and a search for minority ethnic names from the electoral registers for those areas - were used to identify minority ethnic households.

Whilst this study was intended to inform an understanding of the position of minority ethnic homeowners across the whole of Scotland, it was appreciated from the outset that it was virtually impossible to draw a statistically representative sample of Scotland's minority ethnic population - or at least to do so without unlimited resources - because a significant minority is scattered around remote rural areas. Due to financial and practical considerations, the majority of the fieldwork was undertaken in a limited number of areas with significant concentrations of minority ethnic owner occupiers. It is therefore likely that the sample was more representative of the larger minority ethnic groups in urban areas, than other groups in more rural areas.

The study examined the reasons why minority ethnic households were more likely than others to buy, and assessed how far their housing was suitable for their needs. It found that a significant proportion of minority ethnic households had bought a house because of a perceived lack of suitable alternatives. More than a quarter (compared with only 3 per cent of the white control group) said they would have preferred an alternative tenure at the time they became home owners. Echoing the findings in relation to owner occupiers in the first study, some of these respondents felt they had been to some extent forced into owner occupation because it was the only housing option available to them, given that they had been unable to exercise their first choice. It was also notable that white owners were more likely to give positive, aspirational reasons for buying, often related to the inherent value of home ownership, while minority ethnic owners tended to say they had to buy because they needed a bigger house, or to give reasons which were associated with the negative aspects of housing in other tenures.

Minority ethnic owners were more limited than white owners in their choice of houses to buy. Many were constrained by financial limitations, and by the larger than average size of their households. In practice, these constraints meant that they often spent longer looking for somewhere, and ended up buying a house which was lacking in some respect. They were less likely to have found their house via an advertisement in a newspaper or property guide than the control group, and were more likely to have heard about the house from a friend, or to have known the vendor. Furthermore, as in Leith, the study provided fairly strong evidence of a minority ethnic housing sub-market, at least within the South Asian community.

A greater proportion of minority ethnic than white households bought homes in need of major repair or improvement, but were much less likely to have carried out those repairs, or planned to do so in the near future. Evidence that the needs of larger households were not met in owner occupation was also clear; minority ethnic owners - especially South Asians - were much more likely to be living in conditions which were overcrowded according to the statutory definition.

The choice of house may have been further constrained by very specific requirements about neighbourhood. Evidence throughout the research indicated that 'neighbourhood' was particularly important to minority ethnic communities; minority ethnic respondents in this study were more likely than white respondents to mention aspects of their neighbourhoods in relation to both 'likes' and 'dislikes'. The electoral register names search showed that minority ethnic communities often live in identifiable clusters in certain areas - even within certain streets (cf. Scottish Office, 1983). Furthermore, the findings from the survey showed that minority ethnic households were more likely to have moved to their current home from within the immediate locality, and to wish to stay in that same neighbourhood if they moved again. They were also more likely to say they had bought 'this particular house' because of its proximity to family and friends, religious facilities and other amenities, whereas particular features of the house itself appeared to be more important to white respondents.

Minority ethnic home owners were not only living in less suitable housing than their white neighbours, but they were paying more for it. Their mortgage repayments were significantly higher, but incomes were lower and less secure. They often spent a greater proportion of their income on their mortgage, and faced greater difficulties in meeting the monthly repayments. Mortgage arrears were much more common amongst this group than the white control group.

Minority ethnic households were more likely than others to have experienced difficulties finding a place to live at some time, and almost half thought that their difficulties had been related to their ethnic group. Minority ethnic households in this study found the whole process of becoming a home owner - from arranging a mortgage to finding a suitable house within their price range - more difficult than white households in the control group. They also tended to be less satisfied than their white neighbours with their housing.

Overall the findings from this third study suggest that Scotland's minority ethnic owner occupiers faced more limited housing opportunities, and poorer housing conditions than their white neighbours. Many turned to owner occupation because they were unable to satisfy their housing needs in other tenures. While owner occupation tended to be an aspirational move for most white households, for many minority ethnic households it was often a 'last resort' and did not necessarily represent an improvement in their housing circumstances - far less a solution to their housing problems.

Summary of the key findings

All three of the studies described in this chapter showed that minority ethnic households faced a more limited choice of housing options than white households living in the same areas. Although minority ethnic communities were disproportionately affected by poor housing they were - or perceived themselves to be - excluded from mainstream provision in the public sector.

The literature review (MacEwen, 1993) reported that in Scotland, there is greater dependence on the owner occupied sector amongst minority ethnic groups than the rest of the community, and indicated that one reason could be the difficulties in accessing housing in the public sector, which are likely to increase in line with general competition for a residualised housing stock. Clearly, if minority ethnic groups have limited access to council housing, their choice of owner occupation is necessarily qualified; restricted access to social housing has an impact on actual and expressed preferences for other tenure forms. Accordingly, in examining different tenure experiences, assumptions about choice need to be qualified in respect of minority ethnic groups.

A range of other studies have supported the findings from these three studies that in every tenure category (including owner occupation) black households fare significantly worse than comparable white households (Brown, 1984; Smith, 1989). It is also widely acknowledged that currently, most of the stock under management in the public sector is mismatched to minority ethnic group needs and that this can inflate the demand for owner occupation (Bowes, McCluskey and Sim, 1989). Indeed, one of the key conclusions of MacEwen's (1993) literature review, was that:

> the need for larger but reasonably priced accommodation is apparent for large/extended families. While this choice is expressed for such accommodation in the owner occupied sector this reflects, at least in part, lack of suitable local authority and housing association provision and problems associated with access (MacEwen, 1993).

The evidence from the three studies suggests that 'neighbourhood' was a more significant determinant of housing choice and satisfaction for this group than for white households - perhaps even more important than particular features of the house itself. This concurs with other evidence (Bowes, McCluskey and Sim, 1989) which reported that in respect of neighbourhood preferences, minority ethnic groups identified 'good neighbours' and 'unfriendly neighbours' as the most important aspects of locational 'likes' and 'dislikes' respectively.

Minority ethnic households were particularly concerned about the safety of the areas where they lived. The prevalence and the serious nature of harassment in Britain and in Scotland is highlighted by a number of other sources, as is the evidence that harassment - or fear of harassment - is a significant influence on housing choices. Indeed, one of the conclusions of the literature review carried out as part of the first research study was that:

> the widespread experience of racial harassment and its association with both tenure and location, has led to minority ethnic households placing a premium on safety and security. Until effective measures are taken to protect minority ethnic tenants, particular estates and areas will remain highly undesirable (MacEwen, 1993).

Because of financial limitations, the housing which minority ethnic households could afford to buy was often unsuitable and did not meet their needs. Owner occupied housing amongst minority ethnic groups was often characterised by poor physical conditions and overcrowding. This finding is supported by evidence from English research, that minority ethnic groups experience worse housing conditions in the owner occupied sector (generally because of age and location) which carries with it a probability that they require to spend more on repairs and maintenance (Brown, 1984, Smith, 1989, MacEwen, 1991). This is the first Scottish research to confirm that minority ethnic home owners do indeed live in poorer physical conditions than their white neighbours, but that they are less likely to have carried out repairs or plan to do so in the foreseeable future.

Opportunities for policy development

There are a number of areas where strategies should be developed in the immediate future to improve the housing situations and choices of minority ethnic groups. These relate primarily to investment, access, and management of public sector housing. These recommendations for policy are neither new nor radical. Indeed, most are encompassed within the 1994 Scottish Homes Policy Statement *Action for Race Equality*. The document describes itself not as 'simply a statement of principles' but, fundamentally 'a blueprint for action'. One of the primary objectives set out in the Action Plan was 'to improve access to all of the housing which may be appropriate to the needs of minority ethnic households' and clearly the findings of these studies support that objective.

First, the research findings point to an urgent need to respond to the minority ethnic population's perceptions of landlords who appeared not to take on board the needs of minority ethnic communities in housing, and who were unresponsive to problems of harassment. Scottish Homes has recently introduced policy on racial harassment (October 1995). Under this policy, ethnic monitoring is carried out on Scottish Homes allocations every six months. Housing associations are also expected to implement the policy, although they are not yet monitored closely in this respect. Clearly, this represents a step forward, but the performance of housing providers over time will need to show that the policy is being translated into practice at the local level.

Improving the appeal of and access to public sector housing could also include recruiting staff from minority ethnic communities, training staff, and providing written and verbal information in appropriate languages. Indeed to this end, Scottish Homes - through the work of Homepoint and its general race equality policy - have implemented strategies to improve the information and advice available to minority ethnic groups via a variety of means. An example is the appointment of a bilingual worker for a housing association in Glasgow.

Housing management practices can also be refined to help social landlords meet the needs of minority ethnic groups within their areas. For example, allocations policies could play a valuable role in ensuring that applicants from minority ethnic groups are able to gain access to housing in areas close to family, friends and facilities which they use, and in areas where they feel safe. Given the fear of harassment, and the impact which this had on housing choices, immediate action should be taken by local authorities and housing associations in the interests of developing safer neighbourhoods for minority ethnic households. Above all, attention should be paid to policy monitoring, review and evaluation to ensure that minority ethnic groups receive a fair service in all respects as prospective and actual tenants.

The minority ethnic groups involved in the studies were in many ways more similar to than different from the white population in terms of their housing needs and aspirations, but there were important differences which must be recognised if their particular needs and preferences are to be met. In the short term, issues around the supply and location of social housing are not easily overcome, but conscious needs assessment and evaluation in relation to the minority ethnic population should be routinely undertaken in the strategic and physical planning processes. This might include building new housing in appropriate areas and of suitable size, and converting existing stock to accommodate larger families.

Given the small amount of local authority development activity, such provision in the social sector would also need to be made by housing associations, which should include shared ownership opportunities as well as rented accommodation. This is particularly appropriate given the large percentage of minority ethnic owner occupiers in Scotland. However, this raises issues about perceptions of housing associations amongst the minority ethnic community, and there may be some scope for housing associations carrying out targeted marketing exercises within their local minority ethnic communities. It is also important that any local developments which are intended, in whole or in part for minority ethnic households, are discussed in advance with local community groups to ensure that perceived needs are being met and also to help increase awareness of the developments amongst the target residents.

There may be some value in providing advice and information to minority ethnic communities, on the range of housing options available to them, and to offer assistance to them in respect of access. Advice should be available in appropriate languages, and, given the reliance of minority ethnic groups on informal sources of information, should be disseminated via informal networks. Advice in appropriate languages should also be offered in relation to home ownership and mortgages, to ensure that those who do decide to opt for owner occupation receive reliable information and a good quality service.

There is also a clear need for the provision of targeted advice and information to minority ethnic home owners on improvement and repair grants, and on take-up of other benefits. Assistance in applying for available benefits would also be necessary, particularly if application forms are available only in English.

In the light of the under representation of Scotland's minority ethnic groups in traditional social housing, their apparent mistrust of public housing providers and procedures, and the unsuitability of much of the existing stock to meet their needs and aspirations, there is a strong argument for developing new housing, specifically designed for minority ethnic groups. Historically, there has been a lack of specific concern about 'race' issues within the Scottish housing association movement, and an absence of policy and strategy from the centre to deal with these issues. Concern has been building within recent years, and in particular there is a lobby campaigning for a black-led housing group in Glasgow. In response, Scottish Homes is considering strategies to improve the access of minority ethnic groups to housing. One such strategy is the development of a minority-led housing initiative into a more structured organisation to work in partnership with Scottish Homes and other agencies to develop mainstream and other specialist housing in order to meet identified needs of minority ethnic groups in Glasgow.

It has been within the overall Scottish Homes strategy (described above) that the Scottish Homes Glasgow District Office produced its 'Development Funding Strategy' (Dowie 1995) which provides a clear illustration of how the national 'flexible approach' may accommodate the research findings described above within the context of the particular needs and aspirations of communities at a district level. Under this local strategy, the Glasgow District Office allocated £8m out of its local budget, specifically towards meeting the needs of minority ethnic groups within its area, in response to identified local need.

However, what remains much more problematic in the implementation of the adopted policy of Scottish Homes is the extent to which its performance indicators and monitoring procedures will ensure that the housing needs of minority ethnic groups are translated into effective action and positive housing outcomes. This could be especially problematic if district offices are less attuned or responsive to community aspirations. There is a clear danger that local discretion without the necessary closely monitored controls and sanctions will in effect become the status quo of inactivity embedding the disadvantages which these three research reports have illustrated.

Conclusion

The three research studies reviewed here showed consistently that minority ethnic households often faced a more limited range of housing options than their white neighbours, and often lived in poorer housing conditions. Lack of choice was related to a number of factors, including exclusion from housing in other tenures through direct and indirect discrimination, limited and insecure incomes, larger and non-traditional households, and specific locational preferences. Owner occupation was the most common - and generally the most popular - tenure amongst minority ethnic groups, but push factors were often more significant than pull factors. The housing which they bought was usually at the lower end of the market, but was still difficult to afford. Properties were often in need of major repair, and overcrowding was commonplace. Nevertheless, there were pockets of satisfactory housing provision (for example in Leith), particularly where owner occupiers had bought a home in an area which they perceived to be safe.

The research findings lead to an overall conclusion that owner occupation can be a very different experience for minority ethnic than for white households. While amongst the general population, home ownership may imply affluence and freedom of choice for some, this may not be so for households who are forced to buy. Many of those households involved in these three studies expressed a preference for renting, but had found it difficult to do so. Whether the way forward is to encourage specialist provision by a minority ethnic housing movement, or to introduce specific measures to ensure that the needs of Scotland's minority ethnic population are catered for within the mainstream housing movement, the challenge for the future will be to ensure that social landlords' policy commitment to achieving greater equality in housing translates into practice. If the implementation of the policy commitment is to ensure that Scotland's minority ethnic communities are able to exercise a free choice in housing to the same extent as the majority ethnic population, then that target will have been achieved when future research shows that they are just as likely as white respondents to say they are home owners because they want to be home owners.

Acknowledgements

This chapter reviews three studies carried out at the School of Planning and Housing, Heriot-Watt University, and recognition is due to colleagues who worked on those studies. In particular, Sally Wainwright was largely responsible for designing and managing all three research projects, and as such her contribution to the work presented in this chapter deserves acknowledgement. In addition, thanks are due to Hal Pawson who was heavily involved in both the second and third research studies. Finally, we offer our appreciation to the many households who were interviewed for these studies.

5. The housing needs of older people from minority ethnic groups

Helen Carlin

Introduction

According to the 1991 Census, the three largest minority ethnic groups in Scotland are the Pakistanis, the Chinese and the Indians. There are differences between the age profiles of these groups, with the Chinese, for example, tending to have a larger proportion of elderly people than the Indian and Pakistani communities (Scottish Office 1991). Generally the minority ethnic communities are younger than the population as a whole, with 3 per cent over pensionable age, i.e. aged 65, against a national average of 18.5 per cent.

It is, however, generally accepted that due to a combination of circumstances, the 'normal' ageing process may start sooner within minority ethnic communities, and 50 or 55 is a more appropriate age to consider individuals as older (Age Concern 1984, Jeffrey and Seagar 1993). Dowd and Bengston (1978: 427), developing the theory of double jeopardy point out that older people from minority ethnic groups: bear, in effect, a double burden. Like other older people in industrial societies, they experience the devaluation of old age found in most modern societies...Unlike other older people, however, the minority aged must bear the additional economic, social and psychological burdens of living in a society in which racial equality remains....... a myth.

Older people from minority ethnic groups are frequently overlooked; perhaps as Blakemore and Boneham suggest:

A major reason for the non-appearance of older black people on the national agenda is their perceived status as a tiny minority within a minority. Put simply, it is easy to disregard a minority considered to be too small to bother about (1994:16).

Certainly, the housing needs of older people from minority ethnic groups in Scotland have been almost completely ignored by policy makers and housing providers alike. While there is a growing body of research on the discrimination facing people from minority ethnic groups, and more becomes known about the housing circumstances, aspirations and preferences of minority ethnic groups in general, little is known about the specific needs of minority ethnic elders, a point highlighted by Blakemore and Boneham:

> ...compared with the amount of public attention to, and research on, such questions as racial discrimination in housing, employment or education, the lack of research on the ageing of the black population is startling (1994:10).

Without such knowledge it is difficult, if not impossible, to respond to such needs. Indeed, practical responses to these needs have been few and far between, and have generally come into being through the drive and determination of local community groups rather than through any systematic needs evaluation by housing agencies (Munday 1996).

The available evidence points to a neglect of the housing needs of older people from minority ethnic groups, and a very low take up by ethnic elders of specialist housing for older people. It is perhaps the low take up of services which has helped to perpetuate the myth that 'they look after their own', but various commentators have highlighted the changing situation within minority ethnic communities regarding the care of older people by the extended family (ASHIA 1992, Age Concern 1984). Previous research has also demonstrated that low take up does not in itself imply low demand, or an absence of need (Patel 1990, Age Concern 1984).

These needs could be currently neglected for several reasons, including a widespread belief among policy makers and planners that 'they look after their own'; inactivity by housing planners and providers to assess need because of the small numbers of ethnic elders; institutionalised racism; or a lack of ethnic monitoring, leading to discrimination.

From the older person's perspective, a low take up rate of services may be due to various factors, such as ignorance of housing options, and a lack of information on how to gain access to them; exclusion from established referral networks; a fear of being the only tenant from a minority ethnic group, and thereby possibly facing isolation, or, worse, racist behaviour from staff or fellow tenants; housing or support services that are not culturally sensitive to one's needs; or, finally, affordability.

This chapter seeks to explode the myth that 'they look after their own'. It attempts to show that the housing needs of older people from minority ethnic groups are being systematically ignored, and that older people from minority ethnic groups, unaware of the possible options, face a limited housing choice, including accommodation which is not suitable to their needs for the reasons given above.

It includes an examination of previous research. Research on the housing needs of older people from minority ethnic groups is scant, even in the UK context, so this literature review goes beyond those works which solely deal with housing for minority ethnic elders, and also looks at a range of more general research on older people from minority ethnic groups which, due to the very limited amount of information available in the Scottish context (Cranny 1988, Carlin 1994), is by necessity UK wide. It then goes on to look at the Scottish context, utilising the results of two studies by the author, examining current policies and practice in the housing field, and making recommendations about how these issues might be addressed.

Access to services

Throughout the 1980s, a number of community surveys looking at the needs of ethnic elders were carried out. The focus of these surveys was access to services. Accordingly, there was little examination of the cultural sensitivity of the services provided, nor did the surveys address the real aspirations of ethnic elders. However, the studies showed quite forcibly that access to social services and housing was denied to ethnic elders, due to a combination of circumstances, the most prevalent of which was a lack of knowledge of these services and how to access them.

The AFFOR study in Birmingham looked at levels of awareness about certain social services. Perhaps not surprisingly, the study found that awareness was highest among the European group. For example, 94 per cent of the European elders had knowledge of the existence of the home help service, as against only 19 per cent of those Asian elders interviewed (Bhalla and Blakemore 1981). Of the full range of services mentioned, a staggering 64 per cent of older Asian people had no knowledge, as compared to two per cent of the European people.

Previous research in Scotland has found a similar pattern. In a study in Glasgow, only 52.4 per cent of the respondents in the sample had heard of sheltered housing for the elderly, in sharp contrast to 93 per cent of the white control group. However, once its function had been explained to the remainder of the ethnic minority sample, 83 per cent of all respondents thought that it would be useful if sheltered housing was available which provided for the cultural needs of their communities (Dalton and Daghlian 1989).

In the AFFOR study, 88 per cent of the older Asian people surveyed could not speak English, underlining the need for more appropriate information in a variety of languages. However, service providers have to go some way beyond the printing and random distribution of translated leaflets, if they are to be effective in making minority ethnic elders aware of their services, as Patel (1990) points out.

In a study of West Indians in Leicester, Cooper (1977) cites a case of a black woman in poor health, with no relatives, who required practical help, such as shopping. She was entitled to home help but was unaware of her rights; young black individuals with whom she spoke were similarly unaware. This emphasises that language is not the only problem faced by the elders.

Studies have also found differing levels of awareness between different minority ethnic communities. A Coventry survey, for instance, found low levels of awareness of services amongst older Asian people, but found that there was a much higher level of awareness amongst older Afro-Caribbean people. Thus, while 63 per cent of older Afro-Caribbeans had heard of sheltered housing, only 11 per cent of older Asian people had done so (Holland and Lewando-Hundt 1986). Findings such as these were similarly made in other surveys of this type (e.g. Barker 1984, Turnbull 1985, ASHIA 1992).

Access to housing provision is also affected by affordability. Poverty is a fact of life for many older people, with an income at around half the national average (Scottish Homes, 1993a). For minority ethnic elders, this can often be worse. A recent report highlights the differentials in levels of pay and employment between different ethnic communities in Britain. While the average hourly rate of pay for a white male is £8.34, the equivalent figure for a Pakistani or Bangladeshi male is only £6.87. Similarly, within the white community, unemployment runs at 8 per cent, whereas the rate rises to 24 per cent for Afro-Caribbeans, and to 27 per cent amongst the Pakistani and Bangladeshi communities (HMSO 1996). Members of these minority ethnic communities therefore have less opportunity to save towards their old age. In addition, the greater rates of unemployment, together with the higher incidence of lower paid employment, mean less chance to provide for old age by contributing to an occupational pension. Affordability was found to be a crucial element in the failure by minority ethnic elders to apply for housing association accommodation (Jones 1994). There may also be implications for new provision, where higher costs may be incurred through making the accommodation more sensitive to the needs of minority ethnic elders. In her study of sheltered housing for elderly Chinese people in

Edinburgh, Munday (1996) found that there were additional costs incurred by factors including the appointment of a bi-lingual warden, gas cooking facilities and extra large communal facilities. No additional funding was available from Scottish Homes through increased levels of Housing Association Grant, and the additional charges have been passed to the tenants, reflected in the rent and service charges, and offset by donations from the Chinese community and fund-raising activities.

Suitability of services

Knowledge of services does not in itself ensure that services will be used. As stated by Julienne:

> Black elders disproportionately do not go into sheltered housing for the same reason they under-use home helps and meals on wheels. They do not know about these services and, where they do, these services are not sensitive to their particular need. The accommodation is located in an area away from the communities they feel comfortable in; away from the shops catering for their needs and places of worship; staff and residents don't understand and are often hostile to their language or customs; diets are not catered for; and publicity about the schemes is targeted in areas in which they do not live and in a language that they do not understand. (Jeffrey and Seagar 1993: preface: viii).

In the Coventry survey, few of those Asian elders who were introduced to the concept of sheltered housing regarded it as a suitable option for themselves, preferring to find a family housing solution to their problem (Holland and Lewando-Hundt 1986). This contrasts with the findings from the Leicester survey, where over half of those older Afro-Caribbean people interviewed expressed a preference to live in sheltered housing as they became frailer (Farrah 1987).

This highlights the fundamental importance of establishing the preferences of the user, or potential user, of services, before attempting to meet their needs in a way which does not suit them. It also indicates that the social and housing needs of older people are not homogeneous, and will vary according to the individual. This consideration is pertinent to all older people, but particularly to older people from minority ethnic groups. Julienne underlines this point:

> ...their [minority ethnic elders'] housing needs should not be

assumed by providers, and that just because there is a need for sheltered accommodation by one particular ethnic group in one particular area, does not mean that a similar need has to be fulfilled by a similar or different ethnic group in a different part of the country (Julienne in Jones 1994:5).

Fear of isolation and racist behaviour

Fear of isolation from family and community, and the possibility of being exposed to racist behaviour, are recurring themes throughout the literature. The AFFOR study found that concern over speaking and understanding English precluded many minority ethnic elders from participating in social activities such as lunch clubs or day centres, though many elders would have welcomed the opportunity to make more social contact (Bhalla and Blakemore 1981). If this is the case with social opportunities, then it is not unreasonable to assume that it would be of even greater significance in housing, particularly in sheltered housing with its emphasis on community living.

Dalton and Daghlian (1989) found that over half of those interviewed thought that schemes should be mixed, with some respondents fearing that 'separate provision would lead to poorer quality provision for minority ethnic communities', or that developments might become the target for 'white hostility and racism'. One respondent feared that cooking smells might provoke antagonism from other residents, 'which suggested past experience of such complaints'. (Dalton and Daghlian 1989:38). Their research also found that, from the different minority ethnic groups interviewed, the Chinese indicated a particular preference for separate provision, and it is interesting to note that there is now separate provision of sheltered housing for the Chinese elderly in Dundee and in Edinburgh, with a further development planned for Glasgow.

There is evidence from the literature that these fears are not unfounded. Jones, in a study carried out on behalf of four major housing associations in England found that:

> whereas the black and minority ethnic tenants interviewed were generally in favour of living in mixed schemes the response from white tenants was nowhere near as uniform, with some tenants being 'pro' the idea and others being very negative (1994:18).

Language was a major barrier to the interaction between Asian tenants and white tenants, and the smell of Asian cooking was identified as a problem for some white tenants. While the research found only one case of harassment (and stated that this situation seemed to be improving) there was clear evidence of the tensions within some mixed developments, as the following quote amply illustrates:

> The warden made it clear to tenants that racist remarks would not be allowed in the Common Room, and that they will be evicted if they racially harass other tenants. The warden noted that: 'They don't ignore each other....they acknowledge the fact they live here...[they] talk about them behind their backs but are pleasant to their faces'. It is worth noting that the warden has been described as a 'spineless Indian-lover' by several of the tenants because she treats the Asian tenants equally (Jones 1994:119).

Identification of need

In 1982, Age Concern England and Help the Aged Housing Trust sponsored a Working Party to inquire into the housing conditions of older people from minority ethnic groups, and to make practical recommendations as to how these might be improved. One hundred and fifty four housing organisations, based in areas where there was a significant number of minority ethnic residents, were sent a postal questionnaire asking about their attitudes and policies relating to older people from minority ethnic groups. These were followed up by interviews and visits to housing organisations in Liverpool, Leicester, Bradford, Birmingham and London. Minority ethnic community groups who were working with housing associations towards the provision of services for ethnic elders in these areas were also interviewed.
The resulting report stated that:

> Very few local authorities and housing associations had begun to identify the need [of black and minority ethnic elders] and evolve policies to meet it. Hardly any local authorities had any idea of the numbers of ethnic elders in their houses - nor did many housing associations (Age Concern/Help the Aged 1984:25).

Indeed, the research found that all too often (but with some notable exceptions) councillors and officers from housing and social services '...still held to the hackneyed notion that all ethnic elders were cosy in the extended family environment, and were surprised to learn that this was a myth...' (1984:26). The community groups interviewed were aware of the difficulties faced by their ethnic elders, but were frustrated by a lack of financial support, and inadequate knowledge of housing association finance, development procedures or general management.

The absence of a proactive approach by housing providers towards the housing needs of older people from ethnic minorities, led to a situation where:

> Local authorities and housing associations tended to see their problem in terms of the fact that ethnic elders did not approach them for help and they were consequently not aware of their presence in the area.....for ethnic elders in poor housing the problem was how to go about obtaining decent accommodation that was well managed and well maintained (1984:12).

The report set out clear recommendations as to a way forward, stating that:

> The most important recommendations are those which ask housing providers to question their attitudes and assumptions about the needs of ethnic elders, and to communicate with the elderly people themselves and with agencies working on their behalf. This is absolutely essential if the needs of ethnic elders are to be met in a sensitive way (1984:12).

In 1993, a report for the Federation of Black Housing Organisations (Jeffrey and Seagar 1993) adopted a similar approach to the earlier Age Concern/Help the Aged format, and it therefore provides an updated picture of the work being done in this area. Additionally, while the 1984 survey did not include any Scottish housing associations, and only one Scottish local authority, the FBHO report contained responses from 22 Scottish housing associations (though it did not detail how many of the local authorities that responded were Scottish).

In the introduction, Louis Julienne, who chaired the working party overseeing the report, commented that 'the survey provided clear evidence that the neglect of black and minority ethnic elders' housing needs continues virtually unabated, and did not surprise any of us'. Few of the recommendations of the original report had been implemented by any of the organisations participating in the survey. Consequently, 'the assessment of the housing related needs of black and minority ethnic elders was at best based on small scale, ad hoc surveys and at worst based on no evidence at all. The lack of an assessment of need was often accompanied by the lack of an awareness of need'. (Jeffrey and Seagar 1993:1).

The Scottish context

The role of local authority housing departments

Local authorities are required to assess the housing need within their area, and to work with Scottish Homes, housing associations and others to meet these needs. The introduction of community care places on housing organisations, Health Boards and social work departments the duty to work together to assess and meet social, housing and health care needs. However, the available evidence suggests that the housing needs of older people from minority ethnic groups are not being assessed, and will continue to be overlooked. Goodlad (1993: 57), writing about the enabling role of local authorities comments that:

> Only the perception of large-scale overall deficiency in special needs provision has prevented such issues [of planning for small numbers of people with special needs] emerging as problems of resource distribution. The planning for special needs which community care policies now require calls for a 'bottom up' as well as 'top down' element in planning.

Thus, assessments of need are often insufficiently sensitive to local circumstances and to particular groups, such as minority ethnic elderly. Brailey (1991: 81) comments that:

> the housing needs of both ethnic minorities and special needs groups are low down on everyone's agenda. Rectifying this is made harder by the fact that special needs provision requires multi-agency collaboration in assembling integrated packages of care and housing, so there are more agendas to be influenced.

Whether the reorganisation of local government, bringing as it does the social work and housing function within the same authority goes any way towards improving this situation is yet to be seen.

The role of Scottish Homes

The policy of Scottish Homes, the national housing agency, in relation to housing for older people, is to maximise the choices available to older people; encourage flexibility in provision across a range of tenures, types and locations; promote the use of effective planning mechanisms to ensure responses at a local level; and ensure the best possible use is made of all housing resources to meet the changing needs of older people (Scottish Homes 1995:10).

One such way of meeting needs has been in the provision of specialist housing for older people. The emergence of housing specially designed and built to accommodate older people is a relatively recent phenomenon, dating from the early 1960s. Around this time, the very poor housing conditions experienced by vast numbers of older people began to be recognised, as did the inappropriateness of residential care for many of them, although this was the only other available housing option (Townsend 1962).

There are now around 50,000 social housing units in Scotland specifically designed for older people, as well as 4,000 privately owned sheltered and retirement houses (Scottish Homes 1995). Sheltered housing accounts for around 33,000 of these units and is, according to research carried out amongst its occupants, a popular choice for older people, who express high levels of satisfaction about living there (Clapham and Munro 1988). Previous research indicates that take-up of such specialist accommodation by black and minority ethnic elders is very low (Lear 1987, Carlin 1994).

Sheltered housing faces an uncertain future. Only about five per cent of Scotland's older people live in this form of housing, and some commentators have been critical of its relatively high cost, compared to the relatively small number of people whom it assists (Clapham and Munro 1988). Current thinking suggests that, with the exception of certain areas where there is a shortfall, and a clear 'specific local need' for it, sheltered housing will not be a future priority. Instead, the focus will be on the building or adaptation of existing sheltered housing to provide extra-sheltered housing. This is similar in design, but includes more support than is currently available in sheltered housing, such as the provision of a daily meal (Scottish Homes 1993b). However, this shift in policy is likely to have a negative impact on the already inadequate provision for older people from minority ethnic communities, whose needs appear not to have been specifically recognised within most existing provision.

These needs do not seem to be on the agenda of Scottish Homes. Nowhere in the 1995 policy document on the housing needs of older people were the specific needs of older people from minority ethnic groups addressed (Scottish Homes 1995). Similarly, in their 1993 consultation paper on minority ethnic housing, older people received scant attention, although there was recognition that they faced greater language difficulties of access to services than younger members of the minority ethnic community (Scottish Homes 1993c).

But the role of Scottish Homes extends well beyond that of housing provider or enabler, and includes a legal responsibility for monitoring the practices of housing associations with regard to equal opportunities. A report by the Commission for Racial Equality suggested that Scottish Homes had failed to give the question of equal opportunities sufficient weight in its monitoring role. This failure had contributed to the situation in which few of the recommendations of the Commission's Code of Practice in Rented Housing had even been formally adopted by housing associations, let alone become part of their practice (Commission for Racial Equality 1993).

Black associations in Scotland

Calls for black housing associations to be established in Scotland have been met with resistance from Scottish Homes and indifference from many housing providers. The consultation paper from Scottish Homes on ethnic minority housing did not see the setting up of black-led housing associations as the answer in every situation. It promoted a 'flexible approach' and sought 'to avoid a system of separate, designated funding for ethnic minority housing' (Scottish Homes 1993c). Scottish Homes allocated 1.25 per cent of their social housing budget to address the needs of minority ethnic communities, and have commissioned further research. It is too soon to say if this approach will help minority ethnic elders, but the English experience suggests that the needs of minority ethnic elders might be best met by black associations who are best placed to respond to these needs in a culturally sensitive way.

The English experience

South of the border, although there have been recent difficulties, resources have, in the past, been ring-fenced for such organisations. As a result, associations such as ASRA, Carib and Tung Sing Housing Associations have developed sheltered and extra-care schemes for older people from ethnic minorities (Jeffrey and Seagar 1993). These schemes are, for the most part, popular. Apart from some initial difficulties in achieving local authority nominations, and some teething troubles in the initial stages of allocation, the associations which manage them report little difficulty in maintaining low void rates and waiting lists for vacancies as they arise. (FBHO, 1993).

At least on a small scale, therefore, housing which is culturally acceptable to the specific needs of ethnic elders in England is provided by housing associations which are sensitive to these needs. The absence of such housing associations in Scotland perhaps explains why there is a dearth of such housing choice north of the border. The only Scottish provision of this type has been sheltered housing provided by the Glasgow Jewish Housing Association. This organisation, now registered with Scottish Homes, grew out of the Glasgow Jewish Welfare Society, who sought to remedy the problems faced by older Jews (Age Concern Scotland 1994).

This apart, the only other responses specific to the housing needs of older people from minority ethnic groups have been two sheltered housing developments, in Dundee and Edinburgh, for older Chinese people. Both schemes have been developed 'bottom up' by community groups working with local housing associations. An excellent account of the development and early stages of the Cathay Court sheltered housing scheme, developed by Fountainbridge Housing Association in Edinburgh, is to be found in Munday (1996).

Surveys of housing providers

Glasgow has the largest minority ethnic community of any Scottish city. Research was carried out by the author in 1994, to examine how housing associations, as major providers of specialist housing in the city, were addressing the housing needs of black and minority ethnic elders (Carlin 1994).

A short questionnaire was sent to those housing associations which provided specialist (amenity, sheltered or very sheltered housing) for older people in the Glasgow area. Of the 20 housing associations contacted, only nine responses were received, giving a poor response rate of 45 per cent, and comparing unfavourably to the 87 per cent response rate by Scottish housing associations to the 1993 FBHO survey (Jeffrey and Seagar 1993). Between them, however, the associations that did respond had 1061 houses for older people in management.

The questionnaire covered three key areas, namely the ethnic monitoring of tenants; the ethnic monitoring of staff; and the existence of policies on or provision for minority ethnic elders. There was some difficulty in analysing the results because of the variations in record keeping between organisations. For example, one national association was unable to provide figures specific to Glasgow, and therefore provided its figures on a national basis. Another association, which provided mainstream housing as well as specialist housing, was unable to identify minority ethnic tenants by age, but as they had made no lettings to **any** minority ethnic people, this did not present a serious problem in terms of analysis.

Clear guidelines on the implementation and use of ethnic monitoring for housing organisations are contained within the Code of Practice for Rented Housing, and have been available to housing associations for some time. The guidance stresses that any measurement must take into account local factors, such as the numbers of the minority ethnic communities living locally; the number of people on the waiting list; and the operation of the local housing market. It further recommends close consultation with community groups or community relations councils representing the needs of the minority ethnic community (CRE 1991). In spite of this and other guidance, only three of the associations were monitoring the ethnicity of their tenants or applicants in such a way as to be able to make a meaningful assessment of their equal opportunity policy in relation to lettings. In addition, six of the associations had no idea of the numbers of minority ethnic elders living in their area.

Nor are these associations in the minority. Research conducted by the CRE, looking at 40 housing associations in Scotland, concluded that:

> There was little evidence that the associations investigated were evaluating the housing needs of people from ethnic minorities in their area of operation, or translating what information they had into the specific development of schemes (CRE 1993).

Between the seven associations who were able to provide figures for Glasgow alone, there had been 370 new lets in the preceding year (1992/93). If the figure for lets provided by the national associations was included, this rose to 878. From these 878 lettings, only one was to an older person from a minority ethnic group. A similar picture emerged in relation to current tenants, with the exception of one small, community-based housing association, operating in a locality of Glasgow with a well established Asian community, who were represented on the association's management committee. Additionally, the association disseminated information on their accommodation through outreach work with local communities, as well as providing information on their housing in a variety of languages. Seven associations appeared to have no tenants from ethnic minority groups. The large national association had only five tenants from ethnic minority groups in any of its tenancies across Scotland.

Section 3.2 of the Code of Practice in Rented Housing, drawn up by the Commission for Racial Equality in 1991, clearly states that 'any unmet needs in the public sector (e.g. those of the ethnic minority elderly) should be identified and, wherever practicable, action taken to meet them'. Yet, over half of the associations had made no investigation of the number of ethnic elders within their area. It is not surprising, therefore, that the majority of these associations had taken no policy decisions in relation to older people from ethnic minority groups, and had not made any specific attempt, such as outreach work, to make ethnic elders aware of their presence. Most of the associations did not even publish information in any language other than English.

This survey of housing associations in Glasgow was followed up, in September 1995, by a survey of local authorities across Scotland. Forty-three out of 52 local authorities responded (an 83 per cent response rate), to a postal questionnaire, which sought information about policies and practices in respect of older people generally, and older people from minority ethnic groups in particular. Despite the central role of local authorities in the community care planning process, the responses to this survey indicated that information about the needs of older people generally, and the development of policies to meet these needs, was haphazard at best. Five authorities did not even have a clear idea of the number of older people who were resident in the authority area.

The situation was worse in respect of older people from minority ethnic groups. Of the 42 authorities surveyed only one had made any attempt to assess the housing needs of these groups. Of the remaining 41, only five stated that they were considering this as a possibility for the future. Perhaps not surprisingly, these were all authorities who indicated that they did have specific housing policies for older people, and two of them were making proactive attempts to address sensitively the issue of housing needs generally by community profiling or local research.

For many authorities, the housing needs of older people from minority ethnic groups was simply not an issue. As one respondent wrote: '...ethnic minorities make up a small proportion of the population, there is therefore little call for specialised housing'. This theme of small numbers ran through most of the responses as a justification for doing nothing. As Bhalla and Blakemore (1991) point out, however, even where older people from minority ethnic groups live in areas where there are larger numbers, it does not mean that their needs will be met. Indeed, Goodlad (1993) indicates that with 'top down' planning, there is a greater likelihood of needs being overlooked.

Another common theme was that all people were treated equally, and therefore there was no discrimination in operation. This was expressed in one response as 'The needs of every applicant are individually assessed, therefore the cultural needs would be taken into account'. An interesting observation made by one Island authority was that: 'All people are treated equally and there are few minority ethnics here, unless of course you would count the English or the Scots. Should it arise however, care would be given to cultural sensitivity'. This was a somewhat tongue in cheek response, but indicated how the vast majority of respondents felt that the small number of older people from minority ethnic groups on their waiting list or living in their area indicated that all was well. They felt under no obligation to begin to assess whether there was, in fact, unmet housing need, let alone to begin planning to meet it.

The views of ethnic elders

In 1994, research was undertaken into the views of a sample group of 109 older people from the Indian and Pakistani communities in Glasgow (Carlin 1994). (The Chinese elderly were, at the time, being surveyed in detail by Glasgow District Council.) Previous work (e.g. Age Concern/Help the Aged 1984) had suggested a low incidence of older Asians able to speak English, so the interviews were conducted by Urdu and Punjabi speakers. The aim of the research was to ascertain the level of satisfaction people felt with their present accommodation, and if they were experiencing any difficulties with it, such as disrepair or access problems due to stairs etc. It also tried to gauge how aware (or otherwise) individuals were of other housing options for older people, and if they might consider these options suitable for themselves. Each interviewer had translated information on the various housing options for older people, and these were accompanied by photographs of the various sorts of provision elsewhere, in an attempt to establish a common frame of reference.

Over half of those interviewed reported problems with their current accommodation, mainly relating to the stairs. Despite this, only two people had been assisted, through the provision of aids or adaptations, to overcome this difficulty. Not only does this suggest a lack of awareness of this form of assistance, but the low take up rate is in sharp contrast to the rate of take up amongst older people in Scotland generally, which has been estimated at over one third (Scottish Office 1990). When weighed against the large number of interviewees who expressed difficulty in coping with some aspect of independent living, such as bathing, the low level of provision of such assistance seems surprising.

Of those interviewed, 72 per cent said that they had heard of sheltered housing. When asked to elaborate, however, they generally expected sheltered housing to be more akin to 'Part Four' accommodation, housing frailer people who required some nursing care, and thus not likely to be suitable for their own circumstances. Once the nature of this provision had been explained, a significant minority (10 per cent) expressed an interest in sheltered housing, although none of them would consider living in a development where they were the only person from their ethnic group. The majority of those surveyed were happy to be living with their families, though 99 per cent of those interviewed felt that the provision of a community alarm could enhance their quality of life. A note of concern was also sounded by around 10 older people who while happy with their present circumstances wondered if this might always be the case. Similarly, none of those interviewed would consider moving into a scheme where all the staff were white, but almost all would consider a move to a scheme where there was a mix of staff, including people from their own ethnic group, should the need arise.

There was also interest in schemes which would be culturally sensitive, and great emphasis was placed on the location of any potential development by over 90 of those people, who stressed that accommodation should be available in the 'right location', near shops, the mosque and other facilities identified as important. Around ten percent of those interviewed expressed concern at the likely cost of such accommodation,

The factors, referred to earlier, which may lead to a low take up of services, seem to be borne out by these interviews. Knowledge of special housing was limited, and independent living was often confused with 'Part Four' accommodation. Interviewees stated that they had never received any information about the forms of housing that they were discussing. The translated material and photographs of sheltered and extra care schemes that they were shown was for many, therefore, their first introduction to the sort of housing choice that is available to older people in Scotland.

Conclusions

The evidence presented by the previous research, and the more recent research undertaken by the author, shows that there is potential demand among older people from minority ethnic groups for housing which is culturally sensitive to their needs. It is apparent, however, that the work required to identify these needs is not currently being undertaken by the appropriate agencies. The lack of interest in services currently being provided does not imply a lack of need within these communities, and should not be regarded by service or housing providers as an indication that all is well. What is required is more information for older minority ethnic people, to allow them to make their own choices, and the provision of housing which is suitable to their needs, located in areas where they wish to continue living. Guidance on achieving equal opportunities and the elimination of racial discrimination in housing provision is readily available, but as the surveys indicate, very few housing organisations, nationally or locally, feel under an obligation to follow this guidance, and as a consequence, the housing needs of older people from minority ethnic groups continue to be unassessed and unmet.

6. The social work service and elderly Pakistani people

Alison Bowes and Naira Dar

Introduction

For some time now, there has been a concern among researchers and practitioners that elderly Pakistani people have not been using social work services. Some have argued that this is because social work has operated in exclusionary ways, and others that, since Pakistani families are expected to look after older people themselves, they are unlikely to approach services. In this chapter, we report and discuss the findings of a research project, conducted in 1994-5 in Glasgow, which aimed to explore patterns of welfare and mutual care among elderly Pakistani people and their families, with particular reference to their use, or lack of use of the social work service. We focus on the current relationship (or lack of relationship) between a Social Work Department and elderly Pakistani people, and argue that, despite the considerable efforts of the Department to make itself user friendly for this client group, there remain considerable problems, and the very real needs of elderly Pakistani people are often not being met.

There is ample evidence that social work services have not, in the past, successfully addressed the issues involved in working with racialised groups in Britain, although recent years have seen these issues tackled in some areas, and the development of a strong body of anti-discriminatory policy and, to an extent, practice. In Glasgow for example, where our research was based, the former Strathclyde Regional Council was involved in work to promote equal opportunities and service access (e.g. Strathclyde Regional Council 1986, and see McCluskey 1991 on the Ethnic Minorities Project).

Recent literature, such as Chakrabarti and Cadman's (1994) study in Tayside (discussed elsewhere in this volume), the GOAL Project's work in South Glamorgan (South Glamorgan Race Equality Council etc 1994), and Blakemore and Boneham's (1994) review of research in the field, continues to argue that social services are failing to meet the needs of elderly people from minority ethnic groups, despite their considerable efforts at improvement. All argue that there is a need for separate consideration of issues of provision in this area, as services are not currently well supplied to members of minority ethnic groups, who remain ignorant of their availability, and are often critical of services they do receive.

There has been very little work which has looked closely and qualitatively at minority ethnic elderly people's own views in the broader context of their lives and beliefs. For Pakistani people, the continuity and strength of tradition, as Blakemore and Boneham (1994) argue, and we would concur, should not be underestimated: it is unfortunate that some critics, such as Dominelli (1991), have moved debate away from consideration of these clients' own views, by emphasising social work departments' own policies and practices. Dominelli (1991) argues strongly that social work is an essentially racist profession, which reproduces the racism of the society around it. Such a perspective is, in our view, too deterministic, and tends to ignore not only clients' views, but also those of the many social workers attempting to work in non-racist ways. Recent contributors to this discussion, including Chakrabarti (1991) and Atkin (1991) have argued that to acquire research data which will make sense of relationships between minority ethnic groups and social services departments, it is necessary to examine the views both of professionals and clients. In our work, we looked at the views of both service users and service providers, as well as some potential users. The Glasgow context is of particular interest, as community based groups had been set up to provide day care facilities for Pakistani elderly people, and to offer a bridge for them between the community and the Social Work Department. These groups were part of the general welfare scene, and their staff were included in our study in addition to social work staff in area teams.

The apparent difficulties in producing an appropriate service and raising uptake of services by older Pakistani people suggest that issues may need to be identified afresh, through thorough investigation of the viewpoints of the various participants in the interaction (or lack of it) between departments and this client group. To this end, we used an ethnographic style of interviewing, to allow openness to the point of view of interviewees, and to examine these in the context of their everyday lives and professional experiences. The ethnographic approach was also important for challenging the cultural stereotyping which has been criticised, for example, by Ahmad (1990) who argues that the assumptions that Asian families look after all their members throughout life, or that Asian women's problems all stem from arranged marriage, can obviate any responsibility to ask what the needs of Asian client groups may be.

By comparison with the general population, Scotland's Pakistani population is relatively young[1] and the proportion of older people in the population small. As the population ages, however, the proportion of older people will rise. In Glasgow, there were about 1000 Pakistani people over 50, according to the 1991 Census, of whom about 60 per cent were men, and 40 per cent, women. This gender ratio differs from that of the white population in the same age group, which is about 65 per cent female, and is due to the particular patterns of migration, whereby men migrated to Britain earlier than women, some never marrying, and others, marrying younger women.

Methods

The focus of the project was on ascertaining the views of Pakistani elderly people themselves, and of staff in the Social Work Department and community organisations. The lack of take up of services, despite their efforts at improvement, suggested the likelihood of differences of perspective. Staff working in community organisations which catered for Pakistani elderly people had a more or less formal mediating role between the local community and the Social Work Department.

All the fieldwork was carried out in Glasgow. There were three sets of interviews. In all, 30 older people were interviewed, 20 women and 10 men. All defined themselves as elderly, and this was the criterion for inclusion in the study. Their chronological ages varied from 55 to over 90. Four were recent migrants to Britain, and the others had migrated in the 1960s and 1970s. Twenty were attending community organisations which were supported by the Social Work Department, and, of these, six were currently or had been clients of the Department. The other ten interviewees were not attending organisations, and therefore lacked this indirect contact with the Department.

The interviews with elderly people were in Punjabi, and covered the general patterns of welfare and mutual care they currently experienced, how well they felt these were operating, the extent of their knowledge and experience of both statutory and voluntary services, and the degree to which they felt their welfare needs were being met. In some cases, other family members were present at the

[1] The study was funded by the Social Work Research Centre, University of Stirling, and the Scottish Office Central Research Unit. We acknowledge the contribution to the project of Sadia Salim, who carried out some of the interviews with elderly people.

All population figures are from the 1991 Census. Discussion is based on Bailey Bowes and Sim 1995.

interviews, and contributed to them: we were thus able to include some indications of the views of carers in the analysis.

Nine Social Work Department staff were interviewed in two District Offices. Seven were white, two had a Pakistani background. They varied in grade, from Senior Social Worker to Community Work Assistant, and in experience, from a few months to nearly thirty years. These staff were asked about their experience of working with elderly people generally, and with Pakistani elderly people in particular, about their training for such work and their evaluation of it, and their knowledge of and views about both Department policy on working with minority groups, and the Pakistani community in Glasgow. They were also asked to comment on the potential effects of recent policy changes, especially in view of the possibility of Departments buying in services from the voluntary sector for particular client groups.

Seven South Asian staff working in community groups run for minority ethnic elderly people were interviewed. Although the groups were not specifically for Pakistani people, most of their clients were Pakistani Muslims. The interviews for these workers covered similar ground to that of the interviews with Social Work Department staff [2].

The research findings are presented in three sections, each focussing on one set of interviewees, the elderly people, the community organisation workers and the Social Work Department staff. In presenting the findings, we use illustrative quotations from the interviews, which either typify a series of comments, or indicate the degree of variability in views revealed in analysis of the transcripts. Each of these quotations has the interviewee number attached. Where someone other than the interviewee contributed, this is indicated. Generally, these were other family members, especially daughters-in-law or daughters, who were sometimes carers. The interviewer is identified by the initials ND.

Elderly people

There was a strong emphasis in the interviews on the importance of family support and mutual care, but at the same time, there were tensions in some families, and there were some respondents who did not have families. Their isolation was very marked.

Three respondents lived alone, but the rest lived with other family members: there was a variety of family patterns, including couples (three), couples or single parents with adult children (five), and the remainder were living with married sons (14) or daughters and their families (five).

The emphasis on family support was strong:

---

[2] More detail of the methods and the fieldwork is given in Bowes and Dar 1996.

...whenever there is any problem, they all come and help. When my husband took ill, he had to go to hospital and my family came, my daughter and my son came from England. (ELD119) (This woman also lived with her son and his family).

> What do you need someone else for if the family's here? (ELD104)

In some families however, there were tensions, revealed to us despite the conditions of many interviews, in which family members were nearby. For example, one man referred to the lack of space, and his problems in paying rent, which his son was demanding. One couple had moved away from their son's house, due to difficulties in their relationship, and two women were hoping to move out of their relatives' houses for similar reasons.

Within families, roles varied, in that some elderly people were closely involved in family work and mutual care, whereas others required more care themselves, or had, in their eyes, retired:

> I have done my time. Now it's their [children's] turn to take on responsibility. (ELD 118)

Those who required care were not necessarily the oldest people in the sample. People who lived alone could experience extreme isolation:

> I can't do anything...I don't go out alone. I get scared. I don't watch television, because it scares me. So I just stay here. I don't have any family, I don't have any children. (ELD112)

It was relatively unusual for interviewees to talk about direct experience of racism, though one man spoke of an exclusionary and racist society:

> Don't even trust the police, because they lie, and only stick up for their own kids. I've been here since the war. I worked on the machines for the war. I know how the government works. I don't trust them. These people fight for freedom for themselves. What about us, the Asians? (ELD121)

There was a strong emphasis on the importance of Pakistani custom, especially religion, which was often described as central to people's lives:

> We have to hold on to our religion, and the place to do that is at the Mosque, because it teaches us to treat everyone equal, regardless of race, colour, creed. (ELD113)

The emphasis on the family, and the importance of religion was linked with a negative view of residential care for elderly people:

> Maybe if you have no-one, God forbid, then it's OK [residential care], but I have my family around me, so I don't need it. (ELD120)

> If we became ill, our son would look after us, and we would return to Pakistan. (ELD119)

> No, I could not use them. Just the idea that nobody wants you is terrible. If there was no-one else, and you could not cope, then some people might go, but I don't think I would go. I would rather die. (ELD131).

Those who attended the community groups valued them, though there were some respondents who preferred not to use them, and sought other sources of help outside the family.

Community groups were seen as an opportunity to get out of the house by people who otherwise would find it difficult:

> There is nothing else to do here all day. So I suppose at least I get out of the house. And they take me there and bring me back. I go to [x] group on a Monday, and [y] group on a Tuesday and a Thursday. So it gets me out. (ELD102)

Group activities were generally positively received:

> ...we sit and talk and pray, and there's a lunch club. Sometimes we do other things, play games or go out. (ELD116)

> We talk and we have lunch and we pray. Sometimes we have religious discussions or we go out. (ELD119)

Some people were unable to attend the groups:

> How can I go [to a group]? I have so many problems for the last three or four years. I have been very ill. I had cancer.(ELD103)

Daughter: She stopped going because we were scared she would hurt herself going up and down the stairs to attend the centre. (ELD104)

There were others who preferred not to use the groups:

Yes, I know about the groups, but I do not go to them. I have my own group of friends, and we meet every now and again, and that's enough. I am a busy person. There is always something to do. (ELD131)

I have lived here for so many years, it is best to stick to the family. There is community support if you need it, and there are some groups now as well, but I do not go. (ELD129)

Many in the sample were suffering from poor health, which, in some cases, prevented them from using the groups. In some cases, people had stayed at home once their health deteriorated, and were not receiving further social service support. There were some suggestions that the referral system might not be effective in ensuring care as needs increased. In the case of those without family support, health problems could cause great difficulty. A man who lived alone described how a compassionate neighbour had come to his assistance when he was seriously ill:

My neighbours, they came to see me, and I had a temperature and was feeling really ill. They felt sorry for me and took me into their house for about two weeks and nursed me back to good health. They looked after me and cared for me as one of their own. (ELD115)

In several cases, people found their health problems very restricting:

I can't even go out on my own: my eyes are weak, and I have had operations, but they have not made that much difference. There's always someone with me. I can't go out, [unless] my daughter-in-law goes with me. (ELD108)

There was a marked lack of knowledge of the Social Work Department, and some bad experiences of using it, as well as some more positive ones. People who had received services were often unclear about whence it had come. Only two people were able to give accurate information about the location of and services offered by the Social Work Department.

There was a strong element of resistance to help from outside the family:

[My son] has his own business, and he doesn't like getting money from the Government. Once, he was ill...we had no money, but he wouldn't take it from the Government...ND: Is it just because the money's from the Government? ELD120: No, he doesn't like the forms. He says they ask too many questions. He doesn't know why they have to ask so much. (ELD120)

I don't need to [look for outside help]. My family is all here, and my son will live with us. (ELD116)

Others, however, indicated that they would appreciate some help:

What I would really like is some help for my daughter, because she does everything. No-one could look after us like our daughter can. I mean someone else would come and spend their time here and [then] leave. What I would really like is some help for her. (ELD117)

Of those who had received help from the Social Work Department, some were appreciative:

I try to do everything myself, but if it's beyond me, then Mrs X [social worker] is nearby and she's very good. Whenever I go and see her, she has always helped me out willingly. (ELD113)

Others were critical of the service:

Once I asked for a home help. I filled in some forms, but the girl never came back again. I don't know if she's left now.....I haven't been able to go back and find out. (ELD108)

Perhaps the most negative experience was described in a few words:

We went in a taxi, but they asked me to come back on Thursday because no-one could speak our language. (ELD112)

This woman was alone, she had no possessions and no family, and had described herself as too frightened to go out. The woman in whose house she was a lodger had taken her to the office: though she did not describe it at length - she said no more about it than the sentence quoted - the visit had clearly been traumatic.

The perspectives of carers were also noted, and though they were not the main focus of the study, it was clear that they lacked support from outside the family, and that the burden of care could be considerable:

> Daughter: Sometimes, when she becomes really ill I have to be with her all the time, especially if she catches a cold or starts vomiting, but no matter what, she will read her Friday prayers. (ELD104)

A woman caring for a disabled daughter explained how her own difficulties made this harder:

> I suffer from bad health myself and can't go out. I have a heart problem, and I've had this pain for the last six months in my back and side. The rooms are cold, and I can't afford the heating, so I switch it off and put the gas heater on when I need it. (ELD 114)

Community group workers

The community group workers took pleasure in their work, and valued it, especially their ability to work with people whose language and culture they shared:

> I understand their culture. I understand their language, their religion. That's why I think they feel more relaxed when they talk to us. (CWK303)

> We don't have any problems in communicating and talking to people. We understand their background, so we can understand their problems. (CWK306)

They gave detailed accounts of their perceptions of the needs and preferences of Pakistani elderly people, which linked with the accounts given by the elderly people themselves. Needs and preferences were seen as requiring a distinctive manner of delivery, including staff who shared the ethnic background of their clients. The staff raised the issue of lack of knowledge of services among the Pakistani community, and saw the role of the groups as important in trying to improve this.

There was marked frustration among these workers concerning their relationship with the Social Work Department:

> We want to do something for them, but the only thing we can do is send them to other agencies. We cannot do anything. (CWK302)

> I find that my clients could do with more help in the house. It is not that they don't want to accept any help from the social services.....but there are not any Asian people employed. They need home helps from the same background, and from the same religion as them, because they have the idea how to respect these people. (CWK305)

They raised the issue of referrals, suggesting that the Department was not responsive to their cases:

> You try to tell them 'Look, this person has an Asian background, so you do this and you do this and you do this'. I have come across nice white people who provide these type of services, and are flexible to what my referrals [need]. But what happens is because they cannot be a priority.....so very few people end up getting these services. (CWK305)

> Yes, we refer them, but we never get any replies or response. (CWK307)

This worker also felt that her advice was not effectively sought:

> I think [SWD] staff need to be consulting more with the workers about the elderly people's needs. Some people really don't know anything. (CWK307)

The staff also spoke about their position as employees, their lack of training, and what they saw as their lack of prospects. One worker was particularly cynical about his prospects of advancement:

> You see the white people will only tolerate us to a certain level. They will give us the low jobs, but the higher positions, they will keep for white people, either that, or your senior officer will not recommend you for promotion. This is true of the Civil Service, the Social Work Department, of everywhere. (CWK306)

In general, these staff looked towards the Pakistani community for their work satisfaction, and had detailed knowledge of it. They did not perceive their role as part of the broader movement towards community care, and only one was aware of the Social Work Department's anti-racist policy

Social Work Department staff

The seven white Social Work Department staff had very little experience of working with Pakistani elderly people, despite being based in areas of concentrated Pakistani residence. One had seen so few Pakistani clients that she felt they were outnumbered by staff:

> We have more black staff than we have black clients. (SOC207)

Another felt that the clients were there, but confessed that she had not worked with them:

> I think that is because we have, or we did have....a black social worker who dealt with the majority of ethnic minority cases. (SOC203)

One of the two Pakistani workers had extensive experience of working with Pakistani elderly people, previously in the voluntary sector. The other was relatively new to her work.

The white social workers recognised issues such as the possibility of family problems, the need to respect cultural preferences, and the lack of knowledge of services in the Pakistani community, but found it difficult to see how these issues might be addressed:

> Well, I think a lot of it is cultural differences. I think even in our own community, white people, you have got to respect religions, so you have got the exact same in the Asian community. You have got to respect religion. And a lot of that, we are not totally aware of. (SOC203)

> [It's] really difficult. I just feel with the elderly, there is just such a gap. (SOC204)

They suggested that one reason why they were not getting clients might be that they were not getting referrals from the community based groups:

> They should have been referring them over to us. I think what is happening is that they are actually doing [the work] themselves. (SOC201)

Suggestions like this added to the indications in the other sets of interviews that Pakistani elderly people were not getting referred to the Social Work Department. The Social Work Department staff nevertheless felt that the community based groups were an important source of services for local Pakistani elderly people, though they were not all happy that the service was good.

> I don't think we've fully addressed the needs of the black elderly. For example, the initiative that's running, there's no *halal* food. They have fish and chips. They have fish and chips every bloody meal. (SOC201)

There was some questioning of the activities of the groups. One worker was worried about the nature of current provision for Pakistani elderly people, particularly a lunch club in which she was peripherally involved:

> It frustrates me, because I think it could be far better utilised. And it disturbs me a little that the men and women are kept separate, and it seems to be older women that use it far more than men. (SOC209).

They argued that the Department was not providing appropriate services for this client group, and that they themselves were ill-equipped, as staff, to do so. They wanted more training in how to work with Pakistani clients, particularly concerning cultural factors. Some of the anti-racist training they had previously received was seen as important, but not very helpful with their day to day work:

> I think it was helpful to some people. I think some people saw it as maybe one-sided in as much as they were talking about a learning process for us, and it wasn't really geared to the fact that I think we both need a learning process. (SOC203)

> We used to get a lot of anti-racist training, and a lot of people got angry about that. And we got hostile about it...To me, it doesn't seem to matter how much training they get. In fact, the more training they get, the more resentful they become. (SOC207)

The two Pakistani workers appeared to be dealing with the Pakistani clients, and had a clear view of their needs and preferences. One was very enthusiastic about her work:

> I really enjoy working with elderly people....I really enjoy talking to them. And because I think I have confidence with

them....they can talk to us, because we are bilingual....They are very very loving and caring, they miss you if you are not there, and all these things. I really feel proud of these things. They have trust in you. (SOC206)

Using her own experience and knowledge of the local Pakistani community she spoke about the lack of knowledge of social work services:

They are not sure what they [social services] do....if we help them, they think I'm the Social Worker. Anyone helping them, whether they're working or not are [seen as] Social Workers.....They are not clear what we do. One woman approached me. She said 'I need a Social Worker. Can you be my Social Worker?' I say 'I'm not a Social Worker'. And she says 'How can I get one?' It's only those families that have problems that can have Social Workers. It is very difficult for them to understand how the Department works. (SOC206)

The white staff took a rather pessimistic view of the prospects for improvements in services. One worker had come to the depressing conclusion that little could be done, and that a vicious circle had developed, which needed breaking:

Because we do not have the experience, we do not have the people coming forward, [and] they don't have the services for black people. (SOC207)

In her view, therefore, people would not come forward if the services were not appropriate, and the services would not improve because they had no experience. Some saw the role of the voluntary sector in the new care management arrangements as offering opportunities for improvement:

I think we would rely a lot on....other charity groupings to make demands, and to give some indications of.... services they could start to provide because they have seen a gap that we are not meeting, and they could provide it and we could buy into it. I see a partnership developing. (SOC204)

But others were more sceptical:

I think it would be better if it was within Social Work, because it could be monitored - the level of services, their standards, that type of thing. When you're buying in, you're buying in the cheapest, not necessarily the best quality of care. (SOC202)

Conclusions and implications

In common with other studies (e.g. McFarland *et al* 1989, Atkin *et al* 1989, Atkin 1991, Jackson and Field 1989), our work suggests that, though there was a lack of uptake of services, this did not indicate lack of need. Pakistani elderly people in Glasgow needed more information about services, which needed to be appropriately delivered. There was potential for greater use of the community groups, and particular need for support for carers (cf. Chakrabarti and Cadman 1994, Atkin and Rollings 1992, Brownlie 1992).

The problem of lack of knowledge of services required to be tackled in a more positive way. Other studies (Tester and Meredith 1987, Allen Hogg and Peace 1992) have found low levels of knowledge of services among white elderly people, and there is evidence that these are lower for 'Asian' (including Pakistani) people (Atkin, *et al* 1989). Translated leaflets had been used, but it was clear that these had not achieved their objective. There were suggestions in the data that word of mouth was important for spreading information, confirming the findings of other studies (e.g. Jackson and Field 1989, Wardhaugh 1991). Tester and Meredith (1987) recommend the use of personal information, and developed an information pack for use by a range of professionals, including social workers, to convey information personally (Tester 1992). They emphasise the importance of methods of ensuring the accuracy of information given.

The literature suggests that community groups can have a vital role in ensuring the receipt of appropriate services by minority ethnic communities (Fenton 1987, Jackson and Field 1989, Atkin *et al* 1989 Blakemore and Boneham 1992). The community groups in Glasgow were fulfilling a very important role, and should have been a major resource in the development and delivery of appropriate and effective services. Compared with groups elsewhere, they had some advantages, in that they were well distributed through the city, their funding appeared relatively secure, and they apparently enjoyed good relationships with the local community. But there were problems with the referral system, with the relationship with the Department, in connection with referrals and the position of the voluntary group workers, and with the concentration on these groups as the main source of service for Pakistani elderly people.

The anti-racist approach of Strathclyde Social Work Department was important, but needed to be complemented by the development of ethnically sensitive practice. The importance of anti-racist practice has been firmly established (see e.g. Patel 1990, Dominelli 1991), but, as we argued earlier, there is a danger that over-emphasis on it can lead to issues of ethnicity and ethnic sensitivity being ignored. More recent writers, such as Chakrabarti (1991) and Blakemore and Boneham (1994) have argued that social services must be sensitive to people's cultural preferences. The development of ethnically sensitive practice is not a simple matter, but there are suggestions in our, and other work, of appropriate steps which might be taken.

The staff we interviewed asked for further training and support to facilitate their work with Pakistani elderly people, recognising in particular, their ignorance about Pakistani culture, and staff indicated commitment to the principle of ethnically sensitive practice. There were also some examples in the data of insensitive practice, such as the lack of appropriate food at community groups, failure to recognise the importance of religion, and failure to understand the preference for segregating men and women.

Since the Pakistani population in Britain is highly differentiated, the first step in the development of ethnically sensitive practice must be recognition that a checklist of 'cultural tips' cannot be produced (Blakemore and Boneham 1994:125). At the same time however, there exist guides to awareness of the range of customs which may be followed: Blakemore and Boneham (1994) suggest Henley (1979), Mares, Henley and Baxter (1985) and Shukla (1991). Ethnic sensitivity could also be improved in the area of language: allocating all work with South Asians to South Asian workers can lead to a process of ghettoisation, detrimental to both staff and clients. White staff could be instructed in basic elements of local languages, thus enabling them to show respect for their clients, and put themselves at some disadvantage, and they could also be trained in more effective communication with people for whom English is a second language, and in the appropriate and effective use of interpreters. Blakemore and Boneham (1994) also recommend that professional teams should evaluate their work, by following up cases, by collaboration within teams, and by consultation with local minority ethnic communities.

Employment and training issues arose for both community group workers and Social Work Department staff. For Department staff, training issues were linked to the development of ethnically sensitive practice, and a strong case can be made for further training of social workers in the possible cultural preferences of their clients, provided this is linked with an ability to challenge stereotyping. For community group workers there was a need for their work to be more valued, and for professional development to be available: there were indications that the community group workers were somewhat marginalised, that in their view, the basis of their employment was their linguistic rather than their professional skills, and that they did not have opportunities for advancement.

The system of referrals between the community groups and the Department appeared not to be operating effectively. This problem was linked with the issues previously discussed here, namely, lack of knowledge, the position of the community groups, the need for more ethnically sensitive practice and the employment and training issues, and we would argue that movement in all these areas would help alleviate the problem of referrals. At the same time, literature suggests that research focussing on the issue of referrals might be worthwhile, to identify specific areas of practice which might be altered. It should be noted however, that this is a difficult area to research, due to the potential for variation in referral and screening systems (Hall 1974, Rowlings 1978, Petch *et al* 1996).

The pivotal position of the community group workers is clear in this area. They valued their work with clients, and recognised their own abilities to do it, yet they were expected to make referrals to a Social Work Department which they felt was not ethnically sensitive, which marginalised them as workers, and which had proved insensitive to previous referrals. Improvement in areas of difficulty like this seems to be in the hands of Social Work Departments.

7. A neglected problem: minority ethnic elders with dementia

Irene Anderson and Julie Brownlie

Introduction

Other contributors to this book describe the legislative and policy changes which shape current health and social welfare provision, and discuss the general situation of Scotland's minority ethnic population. We focus on a small, but growing, group within that population: minority ethnic elders who suffer from a dementing illness. If, as Norman (1986) suggests, black elders are in a position of triple jeopardy - that is disadvantaged because of age, ethnicity and the fact that services are not accessible to them - then black or minority ethnic elders with dementia face another dimension of disadvantage and, as such, could be argued to be in a position of multiple jeopardy.

The chapter has grown out of an exploratory piece of research carried out five years ago by one of the authors (Brownlie 1991) on behalf of the Dementia Services Development Centre, after a workshop at Stirling University had revealed how little information was available in Scotland about the specific issue of dementia amongst minority ethnic groups. The research used case studies, provided by staff in a variety of settings and geographical locations, to tease out some of the issues of providing appropriate services for this group.

All the staff interviewed were working with minority ethnic elders who had either been diagnosed as suffering from dementia, or to varying degrees had shown signs indicative of the illness. Finding a 'sample' proved difficult, and this seemed to reflect a twofold lack of awareness: of dementia as a possible problem among minority ethnic organisations, and of the special needs of minority ethnic elders among those who were providing dementia services. The unreliability of transcultural diagnosis and the fact that minority ethnic elders were known to have little contact with mainstream services suggested less that such lack of awareness indicated a lack of problem, than that dementia amongst minority ethnic groups in Scotland might be a hidden problem.

Exploration of the issues arising from the 1991 case studies supported this hypothesis. Brownlie found that there were minority ethnic elders with dementia but they were largely invisible; that failure to overcome language problems, or to reach out effectively to minority ethnic families, meant that they lacked information about both dementia and available service provision; that existing services were in general staffed by white workers and geared to the norms and needs of the majority population; and that the failure to recognise dementia as a problem, even within their own communities, could leave minority ethnic individuals and families isolated through lack of support rather than by choice.

Bearing in mind that the case study interviews took place nearly five years ago we set out, in 1996, to answer the question 'What, if anything, has changed since then?'; and it is interesting to note that the first response of many of those to whom we put this question was 'precious little', or words to that effect. In fact our necessarily limited investigation of current practice and research initiatives in Scotland suggests that there have been changes, but that it is difficult to get an overview of their nature or extent. In 1991 the literature on minority ethnic elders with dementia was predominantly American. While there are now British studies in this area, there is still little which relates specifically to the situation of minority ethnic elders with dementia in Scotland.

It is, of course, important to remember that to talk of minority ethnic elders collectively is to mask the enormous differences which exist both between cultural sub-groups and within individual experience (Blakemore 1994); and that the way older people define themselves changes over time (Askham 1993). Much of our material focuses on elders of South Asian origin - the largest minority ethnic group in Scotland - but we use it primarily to identify issues common to all minority groups. The term 'minority ethnic' is used throughout to describe black or minority groups; and 'elders' to refer to those older people defined as such by their own communities.

We begin this chapter by reviewing some literature which locates research relating to services for minority ethnic elders with dementia in the general context of dementia research, and of research on people from minority ethnic groups both as recipients of health and welfare provision generally and as providers of informal care. We identify key issues from the 1991 research, including the need for cultural sensitivity and the dangers of cultural stereotyping, and illustrate them through case examples. Finally, we outline what we have been able to learn about service provision in Scotland in 1996, and discuss the implications for policy, planning and service provision for this particularly vulnerable section of the minority ethnic population.

Reviewing the literature

Writing in 1990, Patel noted that research on black elders could hardly be described as a 'growth industry'. Others have pointed to the scarcity of clinical studies of mental illness and ethnic minorities generally (Glendenning, 1990), and of minority ethnic elders in particular (Manthorpe and Hettiaratchy, 1993). In relation to dementia specifically, Richards and Brayne (1996: 383) comment that:

> the detection and management of dementia among ethnic minority elders has received little attention, even though this disorder is associated with considerable disability and suffering.

Reviewing literature relevant to minority ethnic group elders with dementia, Manthorpe (1994) cites our own study (Brownlie, 1991) as 'the only specific document to focus on dementia and ethnicity' and comments especially on its use of case studies. Tibbs (1996) has since provided a more up to date practice account of the experiences of one minority ethnic elder with dementia. Making a virtue of the continued shortage of this kind of direct focus on dementia and ethnicity, Manthorpe (1994) draws attention to the value of wider discussion which relates ethnicity to health and social care, old age and mental illness.

Health and social care

Studies, mostly in England, in the eighties and early nineties highlighted the extent to which both health services and local authorities were failing to meet the needs of minority ethnic elders through wrongly assuming that this group had information about services, and that the failure to use them reflected a lack of demand (eg. Bhalla and Blakemore 1981). Many of these studies pointed to the difficulties minority ethnic elders have with communication in English, to the lack of interpreters and to the non-availability of translated information. Others, whilst accepting that such factors limit people's knowledge about services, cautioned against the assumption that knowledge of services necessarily leads to use of services (eg. Berry 1981). Research suggested that it often does not - both because services may not be seen as culturally appropriate (Norman 1986) and because minority ethnic elders may have experienced, or fear, racist abuse when using mainstream services (Bhalla and Blakemore 1981). Macleod's (1988) study of Scottish voluntary organisations found that they too were failing, through their open door approach, to reach minority ethnic group users; and Pharoah and Redmond (1991) described voluntary provision as generally 'fraught with problems'. A similar picture, of low service uptake in a situation characterised by a lack of interpreters and culturally appropriate services, was revealed by health service research. The one exception, in terms of service use, was in relation to primary care (Qureshi 1991) but here too a Scottish Office survey found, for example, that 31 per cent of Chinese men and 41 per cent of Chinese women had difficulty in making themselves understood by their GP (Smith 1991).

Patel (1993) is amongst many who point out that the 'market dynamic' established by the NHS and Community Care Act, 1990 has done little to improve the situation, though she suggests that the fact that the legislation does at least recognise the needs of 'minority communities' should be seen as progress. Walker and Ahmad (1994), reporting on research in Bradford, contrast the Act's potential for individualised needs-led care with the danger of increased marginalisation and resource problems for minority groups.

Other recent initiatives and reports have relevance for minority ethnic elders with dementia, but it has to be noted that most do not refer directly to Scotland. Surprisingly, this is true even of Atkin and Rollings's (1993b) Community Care in a Multi-Racial Britain (sic). That Scotland has a small minority ethnic population, that there are as yet few minority ethnic elders, that - even in the future - the actual number of minority ethnic dementia sufferers will never be high, have all been advanced to justify not taking the respective problems of these groups seriously. Not only do such arguments ignore the rights of individuals, but failure to plan and provide properly for these groups is inherently racist (Manthorpe, 1994).

The Race Relations: Code of Practice in Primary Health Care Services (CRE 1992) sets out to promote understanding of the law on racial equality and draws attention to examples of good practice in Britain as a whole. Recommending that both purchasers and providers of primary health care services should keep and monitor ethnic records, it suggests their use 'to assess the situation of particular groups in terms of the services provided' (p.39). Minority ethnic elders suffering from dementia do not seem to have received this kind of attention in either England or Scotland.

A major English study, however, examines how effectively primary care services are meeting the needs of minority ethnic elders generally (Pharoah 1995). Amongst its recommendations are two of special relevance: that the uptake and quality of over-75 health checks for people from minority ethnic groups should be specifically monitored; and that the question of mental health assessment and treatment within primary care for ethnic minority elders 'should be urgently addressed'. This latter point is echoed in a parallel study (Askham et al 1995), which describes and analyses current social and health care services in both mainstream and separate settings and from the perspective of purchasers, providers and minority ethnic elders. Stressing the complexity of communication between minority ethnic elders and professionals, it draws attention to the limited usefulness of translated written information: many such elders are not literate, the information often fails to reach those for whom it is intended, and no opportunity is created for further discussion.

Old age and dementia

Old age and dementia are both difficult to define. Life expectancy is shorter for minority ethnic elders - and it is generally accepted that within the Asian population, for example, people age faster and require services earlier than in the population as a whole (Boneham 1989, Blakemore and Boneham 1994). Wide variations also exist in the expectations which different cultural groups have of their elders and, in particular, in the extent to which deterioration in mental functioning is viewed as part of normal ageing rather than as an indication of dementia.

Pollitt (1996) draws attention to an additional ambiguity in relation to dementia, of where services should be located professionally. This is a factor which besets the problem of service provision, and underlies secondary questions of whether mainstream or separate settings are preferable. Should diagnosis depend principally on GPs or geriatricians or psychogeriatricians or psychiatrists? When should community support be provided by health care and when by social work staff? Should residential provision and its funding be the responsibility of the health service or of local authorities? In the absence of answers to such questions, dementia sufferers and their carers continue to fall between services. The situation of those from minority ethnic groups remains even more hazardous, since each of the service providers may define them primarily in terms of their ethnicity and so fail to take appropriate responsibility for meeting their needs (Scott 1994).

Many of the present generation of minority ethnic elders have come to this country comparatively late in life. They find themselves in strange surroundings, struggling to make sense of a culture and language they do not understand and often feeling alienated even from the younger relatives on whom they depend. It is not surprising that some appear confused, depressed and disorientated, or express their bewilderment and sense of loss in somatic symptoms or withdrawal - signs that may be difficult to differentiate from the onset of dementia (Boneham et al. 1994). Little reliable information has so far been available about either the prevalence or the incidence of dementia within different minority ethnic communities, but Manthorpe (1994) draws attention to current work in his area by the University of Liverpool's Health and Ethnicity Project (see Blakemore and Boneham 1994).

Problems of diagnosis

Difficulty in diagnosing dementia amongst minority ethnic elders has to be seen in the context of the wider situation. An English survey of 700 GPs (Alzheimer's Disease Society 1995) revealed low levels of knowledge about dementia, poor diagnostic practice, and evidence that the early symptoms of dementia are often missed, or misdiagnosed, in the population at large (see also Killeen 1991). Nor is reluctance to acknowledge deterioration of mental functioning as a symptom of illness confined to minority ethnic families (Pollitt et al. 1990). But research has shown that in general minority ethnic groups are more at risk of misdiagnosis, and of inappropriate or delayed treatment, than are other mental health service users; and that this may be particularly true for dementia sufferers.

It is widely accepted (eg. Fernando 1988) that cognitive tests commonly used in the diagnosis of dementia are culture-bound and dependent on language and literacy; that both the social behaviour and physical symptoms of minority ethnic elders may be misinterpreted (Squires 1991); that the so-called 'activities of daily living' used in assessment are culturally determined (Pollitt 1996); and that reticence in talking about their elderly relative, as well as communication problems, make it difficult to obtain the informant history which is normally an important component of dementia diagnosis and assessment (Solomon 1992). Pollitt (1996) describes the recent development in India of culturally appropriate cognitive and functional screening instruments for use with illiterate populations (Ganguli and Ratcliffe 1995), which may contribute to overcoming some of the diagnostic problems.

Cultural sensitivity and racism

Dismissing cultural arguments (Rack 1983, for example) which, at best, excuse clinicians for being culturally ignorant, and, at worst, blame minority groups for their differences Fernando (1988) has argued that clinicians need to take account not only of their personal cultural bias and racism, but also of the culture and racism of their profession and society generally. The historical, cultural, socio-economic and political significance of racism in the experiences of minority ethnic elders is crucial in understanding their perception of relationships with professionals who do not share their ethnic background (eg. White and Kaur 1995).

Racism can come disguised as cultural sensitivity. Blieszner and Shifflett (1988) drew attention to the danger that the reactions of minority ethnic groups may be pathologised so that parallels with the wider population are lost. Similarly, Manthorpe and Hettiaratchy (1993: 173) warn that over-emphasis on individual and cultural responses and explanations can 'divert attention from the power issues of racism and inequalities'. In the same vein, Ahmad (1993: 31), maintaining that the research agenda has for too long been largely defined by white researchers, calls for ethnic minorities ' to reappropriate the responsibility for defining our own realities'. He makes the specific point that there is a need for dementia research which concentrates on the perceptions of health and service delivery of people from minority ethnic groups and with making the system fit their needs. One way to to do this is to explore the experiences of individual dementia sufferers and their families.

Dementia and racism: the experience of minority ethnic elders

No diagnosis of dementia was made in relation to two of the 1991 case study elders: in one because cultural explanations were used to account for confused behaviour; and in the other, because the family denied that any problem existed. In only one case, and only after a residential placement had been tried and had failed, did more than one set of relatives share the care of an elderly person. None of the families had any support from their community, perhaps because dementia was poorly understood and, once it could no longer be denied, was equated with mental illness - leading to feelings of 'shame' for the families and non-acceptance from the community.

For the elderly people in the case studies, their daily lives were constrained first and foremost by the demands of the family's work. Their experiences included being locked in one room when the family was out, eating at strange times, sleeping in the day time and, for one woman who had suffered a stroke some years previously, spending five months of each year in Pakistan. For most it was an environment which provided relatively few clues or reminders of their past, and sometimes actively contributed to their confusion, but at least maintained a bedrock of shared culture and language.

Once their illness progressed, the elderly people found themselves in a variety of care settings - hospitals, day centres, residential homes - where all experienced major problems in communicating their needs. Lack of interpreters or minority ethnic staff leave minority ethnic users in such surroundings isolated and effectively cut off from staff and other residents or patients. Manthorpe (1993) points out how other factors can reinforce the isolation. For example, since elderly men outnumber women in the Asian community, a single Asian day centre user may find himself to be not just the only black person but also the only man. He might, of course, also be the only dementia sufferer. In addition, such users are effectively excluded from reality orientation and reminiscence groups because these groups commonly employ materials that have no meaning for minority ethnic elders.

Stevenson (1989) has noted that, even when there are no language barriers, trying to 'relate past to present' can be problematic if workers lack knowledge of the countries from which older people have come; and finding oneself in strange and institutional surroundings can be a frightening experience for anyone. It is hard for most of us to imagine what it must feel like for someone with dementia who may have lost a sense of their own past and is particularly vulnerable to unfamiliar surroundings, to be surrounded by people who do not speak their language or show any understanding of their background and customs. Language barriers cause problems, but there are difficulties in communication which go beyond lack of a shared language and suggest an abuse of power more indicative of racist practices than of a mere failure of cultural awareness - practices which accentuate the powerless position occupied by confused elders in our society generally.

An alarming illustration of these points came in a passing comment which a worker made about one of the 1991 case study elders:

> Because Mr. P had progressed so far by the time he came to us, there was no problem with his food. Normally he would not eat the same food as us, but like other sufferers he had no hangups about food and would eat what was given to him.

The assumption that people who are ill and appear to be out of touch with their surroundings forfeit the need or right to be treated with cultural respect constitutes a special danger for minority ethnic dementia sufferers.

Especially if they move into residential care, minority ethnic elders with dementia may lose not only their homes or sense of autonomy but also the context in which their cultural values, and hence their sense of self, are reinforced. Arie (1985) has written that people with dementia need security, stimulation and patience. Communication problems and alien surroundings can deprive minority ethnic elders of all three - as happened to Mrs. W.

Aged 92, Mrs. W had spent most of her life on a farm in Hong Kong. She has three sons, two of whom live in Scotland. Her husband died 20 years ago. When she was 86, and still mentally alert, Mrs. W came to live with a grandson in the small town where the family had a Chinese restaurant. Over the previous two years Mrs. W had become increasingly confused: using the floor as a toilet, mixing day with night and wandering out of the house believing that she was still on the farm. The family worked six days a week, sixteen hours a day, and they felt they had no option but to lock their grandmother's room when they went out to ensure her safety. Day care was offered but proved unworkable because of the family's work commitments. Assessment took a long time, partly because of problems in finding interpreters, but eventually Mrs. W was admitted to residential care.

An independent interpreter was sometimes used, but generally Mrs. W's grand daughter did the interpreting and this was the case when Mrs. W was assessed by a psychogeriatrician. Mrs. W's social worker recalled:

> When someone speaks English, the assessment goes on for about an hour; but, in this case, the doctor would ask questions, T would ask her grandmother, she would say something three sentences long and T would say 'no'. I'm not sure if the procedure was right.

Interpretation was a crucial issue in this case, not just in order to carry out a proper assessment but to ensure in the long term that care staff would be able to maintain a dialogue with Mrs. W independent of her family. What was needed, in the words of the social worker, was someone who would 'be there every step of the way'. In the absence not only of this ideal provision, but of an interpreter or any minority ethnic staff, problems arose. The staff were often not able to interpret Mrs. W's behaviour: as when she appeared 'grumpy' to the staff but her grandson was able to explain that she had a headache; or when the staff saw her as aggressive, but later realised that they had reacted to the rapidity of her Chinese dialect. Lack of cultural awareness also created problems: Mrs. W, for example, had always worn trousers and was not used to wearing socks or underwear indoors. Her social worker recalled that in the Home: 'they tried to get her into dresses and to wear underpants....trying to socialise her into the way everyone else is'.

Mrs. W's family never discussed their feelings with the social worker, or complained about any aspect of Mrs. W's care: 'it was as if they feared that help would be withdrawn completely if they did'. On the other hand the residential staff noted that the granddaughter 'did what she could' but that when the family visited they did not stay long. It is not clear if there were different expectations of the family because they were Chinese, or if it was just that this family was more 'visible'. Mrs. W and her behaviour were also visible: people complained more about her wandering into other people's rooms, for instance, though this was by no means unusual behaviour in the residential home.

Chinese food was organised through the family restaurant. The social worker obtained Chinese videos to help keep Mrs. W in touch with her own culture, but attempts to find a Chinese volunteer befriender failed. When the social worker had first become involved she was advised that the Chinese community 'look after their own', an assumption that proved unfounded and racist in its consequences.

The story of Amos: 1996

We turn now to an account, from the Journal of Dementia Care (March/April 1996), of how a particular minority ethnic elder with dementia was successfully cared for by his own community, after the lack of culturally sensitive mental health services had nearly proved 'deadly' for him.

Tibbs (1996) describes what happened to an elderly Jamaican man, living in an English town and suffering from multi-infarct dementia, when he was admitted to a local psychiatric hospital for a three week assessment after an outburst of aggression which alarmed people because it involved a knife. Describing his 'catastrophic decline' (Kitwood, 1989), Tibbs points to the multiple disadvantages which determined the way he was perceived and treated in the hospital: 'He was a man. He was a big man. He was a big black man. And he had a history of aggression'. Very quickly Amos took on the characteristics of someone in the terminal stage of dementia. On this basis, the medical staff refused all requests by the family to have him home, even though he had been admitted as an informal patient.

Eventually a Jamaican friend working in the Social Services Department advised the family on how to make a formal complaint, and to request that care in the community should at least be tried. It was tried, and it worked - thanks to the efforts of the main family care-giver, supported by a specialist social worker for dementia (Tibbs herself), and with 24 hour cover provided by a rota of carers (including one who was the 'lynch pin') from the local Jamaican community and Pentecostal church. The Social Services Department continued to provide home carers to look after Amos' physically frail partner until her death some months later. Amos was helped to deal with this loss and, some time later, to make the transition to residential care successfully. The family remained in close touch with him. They have been actively involved in helping the staff to understand Amos' needs, and how best to manage episodes of agitation or aggression, as well as his previously untreated arthritic pain which came to be seen as a possible trigger for his occasional violence.

Commenting at the end of the article on what she herself had learnt from this case, the author writes (p.21):

> How a system designed to care for people can actually abuse them. How the lack of culturally sensitive services for people from ethnic minorities can be deadly - as it nearly was in this case. How the people who really knew what Amos needed were those closest to him

Some central issues

'Looking after their own'

In focusing on aspects of minority ethnic culture which reduce the demand for statutory services rather than drawing attention to their inappropriateness, two arguments have predominated: that minority ethnic communities 'look after their own'; and that it is the family, as an undifferentiated unit, which does the looking after. Both arguments ignore the many cultural, migratory and social distinctions within and between minority ethnic communities. As the 1991 case studies illustrated, family and network patterns vary widely and caring roles are differently assigned within different minority groups. In some, it may still be common for extended families to live together but this cannot be assumed to be a norm (Smith 1991; Gunaratnam 1993) even in their countries of origin (White and Kaur 1995). Moreover, such intergenerational households are subject, as in the wider population, to family stress resulting from emotional, accommodation and financial pressures as well as from the physical tasks of caring. Again, as in white households, the principal carers are nearly always women; shared family care is comparatively rare; and carers receive little substantial support from either formal or informal sources (Cox 1995). Although it has been suggested that community care may depend more heavily on informal care in minority ethnic communities than in others (Atkin 1992) research on minority ethnic carers is rare (Twigg 1992).

Few studies compare the experiences of minority ethnic carers with those of other carers; or those of people caring for a demented and a non-demented elderly person. Cox (1995), in an American study, found that while for white carers of dementia sufferers the mental impairment of the sufferer was experienced as the major cause of stress, black caregivers attributed stress predominantly to their perceived lack of informal support and a 'sense of incompetency'. Philp et al. (1995) in an English survey, found that the supporters of elderly people with dementia were more intensively engaged in caring, and had higher levels of unmet need for mainstream medical and domiciliary care, than those with non-demented dependents. The nine Asian and Afro/Caribbean dementia sufferers in Badger's (1989) study, though they were more physically disabled, were found to be receiving lower levels of community nursing care than the white sample. Minority ethnic dementia sufferers and their carers, then, emerge from these and other studies as being subject to multiple jeopardy.

One of a small number of British studies of Asian carers was undertaken by Gunaratnam (1993), who interviewed the main carers of 33 elderly people. She reports that only eight of the elders in her study were living in an extended family household. Amongst other findings were that the majority of carers were more concerned with general issues of poverty and poor life conditions than with those directly related to 'caring', that nearly a third were illiterate not only in English but also in their own language, and that half had no contact with service providers.

The 1991 case studies showed that it was often only when families were approaching crisis point that support was offered, or sometimes encountered by chance as when the elderly person was referred to hospital for other reasons. It should be remembered, however, that there is research evidence to suggest that use of formal services does not necessarily relieve the burden of minority ethnic carers and may even, by conflicting with cultural norms, threaten carer well-being (Cox and Monk 1990). Perceived reduction in the need for informal support may also encourage withdrawal on the part of family or community and so leave carers more isolated.

Whilst early diagnosis of dementia does not necessarily lead to significant difference in the level or quality of support, it may lead to greater understanding of the illness as it progresses even when minority ethnic carers do not identify themselves as carers or view their relative's behaviour as worrying. What may appear to be family acceptance of disturbing or eccentric behaviour may actually hide denial of a growing recognition that something is wrong; and families may then be in need of support, if only to talk through what it is they fear. More practically, they need information about entitlement to Invalid Care Allowances and other welfare benefits, about available local services and about their right as carers to have their needs separately assessed under the provisions of the 1995 Carers Act.

Access to services

As already noted, it was apparent in the 1991 study that there was almost no outreach work, or follow up support for the relatives. The fact that the families did not ask for support seemed to be taken as confirmation of agency assumptions that such help was not needed. In the case studies, as in

110

recent discussions with service providers, it seemed that the onus was on minority ethnic families to get in touch with services and not vice versa, and that needs were seen as purely practical. None of the relatives in the 1991 study, for instance, were involved in a carer support group. To assume that minority ethnic families need only relief from the actual tasks of caring fails to acknowledge the emotional investment they have in their elderly relative, and hence the feelings of loss they may be experiencing. It also denies them access to forms of help available to the majority population (eg. Murphy 1993) and effectively means that they are offered a poorer service than other dementia sufferers and their families.

Appropriate services

The 1991 study suggested that, if minority ethnic families of dementia sufferers are to get appropriate and high quality services, the whole notion of professionalism may need to be addressed. In particular, presumptions of time-limited support may have to be reviewed (Bang 1983), both because of the long term nature of the illness and because of the slower pace imposed by the reluctance of some minority ethnic families to admit to problems.

One problem of concentrating on whether or not minority ethnic elders have access to mainstream services is that it assumes, as Patel (1990) noted, that existing services are already satisfactory. Research findings challenge this assumption, and in doing so raise the issue of separate provision. Recent years have seen rapid growth in minority ethnic self-help projects, mainly in response to the lack of appropriate service provision by the statutory and mainstream voluntary sectors. The majority of such projects are small in scale, have limited funding, and cannot hope to meet all the needs of minority ethnic elders including those suffering from dementia. At the same time, specialist provision for dementia sufferers in general has also been increasingly left to independent providers, who argue that their resource restraints mean that they lack spare capacity to undertake outreach work and are in no position to develop additional services tailored to minority ethnic elders' needs.

A major concern about separate provision is that it will relieve mainstream services of the need to change, providing what Patel (1990:131) describes as a 'buffer' against criticism directed at their failures, and that the minority ethnic voluntary sector will continue to play a substitutive rather than supportive role in relation to mainstream provision. The overall result, of course, would be that minority ethnic needs will continue to be marginalised, the structural context which denies minority groups access to mainstream services will be ignored, and issues of racism and discrimination will fade into the background.

The families of minority ethnic elders with dementia, who have been found to turn to outside help only in periods of extreme stress, are unlikely to have the time or energy to criticise separate provision as a compromising short term solution. In any case, many may see separate provision as the only way of ensuring that the cultural identity of their relative is affirmed.

Manthorpe and Hettiaratchy (1993:175) point out that: 'key decisions are increasingly made at the level of assessment, and involve the composition of a service package and who will be the care manager.' Patel (1990) stresses that such assessments are meaningful only if they take account of poverty and racism, and provide real choices between mainstream and separate services. In other words, assessments of minority ethnic elders with dementia must take account of all the other factors which commonly create problems for dementia sufferers and their carers - isolation, physical disability, lack of mobility, incontinence, visual or hearing problems and so on - while recognising that these vulnerabilities are accentuated by belonging to a minority ethnic group. As Marshall (1990: 32) has put it: 'Whatever elderly people in general suffer in this society black elderly people suffer more'.

Training needs

Whether at the point of assessment or in the provision of ongoing care, to define and react to people with dementia only in terms of the illness, rather than as people with personal identities, circumstances and histories, is bad practice whatever their ethnicity. So, too, responding to the families of minority ethnic elders with dementia in ways which accord with their world view, and tailoring support services to cultural expectations, should be seen as an extension of normal good practice.

Whilst attempts were made by some of the workers interviewed in the 1991 study to respect individuals' cultural backgrounds and to provide culturally appropriate stimulation and support, such practices seemed to depend on the initiative of particular workers. None of the staff interviewed at that time had received any specific training for work with minority ethnic dementia sufferers or their families. More basic, however, is the need for staff to develop awareness of their own values and assumptions about 'normality', and to learn to apply cultural knowledge sensitively rather than to reinforce racial stereotypes. As Manthorpe (1994) points out: 'Empathy and what Ahmad (1990) terms authenticity (a sensitivity grounded in an anti-oppressive approach) may be factors that need continually restating...'

Scotland 1996: has anything changed?

In early 1996, lacking the time or resources to undertake a systematic survey, we used a snowballing approach to contact over twenty agencies, individual workers and projects which, given their stated remit, might be concerned with the issues of service provision for minority ethnic elders with dementia. We are grateful for the ideas and information people shared with us, and have used these - like the case studies - to draw out issues which it seems important to think about further.

The 1991 research had found staff at all levels, and in every kind of organisation contacted, to be largely unaware of dementia in the minority ethnic population. In 1996, by contrast, most service providers we talked to had some personal knowledge of individual minority ethnic dementia sufferers; and many recognised that appropriate services for this group were not being provided by their own or other organisations. Awareness, however, does not of itself translate into action. The following points in particular stand out.

Lack of strategy, leadership and resources

In 1996, there is still no one agency or organisation taking a lead responsibility for raising awareness of dementia within minority ethnic groups, or of ensuring that the needs of minority ethnic elders with dementia are met; and this point is closely linked to that of resources. Minority ethnic projects and dementia projects both occupy precarious positions within wider organisations. Not only do they have low priority in the competition for resources, because they cater for small numbers of service users with needs different from those of the majority, but their successful operation often depends on the commitment of particular managers or workers and may not survive when they move (or, more often, are moved) on. On both counts what is said to be missing is commitment from 'the top'.

Similarly, when projects set up with Urban Aid or other short-term funding are not taken over by other reliable funding sources they either come to an end, or survive on a hand-to-mouth basis which makes service development virtually impossible. This situation is now further exacerbated in Scotland by the recent disaggregation of local authorities. In the absence of funding from smaller new authorities which are unable to afford to support them, some projects are being forced to provide only for the needs of minority ethnic elders in the city areas. This is particularly worrying, given that it is often the minority ethnic elders in outlying areas who are already the most vulnerable and isolated; and it may suggest a need for careful monitoring of organisations whose funding is linked to encouraging greater minority ethnic use of services.

The general picture is of some concerned individuals, and a handful of encouraging projects, struggling to overcome problems of isolation, prejudice and resource shortages in a situation characterised by the absence of an overall strategy, or the information necessary for developing one. Perhaps it is time for another workshop, or the establishment of some kind of network to enable those who are taking seriously the problems of minority ethnic dementia sufferers to take stock of the situation?

Minority ethnic staff

The continued lack of minority ethnic staff working directly or indirectly with minority ethnic elders with dementia is still very evident. There have, however, been some encouraging developments. In Glasgow a Multicultural Health Team, staffed by health care professionals from a number of different ethnic groups, is working closely with social workers and voluntary organisations to improve mental health services for people from minority ethnic groups. Particularly helpful for dementia sufferers and their families are moves to make mental health and other relevant services available in centres already used by minority ethnic elders. Such initiatives recognise the reluctance of these elders, and especially of older women, to take problems other than physical ones outside the family and into unfamiliar settings. Another positive development is the appointment in some areas of link workers or other staff with special responsibility for the minority ethnic population.

It remains true however, in 1996, that most mainstream dementia services have no minority ethnic staff at any level; and that there are said to be no applications from minority ethnic candidates when posts are advertised. Consideration needs to be given to positive recruitment policies to remedy this situation, whilst recognising that the employment of minority ethnic staff will not in itself bring about change except as part of a coordinated strategy.

Making information available

Access to interpreters and translated information about both dementia and services is now more available than in 1991. But it remains patchy, and its production uncoordinated. The Alzheimer's Disease Society (England) has information leaflets in a wide range of minority languages. Gunaratnam's (1991) excellent guide for minority ethnic carers Call for Care is available in Urdu, Punjabi, Bengali and Gujarati as well as in English, but does not address the problems of dementia care specifically. The helpful guide for dementia carers produced by the Health Education Board Scotland (new edition, 1996) gives clear information and practical advice on the care and

114

management of dementia, but is available only in English. Some individual projects have had leaflets translated into the languages of potential users, which combine general information with details of the specific services offered. Other material undoubtedly exists also, but its availability needs to be publicised - perhaps through a national data base?

A similar information gap exists in relation to interpreters, whose unavailability when needed can add immeasurably to delays and distress for minority ethnic elders and families. All service providers should have access to information about where they can be found, and about national networks such as Language Line (120 telephone interpreters available 24 hours a day, seven days a week).

Use of services

The availability of translated material does not ensure its use or its usefulness, especially if it is not integrated into a programme of outreach work. Some mainstream service providers in 1996 sounded puzzled and rather hurt that, in spite of their best efforts, minority ethnic elders and their carers mostly stayed away, or used services in a very limited way. One local authority day centre, in an area with a substantial minority ethnic population, has had no minority ethnic user in the six years of its operation. Such experience seemed not uncommon, and was at once both normalised as a reluctance common to all groups in the community to become involved with Social Work Departments, and culturalised as the widespread failure on the part of minority ethnic groups to take up any kind of health and welfare service. Another manager expressed frustration that minority ethnic elders do not use his day centre, adding that if they did the Centre would have to change the way it operates!

In the absence of resources enabling them to undertake outreach work, voluntary dementia projects, too, sometimes seemed to be expecting minority ethnic dementia sufferers and their carers just to fit into the existing provision. But we also found, within the voluntary sector, staff who recognised that fundamental changes in the way they operate are essential if they are really going to succeed in making their special expertise in dementia care available to minority ethnic elders.

Organisations specifically for minority ethnic elders, on the other hand, which have staff who are able to meet linguistic and cultural needs, are offering a very wide range of general services. This means that, with limited resources, they find it impossible to provide a special service for particular small groups such as those with dementia. It would seem, then, that joint initiatives might usefully be developed between dementia projects and minority ethnic elder projects, to draw on the strengths of both and to close the gap created by the limitations of each.

Training initiatives

In an overall situation in which most of the staff working with minority ethnic dementia sufferers still receive no specific training, we heard of examples of cultural awareness training for health service staff, and of dementia training for minority ethnic organisations. As in 1991, there still appears to be no culturally appropriate training in Scotland in areas such as reminiscence therapy, though it should be noted that the London based Age Exchange has been working in the area of culturally appropriate reminiscence work with ethnic minority elders since 1983, and provides a source of relevant and available materials.

There are gaps in some otherwise encouraging training initiatives, which demonstrate continued failure to bring together awareness of an individual's dementia with awareness of their ethnicity. Murphy (1993), for example, describes a comprehensive training programme, designed to provide home care assistants in a Glasgow dementia project with 'the necessary attitude, skills and knowledge required to support people with dementia and their carers in the local community', but makes no reference to the heterogeneity of that community. Nor, in spite of the title, does McLennan's (1993) *Dementia Touches Everyone: a guide for trainers and trainees in general practice*. This is particularly disappointing, since GPs may often be the only health or social care professionals in contact with minority ethnic families, and their role in the early identification of dementia is crucial.

Research in Scotland

We have drawn attention already to the lack of information in Scotland both about the needs of minority ethnic elders with dementia and their carers, and the nature and quality of the services available to them. We learned of only two relevant ongoing Scottish research projects: one on the mental health needs of Asian women including some with dementia, and the other on the needs of minority ethnic carers. Both will make a valuable contribution, but neither focuses specifically on dementia. The information needed for service planning for this group should be identified and a research agenda drawn up.

Towards better services

An Asian community care worker stressed the point that service providers, including those who themselves belong to minority ethnic groups, must avoid assuming that they know what help people want. Access to information, appropriate food, and culturally relevant reminiscence material is important. But minority ethnic elders with dementia also have other needs and priorities, in relation to home care as well as to day centre and residential provision, and service planning must take account of these. Important amongst them, it was suggested, are the central importance which minority ethnic elders attach to spirituality and religious observance, and to social contact with their elderly peers. Such insights are vital to sensitive service planning. The first step, however, is that service provision and community care planning must cease to marginalise minority ethnic elders with dementia.

In conclusion we would say of the present situation in relation to services for minority ethnic elders with dementia in Scotland, as Naina Patel (1993:132) said about the wider issues of specific services for black elders, that:

> the crucial point, it would seem from anecdotal evidence, is a general lack of urgency as far as the authorities are concerned .... : those that are doing something are doing too little; the others are not doing anything at all.

8. Minority ethnic elders in Scotland: facing the challenge

Mono Chakrabarti and Mel Cadman

Introduction

If it can be argued that social work services to elders and their carers generally fail to meet needs either as generously or as imaginatively as they might (Marshall 1990 for example), what prospects are there that the needs of minority ethnic communities will be effectively addressed? A number of sources imply that the prospects are very limited indeed. Firstly, research has demonstrated that social work services to black and minority ethnic people in Britain are seriously deficient at all levels. Surveys carried out by the Commission for Racial Equality (CRE), in 1978 and in 1989, indicate that '....even among the few departments that have committed themselves to promoting equality of opportunity in service provision, policy implementation is still in its early stages....there is little evidence that [they] are doing much more than making *ad hoc* arrangements' (CRE 1989). Similarly, Social Services Inspectorate reports in 1986 and 1987, designed to examine in detail how social services were being targeted to minority ethnic communities concluded that: 'Few social services departments have made much progress in developing their services.....policies are virtually non-existent and service development is at a very low level.' (Social Services Inspectorate 1987:.3). Both reports emphasise their concern that such failures contravene Section 71 of the Race Relations Act 1976.

A more recent report from a combined inspection of community care services by the Social Services Inspectorate and National Health Services Management

Executive in 1994 also indicated that '.....there was poor understanding of race and equality issues in some areas.' (SSI/NHSME 1994). These diverse reports attested to two crucial features of social services and 'race'; first, that the adoption of equal opportunities policies alone may have no beneficial impact on the delivery of services to minority communities, and, second, that the commitment and interest of practitioners in the absence of effective policy and managerial support has little impact.

The specific needs of minority ethnic elders have also been researched, albeit outside Scotland (Bhalla and Blakemore 1981; Holland and Lewando-Hundt 1986; Ahmad and Atkin 1996; Williams 1990). This research indicated that black elders experienced considerable discrimination of access to social services, because of a combination of factors connected with language barriers, lack of familiarity with social service provision and apprehension about the relevance and suitability of the services on offer. Writers such as Patel (1991) analyse the source of these difficulties as being racism, particularly institutional racism, in which a complex of individual and cultural assumptions and stereotypes become embedded in agency policy, procedures and practices, so that the particular needs of black and minority ethnic people are ignored.

While research on welfare services in Scotland has been more limited, McFarland et al (1986) , Dalton and Daghlian (1989) Bowes, McCluskey and Sim (1989) and Cadman and Chakrabarti (1991) confirm that similar problems prevail, although the size of the population, ethnic origins, demographic characteristics and pattern of migration and settlement of black Scots have created some variation.

The cumulative picture in Scotland by the early 1990s suggested that many of the sources of discrimination for black and minority ethnic service users were similar north of the border, and that the impact of public service policies was broadly similar both in impeding access to existing services and in hindering the development of services adapted to the needs of minority groups.

If one factor can be singled out as playing the primary role in challenging existing patterns of social work provision for elders, it must be the advent of the NHS and Community Care Act 1990, and in particular its requirement to prepare and publish regular plans following full consultation with interested members of the public and service users. If this requirement did not, in itself, compel recalcitrant local authorities to review service provision, for those authorities which had begun to establish dialogue with the minority communities, it provided a welcome statutory impetus to strengthen and extend this dialogue. Consultation with minorities tended to confirm the uncertainties about social work services, about the needs of vulnerable citizens and the difficulties of ascertaining the views of those whose first language was not English. Together with the results of the 1991 Census, an unrivalled opportunity for systematic planning and development of services to minority communities presented itself.

One social work department in the central belt of Scotland used this opportunity to review its services to elders, spurred in part by a general concern that minority communities seemed reluctant to use services but also by concerns, articulated by community representatives, that their elders were particularly vulnerable to poverty, boredom and, on some occasions, isolation. A research team, led by a black worker, was asked to survey their needs with a view to helping inform future service development.

The results of this survey are summarised in this chapter. Through comparison with other research, both within and outwith Scotland, it is argued that the findings are likely to have implications for authorities elsewhere in Britain.

The survey defined an 'elder' as anyone 50 years of age and over, partly because the age distribution of the minority communities skews in favour of younger people and partly because this reflects an increasingly accepted convention. 78 elders were interviewed in late 1993 and early 1994, using a questionnaire administered by a person from one of the principal minority communities, and the interview was conducted in a language of the respondent's choice. There was substantial consultation with representatives from the local minority communities and a pilot questionnaire was undertaken. Those interviewed represented an 'opportunity' sample known to workers in the various agencies working with the minority communities in this authority.

In the next section, the demographic, social and family characteristics of the minority communities and of the sample are noted. Then, the data on elders' knowledge, understanding and perception of various welfare services, especially social work, are discussed and brief reference made to the limited evidence about carers. The implications of these findings for the development of social work services in Scottish and similar authorities are then analysed. In the final section, the recommendations which follow from the survey are discussed.

Elders: characteristics of minority population and sample

As Table 8.1 indicates, minority ethnic groups represent a slightly smaller proportion of the population within the authority studied than in Scotland as a whole but the prevalence of particular minority groups is similar. In the city in which the majority of the sample lived, the minority ethnic population approaches two per cent of the population, with the prevalence of different ethnic groups varying slightly from the rest of the authority and Scotland, although people of Pakistani, Indian and Chinese origin represent the most discernible, relatively discrete groups. Table 8.2 illustrates the stark differences between the age distribution of the white and minority populations; while 34.8 per cent of the white population is elderly, this proportion drops to between 10 and 15 per cent for minority ethnic groups. As demand for support services tends to increase, as the population ages, these figures suggest that the demand for social services is likely to be very limited at present. Although the sample of respondents, as represented in Table 8.3, does not completely mirror the make-up of the various groups in the city used in the survey, it reflects it reasonably closely.

Table 8.1
Population in Scotland and sample authority by ethnic origin: (OPCS, 1991)

	White (%)	Black & Others (%)	Indian (%)	Pakistani (%)	Banglad-eshi (%)	Chinese (%)	TOTAL (%)
Scotland	98.7	0.3	0.2	0.4	0.0	0.2	100
Authority	99.2	0.1	0.2	0.3	0.0	0.2	100
City	98.2	0.6	0.4	0.7	0.0	0.2	100

Table 8.2
Population of elders in city: age by ethnic origin: (Census 1991)

	50 - 64	65 - 84	85+	Totals	(50 - 85+ year old as % of own ethnic group)
White	28,764	25,380	2,530	56,674	34.8
Pakistani	102	16	0	118	10.2
Indian	81	16	1	98	15.6
Chinese	43	9	0	52	13.1

Table 8.3
Ethnic origin and age (Sample) (N=78)

	50 - 64	65 - 84	85+	N.R.	Total
Pakistani	31	7	0	1	39
Indian	20	3	0	1	24
Chinese	10	3	0	2	15
Total	61	13	0	4	78

As might be expected from a sample group of this age, the survey showed English to be the customary language of communication in only 1.3 per cent of cases, primary languages reflecting countries of origin. Although no direct attempt was made to evaluate fluency in English, it became evident to interviewers, especially those in contact with the Chinese community, that language was an obstacle, when seeking advice and support. Data on employment patterns indicated that there was a higher incidence of unemployment and a marked skewing in favour of employment in catering, retailing and other self-employment. Unemployment and partial employment appeared very marked for those aged 50 - 64. Cumulatively, the picture emerged of a group of people likely to face their later years with substantially reduced financial resources in the way of earned income and, ultimately, pensions, than those of a comparable white group.

No independently verifiable account of elders' capacity to care for themselves was established, although a self-assessment of ability to cope independently indicated that about 70 per cent felt they could. Approximately 25 per cent of respondents required occasional help, but interviewers' impressions were that these needs mainly reflected elders' difficulties in communicating with agencies where relative fluency in English was necessary. Just under four per cent of respondents reported substantial dependency.

Household size and adequacy of accommodation varied according to ethnic origin. Families of Indian origin tended typically to live in rather smaller, apparently nuclear families and were reasonably satisfied with their accommodation, while those of Pakistani origin lived in the largest family groups and often expressed dissatisfaction with their accommodation. Help in time of need was estimated to be available from members of the immediate and extended family to most elders, and over 80 per cent of the sample believed that help would be readily forthcoming. However, this image of positive and helpful bonds between family members should not divert attention from the small proportion who appeared to have no family able or willing to help, or from the 18 per cent who believed some difficulties in providing help might be encountered. Significantly, the overwhelming majority of elders in the sample were relatively young and independent, and this suggests that helping resources had not yet been seriously tested.

The impact of welfare services on elders

Studies of minority ethnic elders (e.g. Patel 1991) have shown that their use of public services and resources tends to be minimal, and there have been various attempts to identify why the take-up is so low. Given the relative age of these studies and the differences in the composition of ethnic groups between England and Scotland, some exploration of these issues was relevant, first to establish the sources of information and advice to which elders would turn, should family support be unavailable or inappropriate; second, to assess elders' knowledge about the range of social services available to elderly people. Finally, examining elders' impression of social services agencies and the developments they wished to see in the future was important, especially amongst a group whose use of services had so far been minimal.

Previous research suggests that any minority group's confidence in existing services was likely to be low; any attempt to remedy such a problem would benefit from more detailed knowledge of the sources of this image deficit.

Elders were asked about the sources of information they would use to help deal with a range of problems they might encounter; their responses held few surprises and are summarised in Table 8.4. Information on housing or welfare benefit matters was sometimes sought from the appropriate agencies, although dependence on family/friends and other minority community agencies was more significant. People of Chinese origin in particular, few of whom appeared able to communicate fluently in English, were almost wholly reliant on others for access to sources of information.

The importance of establishing the role and function ascribed to the Social Work Department by elders was illustrated by responses to questions about who, or which agency, should be approached if illness/disability precluded their being able to cope on their own.

The Social Work Department was clearly identified as the appropriate source of information about help with shopping for a substantial minority, with 'other' agencies, especially those working for minority ethnic communities, being the next most popular choice.

Not surprisingly, the family featured as the first point of reference for discussing personal problems but, again, the Social Work Department was the agency most often identified as appropriate by a significant minority of respondents.

In responses to a question about help with self-care, the family's dominance as a source of information gave way to agencies, although, on this occasion, health agencies and their workers featured more often than the Social Work Department. The question about which agency would be approached in relation to a need for full-time care elicited a very similar response, emphasising the dominance of health agencies and workers as primary sources of information. This response, and evidence from other parts of this survey, tend to point to the clear association which elders and carers form between health and welfare functions and services and emphasise the need to ensure health professionals have accurate information on social work services.

Finally, the survey focused on the question of where elders would go if they felt lonely and isolated. While 'family' features as first choice for a majority, perhaps surprisingly the Social Work Department emerges as the agency to which most elders would turn.

The contrast between responses which portray health agencies as the primary source of information in relation to the provision of practical, essentially social care, resources and those which place responsibility on social work agencies for problems associated with needs for emotional support, raises issues about how information on services is promoted to, or is perceived, by members of the minority communities.

Table 8.4
Sources of information as received by survey respondents (%)

	Family etc	CAB	Social Work Dept	DSS	Media	Hs-G Dept	Health Profs.	Other	NR
Welfare benefits	18	13	10	35				19	5
Hous-ing	19				12	38		30	1
Help with shopping	14		39		12			26	9
Personal problems	35		22		14			17	12
Self-care	12		24		12		36	7	9
Full-time care	12		14				36	26	12
Loneliness & isolation	31		30		14			13	12

Notes: CAB = Citizens Advice Bureau; DSS = Dept of Social Security; NR = No response

There were stark differences between elders of Chinese origin and those from other ethnic backgrounds. Very few of the former were able to identify the agency responsible for different services, and dependence upon both family members, and especially the nearby minority ethnic community organisation, was substantial, mainly because of language difficulties. This also demonstrated that such difficulties had seriously hindered the ability of Chinese elders to acquire essential knowledge about even the most basic services, let alone access them.

Respondents were also invited to identify other issues/difficulties which had arisen and to indicate the sources of information they had used. Seven people indicated that racial harassment had been a problem for them; six identified loneliness, and five medical care. Of those who identified their source of information, six (nearly all from the Chinese-speaking community), had sought advice from a local translation and interpreting service, and three each from either the local Racial Equality Council or police. The reporting of racial harassment is depressingly similar to other surveys carried out in Scotland (see Bowes and Sim 1991, for example) and serves to underline the role which racism plays in affecting elders' access to services.

The inaccessibility of social services to minority ethnic communities is normally compounded for elders by their unfamiliarity with the social welfare system as well as by language barriers. The survey sought information about respondents' knowledge of social services. They were asked about various specified services; whether they knew the criteria governing eligibility for the service; whether they knew where it was provided; and whether they knew how to apply for it.

Table 8.5 lists their answers. Column 1 gives the various types of social services, about which elders were asked, in abbreviated form. Column 2 gives the percentage of respondents who claimed to know nothing about the service; and in the remaining columns are the percentage who knew about various aspects of the service.

Table 8.5
Knowledge about key social services (%)

	No Knowledge	Know what it is	Know when eligible	Know where to go	Know how to apply
Home Helps	41.0	57.7	42.3	34.6	24.4
Laundry Service	65.4	34.6	24.4	18.0	14.1
Meals on Wheels	62.8	37.2	23.1	17.9	14.1
Alarm Scheme	80.8	19.2	14.1	10.3	7.7
Day Care	62.8	37.2	25.6	20.5	16.7
Respite Care	69.2	30.8	23.1	23.1	19.2
Sheltered Housing	32.1	67.9	53.8	39.7	28.2
Residential Care	65.4	34.6	26.9	21.8	16.6
Aids & Adaptations	70.5	29.5	26.9	15.4	12.8
Financial Help	76.9	30.0	16.7	15.4	14.1
Help - Housing costs	75.6	23.1	17.9	14.1	12.0

Of these key social services to elders, only in the case of home helps and sheltered housing, did a majority possess even the most basic information. Even here, only a small majority knew something of the criteria for eligibility (in the case of sheltered housing), but a minority knew how and where applications could be made; in the case of the home help service, a large minority knew about the eligibility criteria. In all other cases, the majority who appeared to know nothing about the service ranged from 62.8 per cent who knew nothing of 'Meals on Wheels' to 75.6 per cent who knew nothing about 'help with housing costs'. None of these services could be described as other than fundamental and it is possible that substantial numbers of eligible elders are foregoing support vital to their well-being.

Variations attributable to ethnic origin appear to be significant, and surprisingly consistent. With the marked exception of sheltered housing, elders of Chinese origin tended to know least about the range of services, and not uncommonly, none of the Chinese elders in the sample knew anything about some key services.

Additional comments were made by respondents in relation to this section. Seven people indicated that they never used social work services, two stated that services should be better publicised and one mentioned that Meals on Wheels did not provide suitable food.

Views on social work services and future developments

In the authority being studied - and certainly elsewhere - minority ethnic people generally use services less than white people in broadly comparable situations. Obstacles can be as obvious as language barriers, but other factors, such as concern over the approachability and responsiveness of staff can all play their part (Cheetham 1981; Denney 1987). In an attempt to pinpoint the obstacles to service access for minority ethnic elders, respondents in the sample were asked to indicate the strength of their agreement with a number of statements made about aspects of the service currently provided, and to express opinions about options for future service development. A summary of elders' responses to these statements is given below. Each statement also offered opportunities for elaborating on the reasons for making particular choices, in the hope that these narrative accounts would provide some further insights.

The first question related to how well elders believed the local Social Work Department had targeted its services to minority ethnic people. Fifty-six per cent thought it had done so effectively, with 34 per cent answering negatively.

It is a consistent complaint from minority communities, reflected by writers in this field, that social work and other services fail to target in a way which is appropriate to minority people. There may be grounds for relative satisfaction, therefore, that the survey showed a clear majority believing that the Department had targeted services reasonably well. In fact, the authority, not long before this survey was carried out, had engaged in a substantial programme of distributing information about services in the principal minority languages; it is to be expected that this will have increased levels of awareness.

Significant additional comments were made. Nine per cent of respondents thought more publicity was needed; four per cent mentioned language barriers, while a couple of respondents indicated that the Department was unable or unwilling - it was not made clear which - to deal with complaints about racism. Two respondents indicated that more minority ethnic staff were needed in the

Department.

The second question concerned the approachability of local social work staff to minority ethnic people. Again a majority, 62 per cent, answered positively while 30 per cent answered negatively.

The impression people have formed of a social work service is vital to understanding the base from which any attempt to improve service take-up has to start. In this case, a very substantial majority had a favourable impression of the service they would receive from staff, although the minority view should not be ignored.

The question attracted a range of additional comments. Five per cent indicated that they had been in contact with social work staff and had found them helpful, whilst one respondent indicated that, in his case, the staff had been more friendly than helpful. Concerns about language barriers and the problematic location of services were mentioned by four respondents.

Two questions related to residential care. First, elders were asked if they thought residential units would make it easy for family and friends to visit them. Seventy-one per cent indicated they thought there would be no problem, with only 16 per cent indicating the contrary. It had been envisaged that elders might be anxious that residential care would result in enforced isolation from family and friends, but, on the basis of this evidence at least, this assumption was not borne out.

However, a related question asking how easily minority ethnic residents might socialise with other residents, prompted a very different response. Sixty-eight per cent answered that they would expect to face problems, sometimes serious, in socialising, with 29 per cent indicating otherwise. Given the sparse distribution of the minority population of elders within this locality, the likelihood is that they would encounter no other person from their own ethnic group. The additional, narrative, responses to this question indeed confirmed that language barriers and problems with culture and customs were anticipated as the main obstacle by 39 per cent of respondents. Perhaps surprisingly, none indicated that they would expect to face any racially motivated harassment.

It seemed important to find out what impression elders had formed about day care, a resource which has been increasingly developed to meet the needs of elders for whom residential care is inappropriate. The often asserted, if frequently misinterpreted, view that South Asians would much prefer to support elders in a family setting, could be argued to give day care greater prominence as a possible resource, though it is more commonly argued that family care is preferred over day care. The question was, therefore, asked what picture elders had of a day care centre and a brief description of its function and purpose was included in the question. Sixty-two per cent answered they had a generally positive view, only nine per cent indicating they did not, but 29 per cent felt unable to answer.

Despite the statement's containing a very brief description of its functions, this substantial proportion of non-response is a direct indication that the concept of a day care centre is not well understood. The overwhelmingly positive response to the idea from those who understood something of its potential or purpose indicates that such a development would be welcomed. Indeed, eight per cent of respondents added that they positively welcomed the idea of this resource; two respondents indicated that the mosque provided this kind of support to them, and one or two qualified their support for the principle by indicating that either separate provision or greater numbers of minority ethnic staff were needed to make it more attractive.

A question about domiciliary support focused on the importance to elders of home helps belonging to the same ethnic group. As might be expected, the vast majority agreed that this was either very important or important. Ethnic group was not defined, but 45 per cent of respondents indicated that the reason for their reply was because they wanted somebody who could communicate in their language (27 per cent) or understand their culture and customs (eight per cent) or both (ten per cent). One respondent indicated that a home help from the same ethnic group would make him concerned about the issue of confidentiality; this question of confidentiality, while alone in this sample, serves to caution against making any stereotypical assumptions about 'ethnic matching'.

As one of the main purposes of this survey was to ascertain whether elders had formed a particular view about the Social Work Department, a question was asked regarding the Department's commitment to the needs of minority elders. The answers indicated that a small majority, 51 per cent, felt positive, with 38 per cent indicating otherwise. Very few respondents elaborated on their answers. These responses give no grounds for complacency, but need to be interpreted in the light of other responses, which have generally indicated a positive impression of existing services and intentions. Again, the fact that the authority had made substantial efforts both to publicise its existence and services and had been engaged in formal dialogue with the minority communities for some time, probably generated a more favourable response than would be found in other areas of Scotland with no such track record.

Two final questions focused on possible options for the future development of services. It is worthwhile trying to understand how elders might wish to see services develop, although there are grounds for believing that these questions were less well understood than others; the responses must therefore be treated with some caution.

First, elders were asked how positively they felt about day care and residential services being provided separately for minority ethnic groups. A clear majority, 62 per cent, stated they were in favour, with 30 per cent indicating to the contrary.

The reasons given by 21 per cent of respondents in favour of separate provision were, again, focused on language, culture and customs, with another five per cent reaffirming their positive support for the principle. Only four per cent expressed opposition in principle to the idea, some of them quite forcefully rejecting the idea of 'apartheid', with a very small number expressing concern about either costs or the necessity for the service at all, given their family's commitment to supporting them through their old age. Four per cent suggested that more minority ethnic staff in existing centres would deal with the problems they might expect to face. It seems reasonable to bear in mind that others might have supported this as an acceptable, perhaps even better, alternative to separate provision.

The second question asked if social services to minority people would improve only if run by minority groups themselves. Given the generally positive impression respondents appear to have about the willingness and ability of the Department to provide services, it is something of a surprise that 59 per cent supported this principle. Only about a third of respondents elaborated on their choices, but these reflected divergent views. Those supporting the view that services would improve if run by minority groups mainly gave reasons of communication, culture and customs. Of those who did not favour this option, eight per cent of the sample expressed serious doubts about the minority community's ability to offer services properly, with another eight per cent indicating that the provision of minority ethnic staff in existing centres would be a preferable alternative.

Analysis of elders and social work services

Given the relative youth of the sample, it is not surprising that there has been so little use of welfare services by the elders in this survey, although it is possible that there is some unmet need. The impression created is of a group which is not overwhelmed by poverty or poor housing, although there was no attempt to focus on this in the survey and it would be unwise to draw firm conclusions.

At another level, however, elders' lack of knowledge about the wide range of services designed to support them with financial, practical or emotional assistance, can only be described as a matter of concern. If, at present, their needs for these services are very limited, it is important not to overlook the fact that the ageing of this population will generate greater levels of need in the foreseeable future.

If their current lack of information were to persist into this stage of greater dependency, the best they could look forward to is an old age deprived of some of those resources which make it more comfortable; the worst, an old age marked by substantial deprivation and misery. Families provide an important potential source of information and advice to all elders. In the case of those from the minority communities of South Asia, where differences in language compound the problems created by their unfamiliarity with Britain's welfare system, carers will often act as a vital link to this external support system.

Although the survey was unable to identify an appropriate sample of carers, some impressions of the particular issues and difficulties which carers might expect to face were obtained. In general, there seemed little reason to believe that carers were any better informed than elders about the nature and scope of social work services. It appeared that elders could reasonably expect family members to offer them substantial support as dependency increased, although changes in household and family structures in the longer term (Bowes and Sim 1991) suggest caution. Overall, elders might expect to share some problems with their white counterparts in getting support from family members but, arguably, with the added difficulty of being unable to communicate their needs in many instances.

Implications of findings for social work

The composition and age distribution of the minority ethnic population in the city where the survey was carried out creates little demand for services to elders or their carers at present. This, perhaps welcome, opportunity to take stock and plan services thoroughly and systematically should not, of course, detract from the pursuit of devising properly responsive services even for the small number who may require them now. Nor should it obscure the fact that some elders, particularly those of Pakistani origin, will eventually form an even larger proportion of their ethnic group than white elders do now, because of the ageing of larger families.

The clear impression which emerged from this survey, confirmed by others (Bhalla and Blakemore 1981) is that members of the extended family expect to support their elders into and through old age, probably to a greater extent than is true for their white counterparts. While there is no reason to question the sincerity of such intentions, three difficulties need to be acknowledged. First, elders may have unrealistic ideas about the availability of family members to support them, and potential carers may be unaware of the acute demands which caring could place on them. Second, minority ethnic families live with the kinds of inexorable pressures which have played such a large part in causing the dispersal of extended family networks in Britain, like employment demands, unsuitable housing and family breakdown through separation and divorce. A third and less tangible factor is that the mainstream culture in which minority families live in Britain attaches much less prominence to supporting elders than that which minority communities have experienced in their countries of origin; it is probable this influence will have had some impact.

If there are few immediately pressing problems at present, younger elders in this survey, that is between 50 and 65 years of age, appear to experience both significant under-employment and unemployment. The fact that prior employment was often in the catering and retail trades or in other self employed capacities suggests that there may be financial difficulties in older age owing to the lack of adequate pensions. The survey also pointed to a significant lack of knowledge about welfare benefits to which elders might be entitled in part recompense for unemployment. Whilst Social Work Departments would not normally regard this age range of people as being in priority need, there is nevertheless an opportunity to establish and support day care centres run by minority communities themselves, under Section 10 of the Social Work Scotland Act 1968. Certainly this would provide a very useful platform from which to launch the dissemination of information on welfare benefits and, of course, relevant social work services.

Ensuring leaflets on social work services are translated into the principal minority languages has only a limited impact on potential service users. The survey interviewers became particularly aware of the difficulties of describing accurately and effectively the purpose and function of a number of welfare and social services. Together with the fact that not all elders could read literature in their spoken language, the value of making personal contact and using more accessible media, like video, is suggested. Health centres were frequently regarded as the prime source of information on a wide range of services, and this suggests they should be used extensively to publicise service availability.

The generally positive image which elders and carers had formed of their local Social Work Department may well reflect the substantial efforts which had been made to establish dialogue with members of the minority community and to publicise services; it may not apply to minority people living elsewhere in Scotland. However, as other research would imply, minority elders and carers often expressed some concern about how sensitive existing services would be. Many of the changes proposed echo the relatively familiar themes of; ensuring that translation and interpretation is available to ensure wishes and needs are fully communicated; responding positively and knowledgeably to the differing customs, cultures and religious beliefs of minority people; employing more minority people in key posts. Even here, though, it is important to recognise that views were far from unanimous and that differentiation between individuals and ethnic groups is to be expected and acknowledged.

Opinion about whether improvements in services could be achieved most effectively by providing them separately for minority ethnic people was clearly divided. The provision of minority-led dedicated care and support to minority elders has to take account of three factors. First, the already small minority ethnic community is significantly differentiated by country of origin, language, religious belief, customs and culture. Any minority-led provision will, therefore, face formidable problems in accommodating such diverse interests. Second, minority-led provision calls for considerable expertise in designing and running services and may require substantial capital (Institute of Race Relations 1993). Third, the relatively dispersed minority population in this authority, (typical elsewhere in Scotland), makes it difficult to provide sufficiently responsive services throughout; concentrating these in one or two areas either precludes use by many or creates major access problems. At least initially, it may be more realistic for the local Social Work Department to maintain full responsibility for services, but

131

to develop them in a way which takes account of the need to meet elders' and carers' needs more effectively. In the longer term, particularly as the population's needs for formal care and support grow, the possibility of alternative and complementary minority-led provision could be seriously examined.

The likelihood that substantial support to minority elders will be offered by families presents a challenge to design services which recognises that the traditional models of day care may be inappropriate. Crossroads in Glasgow appears to have developed a model which offers a centre base for some services to elders but which also openly welcomes and encourages other members of the family to accompany them. This model may not be appropriate for all, of course, but the opportunity to make contact with and support carers in this way has some clear attractions. Otherwise there is no basis for assuming carers' needs are different from those of the majority population ; providing a mix of services which offer support, information and advice and also respite, providing this is also ethnically responsive, should meet these needs effectively.

Conclusions

The pursuit of racial equality in the provision of social work services in Britain has been prompted by a growing concern, crystallised by Dominelli (1988), that black and minority ethnic people suffer exclusion from services which are intended to promote well-being, whilst at the same time being too frequently the object of interventions which are intended to control and contain. Even a passing familiarity with the developing debate about the combination of forces which shape racism will recognise that this process and the inevitable outcomes have their counterparts in other public services, such as health (Ahmad 1992) and housing (Bowes, McCluskey and Sim 1989). If there were earlier evidence of an assumption that the very nature of the social work task, and its professional training courses, tended to preclude practice which was racist in outcomes, studies from the 1980s onwards have laid this shibboleth firmly to rest. Perhaps inevitably, the location of the social work task , within some of our most orthodox institutions, such as local authorities, the law and health services, ensured that it would absorb at least some of the taken-for-granted assumptions and traditions which permeated these institutions' practices, as some writers have suggested (Cadman and Chakrabarti 1991) . If the advent of a 'new' professional qualification in social work in 1991(CCETSW 1991) represented the clearest commitment yet made by a professional body to confront and challenge racist assumptions, the revised qualification, introduced in 1995 (CCETSW 1995) demonstrates the impact of a substantial backlash against this challenging approach to training. If any evidence were required of the need constantly to guard against complacency or undue optimism that racial equality is within grasp, this one example provides it. The need constantly to reiterate, re-emphasise and re-state the case for racial equality cannot be overlooked.

In Scotland, the evidence available suggests that racism in all its manifestations, including the institutional level in public and social work services, is as formidably embedded as in England and Wales, where the greatest body of research has been conducted. While over the past decade various initiatives have slowly developed to adopt equal opportunities and to enhance the appropriateness of social work services, the community care legislation should provide a further stimulus to service diversification which reflects the principles of equal opportunities. If the development of a service which recognises in full a racial equality dimension must necessarily develop from continuing dialogue with members of the minority communities, the following broad principles represent a basis on which such developments can be built.

First, minority ethnic elders need to know what services are available and how to access them. Providing literature in the principal minority languages is a good start, but the evidence suggests that other media, such as videos and oral material, is needed to supplement this for those who cannot use written information. The creation and support of minority-led day centres provides an ideal opportunity for the promotion of this information, as well as providing useful recreational and social support to a wide range of elders. Health centres and hospitals appear to be a particularly well recognised source of information and advice on a range of benefits and services.

Second, elders' employment patterns, characterised by self-employment in catering and retail trades, often with substantial under-employment and unemployment, leaves many with minimal financial resources for their retirement. Given the frequent lack of knowledge about entitlements, the provision of effective welfare rights advice seems particularly apt.

Third, continuing support to, and development of, minority-led organisations recognises the crucial role which they play in supporting minority communities. The evidence from this survey indicates that existing minority led organisations are hard pressed to meet their current commitments and their role is too circumscribed to meet the very diverse and complex problems of the communities they serve. The placement of professional staff within these organisations could help them acquire and develop their role more effectively.

Fourth, minority communities may have a more extensive role to play in service provision than hitherto, and current developments in Scotland, such as the development of the Positive Action in Housing initiative sponsored by Scottish Homes would suggest that the prospects of developing models for future provision should be explored with members of the minority communities in the near future.

Fifth, the process through which changes in policy and practice are identified and implemented needs to take account of the substantial disempowerment of minority ethnic communities. It is, therefore, essential that members of these communities are widely consulted so that their perceptions, needs and aspirations are fully embraced in the move towards promoting racial equality.

Finally, local authority departments have a clear responsibility to make services more accessible, more attractive and more responsive to minority ethnic service users. The evidence from this survey indicates that a substantial level of confidence in local authorities' willingness to provide services exists and that the degree of diversity in services needed to meet the rather modest aspirations of minority elders is not enormous. Certainly the additional financial pressures created by local government reorganisation are potential adversaries to the development of services to minority communities, but it is to be hoped that the growing voice of minority ethnic people and the developing recognition of their rights to equal treatment will ultimately prevail.

9. 'No one has asked us before': the welfare needs of minority ethnic carers of older people in Lothian

Gina Netto

Introduction

The White Paper *Caring for People* (Department of Health 1989) and the ensuing legislation, the NHS and Community Care Act (1990) and associated policy guidance have irrevocably altered the nature of health and welfare provision. The change in emphasis for services to be delivered in the home or in 'a homely environment' in community care policies (Cmnd 849) has also led to a new recognition of the role of carers. This has culminated in the passing of the Carers Recognition and Services Act (1996), making it a duty for local authorities to carry out an independent assessment of the needs of carers in addition to those of the people they look after. Further, the legislation gives local authorities the discretionary power to provide services which are identified as required by the assessment.

Much has been written on the nature of informal care in the past decade (Qureshi and Walker 1989, Twigg 1992) which demonstrates the heavy costs of caring in financial, emotional and physical terms. Finch (1989) found that care in the community increasingly resulted in care provided by the family. The General Household Survey on Informal Carers (Green 1985) also provided vital information on the extent and pattern of care-giving in the community which was updated in 1990. Organisations such as the Carers National Organisation and Carers Impact have campaigned to push carer issues onto the policy agenda and lobbied for support for those providing informal care. In recognition of the pressures on carers, the

King's Fund Centre published *Carers Needs: A 10 Point Plan for Carers* in 1989. This plan is based on seven identified needs of carers: information, respite and sitter services, emotional support and counselling, support in a crisis or emergency, practical help, health care, and education and training.

One of the most fundamental elements which characterises informal care is that it takes place within the context of an existing relationship with the cared-for. Thus, discussions with and about carers are inextricably bound to the person they are providing care to and it is difficult, if not impossible, to consider one without the other. The disability movement has argued that the prioritisation of carers on the policy agenda takes place at the expense of treating disabled people as individuals in their own right and does little to promote their independence and autonomy. However, as Twigg and Atkin (1994) argue, to focus solely on disabled people, ignoring those who provide care to them is also unacceptable. Not only are carers entitled to services in their own right but the welfare of those to whom they provide care depends, to a large extent, on the continued well-being of the carer. Thus, both the needs of carers and the people they look after must be incorporated in public policy.

Many research studies have been carried out in England on the experiences of minority ethnic carers (Begum 1992, Coles 1990, Kalsi 1993, Lambeth Social Services 1990, London Borough of Camden 1990, McCalman 1990, Sage and Sangavi 1992, Walker and Ahmad 1994). Consultations with carers from multi-racial backgrounds have also been documented (Griffiths 1992, Black Carers Forum 1992).[1] These studies report the many problems which minority ethnic carers share with white carers as well as identify their particular difficulties. They also reveal that the former have tended to have their needs overlooked in community care planning. Some of the problems which have been revealed by these studies include low awareness of services, inaccessibility and inappropriateness of existing services and a fear of racial discrimination. However, thus far, the needs of minority ethnic carers in Scotland and the extent to which their needs have been met has not been considered in depth.[2]

Widespread uncertainty and ignorance about the community care needs of minority ethnic carers persists. Myths such as 'they look after their own'

---

[1] A few useful handbooks for professionals working with minority ethnic carers have also been compiled (Yee and Blunden 1995, Yee 1996).

[2] Chakrabati and Cadman (1995) included a small sample of nine carers in their study which mainly focused on the needs of minority ethnic elders in Tayside.

prevail in spite of accumulating evidence that traditional family ties are being broken down due to factors such as geographic dispersal of relatives in search of employment, economic pressures and changing values. Unless attention is drawn to the needs of minority ethnic carers, those who control resources and services may continue to be unaware of the extent of unmet need which exists. Additionally, even if steps are taken to increase service uptake among minority ethnic carers these may not succeed unless prior investigations into specific service requirements have been carried out.

This paper is based on the findings of a research project which investigated the needs, use and preferences for delivery of health, social services and other essential forms of support for minority ethnic carers of older people in the Lothian region. It concentrates on carers' interest in using existing social work and community services, suggests ways in which these services can be made more appropriate, and reveals gaps in provision. The paper concludes by considering some implications for social work departments on how minority ethnic carers may be supported in looking after older people.

Context and scope of the research

The research was originated by an expression of willingness on the part of the Scottish Ethnic Minority Research Unit (SEMRU) to Lothian Racial Equality Council (LREC) to co-fund a project. LREC recommended a project proposed by VOCAL (Voice of Carers Across Lothian), a voluntary carer-led organisation, which aims to raise awareness and represent the needs and interests of carers in Lothian. The specific research initiative stemmed from a perception that little had been done to identify and support minority ethnic carers who were likely to face not only the same difficulties as white carers, but also specific difficulties associated with their ethnic origin. The proposal targeted carers of older people, a group which was likely to grow as the currently young minority ethnic population ages.

The study focused on the 'visible minority ethnic communities', that is, those whose skin colour marks them as distinctly different from the majority white population and who are thus most likely to be victims of direct racial discrimination. However, it was also recognised that these groups may also suffer from indirect discrimination through a 'colour-blind' approach in service-planning which failed to take into account their specific needs.[3]

---

[3] This concentration of the study was not intended in anyway to discount the needs of white minorities, such as the Jewish and Polish communities, but rather to carry out a comprehensive assessment of the needs of a particular group of carers and the services available to them.

It was further decided to concentrate on the needs of those minority ethnic carers who were caring for people over the age of 50. This age was chosen for two reasons. Firstly, it has been recognised that the onset of age-related diseases occurs earlier in the minority ethnic communities, due to ill-health and poor social and economic conditions. Secondly, the minority ethnic projects working with older people, including the two who participated in the project, tend to cater for those aged 50 and above. The geographical focus of the project was confined to the Lothian region and included the city of Edinburgh where the largest number of minority ethnic people reside, as well as Mid-, East and West Lothian.

Both Lothian Health and what was then Lothian Social Work Department were approached for representation on the project. Two voluntary organisations which supported older people in the minority ethnic communities were also invited to participate. These were the Edinburgh Chinese Elderly Support Association (ECESA), and MILAN (Senior Welfare Council) which works with the Bangladeshi, Indian, Mauritian and Pakistani communities. The collaboration of these organisations and Lothian Racial Equality Council was sought because of their key involvement in the area and the need to raise the profile of the project within the minority ethnic communities, thus facilitating access to carers. The research was funded by SEMRU, VOCAL, Lothian Social Work Department, Lothian Health, the Edinburgh Healthcare Trust and various other trust funds.

Research aims

The specific aims of the research were: to identify service needs and preferences for service delivery; to identify barriers to services and examine the extent of direct and indirect discrimination in accessing existing forms of carer support; to identify gaps in current service provision and make specific recommendations for changes in current service delivery patterns; and, finally, to inform the process of future planning and consultation.

Methodology

Arriving at a sample of minority ethnic carers of older people in Lothian

The number of carers identified and invited to participate in the project was informed by an estimate of the total number of minority ethnic carers of older people in Lothian and by the 1991 Census figures for people above the age of 50 in Lothian. The General Household Survey on Informal Carers found that one adult in seven was an informal carer, and, of these carers, 90 per cent were looking after adults above the age of 45.[4] Applying these trends to the minority ethnic population of 9,782 adults in Lothian, an estimate of a total of 1257 carers of people above the age of 45 was obtained. Adjusting this for the relatively younger age of people in the minority ethnic communities (11.3 per cent of the minority ethnic population are above the age of 45) as compared to the white population (36.8 per cent), we obtained an estimate of 384 minority ethnic carers.

Every attempt was made in the study to reflect the proportions of each of the minority ethnic communities in Lothian within the group of carers interviewed. Since data on the number of carers in each of the minority ethnic communities were not available, the numbers of people over 50 in the minority ethnic communities, as recorded by the 1991 Census, were used as a basis for estimating the target proportion of carers to be interviewed from each minority ethnic community (see Table 9.1).[5]

Table 9.1
Number of people over 50 in Lothian by ethnic group (1991 Census)

Ethnic group minority	No Above 50	Percentage of minority ethnic elders
Afro-Caribbeab	107	10.6
Bangladeshi	23	2.2
Chinese	273	27.2
Indian	165	16.5
Pakistani	358	35.7
Other Asian	76	7.6
Total	1002	100

A total of 45 carers was identified and interviewed. A third of the carers were Chinese, another third, Pakistani and the remainder were of Afro-Caribbean, Bangladeshi, Indian, and Other Asian backgrounds. Comparing the breakdown of carers by ethnicity against the 1991 Census data, we found that Bangladeshi, Chinese and Indian carers were slightly over-represented while Pakistanis were slightly under-represented. The proportion of Afro-

---

[4] The General Household Survey did not reveal any figures for the number of carers looking after someone above the age of 50.

[5] The assumption made was that the proportion of those above 50 who are dependent on informal care is likely to be the same in each of the minority ethnic communities.

139

Caribbean and Other Asian carers were noticeably under-represented, reflecting the researcher's difficulty in identifying carers in these communities. This sample is statistically reliable with regard to the minority ethnic population in Lothian as a whole but less reliable for some of the smaller groups of minority ethnic communities. Carer responses are thus considered as a total rather than disaggregated into minority ethnic communities.

Table 9.2

Number of carers of those aged over 50 by ethnic group in sample

Ethnic group minority	No Above 50	Percentage of minority ethnic elders
Afro-Caribbean	2	4.4
Bangladeshi	3	6.7
Chinese	15	33.3
Indian	8	17.8
Pakistani	15	33.3
Other Asian	2	4.4
Total	45	100

Approximately half of these carers in the sample were in touch with MILAN and ECESA either directly or through the people they were looking after, thus ensuring some feedback on the appropriateness of current service provision by these agencies. However, carers who were not in contact with these organisations were also identified to provide a more accurate overall picture of the experiences and specific needs of minority ethnic carers.

Contacting carers

Carers were identified with the co-operation of MILAN and ECESA and by outreach work through community leaders, women's groups and professionals in medical and social work departments including some who themselves belonged to minority ethnic communities. Information leaflets were printed in Bengali, English, Gujerati, Hindi, Mandarin, Punjabi and Urdu providing information on who may be seen as an informal carer of an older person, the aim of the project and how to get in touch with the researcher. The anticipated method of identifying carers through 'snow-balling', that is through carers who were already identified and interviewed, achieved only limited success. This may be due to the isolation which carers often experience by virtue of their caring responsibilities or to a reluctance to pass on the names of friends or relatives without knowing their willingness to be interviewed. In many cases, carers were identified by professionals who were providing services to those in receipt of care.

The questionnaire

In designing questions which aimed to assess carers' need of available services, an important consideration was the likely possibility that carers would not have heard of some or all of the services on offer. To counter this lack of familiarity with existing services, questions which aimed to elicit needs in certain areas were followed by those which elicited carers' interest in using related services. For example, questions which elicited carers' ability to take breaks from caring were followed by questions eliciting their interest in respite services. Further, services were referred to in functional terms, rather than by the terms they are generally known by. Thus, rather than asking 'Would you like the person you are looking after to go to a lunch club?', the question used to elicit this information was 'Would you like the person you are looking after to go to a place where s/he could have lunch with other people on a regular basis?'.

Working with interpreters

It was anticipated that gathering information from carers would require working with a team of interpreters who were collectively conversant in the range of languages used by them, familiar with the project and who would be available for the duration of the study. To ensure that interpreters were clear about their role and used consistent terminology, a briefing and training session was held. The session detailed the purpose of the project, areas covered in the questionnaire, key terminology and training in the process of interpreting.[6] It was emphasised that interpreters were to enable carers to speak for themselves rather than speak for them. The pool of interpreters included both male and female interpreters for each community. When interviewing Bangladeshi, Indian and Pakistani female carers, only female interpreters were used.

---

[6] Some training in interpreting was also included because while some of the interpreters were professionals from Lothian Interpreting and Translation Services, others were chosen for their familiarity with the community and had not been previously trained in interpreting skills.

The interviews

A pilot study to test the process of eliciting data from the questionnaire was carried out with two carers, one English-speaking and one through working with an interpreter. Since this did not reveal any major problems, after a few minor adjustments, the main study commenced. Almost all the interviews were conducted in the homes of the carers. the advantage being that the carer did not have to make alternative care arrangements during the time of the interview. A disadvantage of this decision was the possibility that in some cases, the carer was inhibited by the presence of the person they were caring for. However, it was felt that on balance, the advantage of interviewing carers in the home outweighed the disadvantage because it minimised inconvenience to the carer.

Interviews generally lasted from one and half hours to two hours. Often, the interview session was halted to allow the continuity of caring, such as checking on the older person, getting a drink for them or taking him or her to the toilet.

Analysis of the data

Data were collated and analysed by computer using the Statistical Package for Social Sciences (SPSS). The methodology also included the organisation of focus groups of Asian and Chinese carers. These discussions validated the findings of the survey, obtained more useful information for service providers, yielded a consensus of opinion from carers who had been individually interviewed, and tested out the appropriateness of some of the recommendations. They also formed the basis of future carer support groups. Due to limitations of space, only the findings of the survey are reported here.

Research findings

Characteristics of carers in the sample

About three quarters of carers (76 per cent) were women, and the peak age of caring was from 21-40 years which was relatively low in comparison to the peak age of 45-64 years found in the General Household Survey. This may reflect both the generally younger age of the minority ethnic communities and the early onset of age-related diseases in these communities. The younger peak age of caring suggests that these carers will spend more years caring than their white counterparts.

Only about half of the carers (53 per cent) were able to speak English. Many carers had considerable responsibilities in addition to caring for at least one older person: 29 per cent had a minimum of three young children under the age of 16. Carers themselves were often not in good health, with 31 per cent rating their own health as either quite poor or very poor. Over a third of carers (36 per cent) took on the task of caring for an older person in addition to undertaking a paid job. Caring for an older person also had financial implications: 49 per cent of carers had their work affected or chances of taking up employment reduced by caring for an older person and 31 per cent financially supported the people they were looking after.

A striking characteristic of care in the minority ethnic communities was that 72 per cent of carers were looking after someone within their own household, whereas the General Household Survey suggested a comparable figure of 4 per cent in 1990. While those living with minority ethnic carers are more likely to benefit from continuous care than their counterparts in the white population, the carers themselves are much more likely to be in need of services which allow them a break from caring. Apart from affecting work or limiting the chances of employment, caring for an older person also limited social activity, brought about physical and emotional stress and restricted the possibilities for respite.

Characteristics of the cared for

The extent of responsibilities undertaken by the carer was closely related to the condition of the cared for. Certain characteristics of those receiving care are thus worth noting: 50 per cent had difficulties in a minimum of three areas of physical functioning, 61 per cent suffered from at least one physical and one mental difficulty and about 40 per cent suffered from depression. All of these factors suggest a heavy dependence on informal care. In addition, the inability of 83 per cent of the cared for to speak English meant an increased reliance on the carer for communication in the wider community.

Other characteristics worth noting were the relatively young age of those receiving care: about a third of the cared for were between 61-70 years. Seventy per cent of those receiving care were female. Cultural expectations on the female seclusion of women may also increase their reliance on the carer.

The nature of care

More than a third of carers (35 per cent) were involved in two of the most strenuous aspects of care-giving: providing personal care such as bathing and dressing, and providing physical help in walking and climbing up and down stairs. Other caring responsibilities included household chores (undertaken by 83 per cent), providing medical support (65 per cent), entertaining (70 per cent) and regular checking on the condition of the cared for (96 per cent). Aspects of caring which take on added significance in the communities are those such as dealing with paperwork which require the ability to speak, write or read English (41 per cent). Significantly, 39 per cent of carers acted as interpreters for the people they were looking after.

More than four fifths of carers (81 per cent) provided care seven days a week, with 31 per cent providing continuous care all day long. Over half (53 per cent) had been caring for more than five years. Adding to the accumulating evidence in the literature on the inability of the extended family to care for the elderly, the study also found that 40 per cent of the cared for were looked after by a sole carer. About two thirds of carers (70 per cent) reported that they had little or no family support in caring for the older person/s and 47 per cent reported that they had no time off from caring. In the event of an emergency, 33 per cent of carers would either be unable to make alternative arrangements without difficulty, or would be unable to make them at all. The picture which emerges is one in which a substantial proportion of minority ethnic carers routinely manage entirely on the strength of their own resources.

Overall use of social work and community services

About 70 per cent of carers did not use any of the services provided by social work or voluntary organisations. The main reasons given for this were lack of information on their availability and difficulty in accessing them. Eighty per cent of carers felt that there were gaps in service provision, which if filled, would make the task of caring easier. However, only 24 per cent of carers had been in contact with the Social Work Department. The most common reason given for not contacting the Department was lack of knowledge of its role. Only nine of the 45 carers said that they did not need any services.

Use and interest in domiciliary support

Only six out of the 45 carers in the sample were using home helps. They reported varying levels of satisfaction while six other carers had discontinued the service. Positive comments on the service included satisfaction with the performance of household tasks, the provision of the service at no charge, the opportunity it afforded for a break to the carer and social interaction for the cared for. Those who were unhappy with the service or had discontinued it expressed dissatisfaction with the number of changes in home helps, limitations in what home helps would undertake and its lack of affordability. Forty-two per cent of carers currently not receiving the service indicated that they would like it provided.

Only four of the 15 carers were receiving the meals on wheels service for the person they were looking after. Again, varying levels of satisfaction were reported and two of these had discontinued the service. Satisfied carers reported that it lightened the burden of caring and the food was culturally familiar. Dissatisfaction with the service stemmed from lack of suitability of the food for the cared for and a lack of conviction that it complied with religious requirements. A fifth of carers currently not receiving meals on wheels would like the service to be provided, preferring food which reflected their ethnicity. In addition, those who were Muslims required the food to be halal while others required it to be vegetarian to comply with the requirements of other religions.

As far as personal care services are concerned, only one carer in the sample was receiving the services of a bath nurse with whom she was satisfied, although she would have preferred a male nurse to tend to her father-in-law. Twenty-four per cent of carers reported that they would like help with providing personal care such as bathing, taking the person out or giving them a massage.

None of the carers were currently receiving a sitter service, although a third of the carers interviewed expressed a desire for it. Many of these carers strongly emphasised the necessity for the sitter to be able to speak the same language as that of the person being looked after.

Crisis support

None of the carers had used a crisis support service before and the concept was new to almost all the carers who were interviewed. However, 42 per cent of carers reported that they would use a crisis support service in the event of an emergency. This is consistent with the finding that a substantial proportion of carers would not be able to rely on family members even in an emergency.

Support outside the home

In terms of day care provision, 42 per cent of carers were familiar with the day care service provided by MILAN and ECESA either through direct experience or through the experience of the person they were caring for. Satisfaction levels of these services were generally high: of the 19 carers with experience of the service, 14 were very satisfied, four quite satisfied and only one dissatisfied. The main reasons given by carers for their satisfaction was the opportunity it afforded for social interaction. A few carers expressed dissatisfaction over the lack of transport arrangements which made it difficult or impossible for the people they were looking after to attend the lunch club and a few had concerns about the food meeting the health requirements of the person they were caring for.

Of the carers who were looking after people currently not using day care provision, about a quarter expressed interest in the service. All thought it important that at least some members of staff and some users of the service should speak the same language as those being cared for. They also expressed concern that the food provided was culturally familiar as well as compatible with dietary requirements. Many carers also stressed the importance of suitable transport arrangements. Other amenities which carers thought important were accessible toilets, staff who would help the older person move about if necessary, and for some Asian carers, separation between men and women.

As far as residential respite care was concerned, none of the carers had used it and interestingly, only 11 per cent expressed an interest in doing so. The main reasons given for this were a lack of willingness of the cared for to use such a service, and their own desire to be with the cared for. Carers also had concerns about whether the cared for would be able to communicate with others.

A few carers, mainly Asian, expressed their reluctance in terms which could be related to their cultural beliefs:

> My mother has a daughter and a son. When people don't
> have children, they go to nursing homes.

As far as long term residential care was concerned, only three carers were looking after people living in nursing homes. Of these, two were positive about the service provided:

> It's small, run like a home. Care is good, they have
> organised activities, good meals. They take them out to
> various places, shopping, get people into recreational
> things. She is not isolated by being black, she's pals with
> the others.

One carer was not satisfied with the quality of care which his mother received, or the lack of availability of Chinese food but having discussing it with friends, had resignedly come to the conclusion that the standard of care in all nursing homes was similar.

Asked whether carers would consider long-term residential care for the people they were looking after, 72 per cent responded negatively. One of the most common reasons given for this was the latter's unwillingness to go:

> He wouldn't like it, likes to sleep in his own bed, in his
> own home.

> If you take her away from her son, it would be the end of her world. She likes to be in the family unit, feel wanted.

Other carers, mainly Asian, explicitly mentioned cultural and religious beliefs:

> I would not send her there, our culture stops us from doing this.

> We want to go to heaven: when we look after her, we are all the time getting blessings.

Other reasons given for not considering residential care included the choice of the carer to be with the cared for, the reluctance of the cared for to go into residential care and the inability of the person they were caring for to communicate with others. Of the seven carers who stated that they would consider using the service, two older carers said that it would be imperative in the event of their death. Two other carers responded that they would consider this option if the condition of the person they were looking after worsened.

Other services

Other services used by both carers and cared for were provided mainly by minority ethnic voluntary organisations and included lunch club provision, aromatherapy, and massage. Only two carers had been in touch with mainstream carer agencies to obtain information.

Preferences for service delivery

Asked about their preferences with regard to contact with professionals, 69 per cent of carers felt that it was either very important or quite important for professionals to be the same gender as the person they were looking after. With regard to the ethnicity of professionals, 56 per cent felt that it was very important or quite important for professionals to belong to the same ethnic group as the cared for to allow for improved communication. Significantly, 64 per cent felt that it was very important for professionals to communicate in the same language as the cared for. Among the 29 per cent who felt that it was not important were carers who could speak English or who were looking after people who could speak English.

Asked how important it was for the people being looked after to be in contact with others from the same minority group when carers were not at home, 56 per cent felt that it was very important and 24 per cent that it was quite important. Access to familiar food thought to be very important by 76 per cent of carers. These findings have obvious implications for the placement of minority ethnic older people in lunch club and day care services, respite care and long-term residential care.

Implications for social work and community services

The study clearly shows that the current low uptake of social work and community services cannot be attributed to lack of interest or need on the part of minority ethnic carers. The extent of unmet need which has been revealed is likely to increase as the minority ethnic population ages, unless measures are taken to address those needs. As in other similar studies elsewhere, this study demonstrates a low awareness of existing services among minority ethnic carers as well as the inaccessibility and inappropriateness of existing services to these carers' needs. It is difficult to ascertain the extent of direct discrimination which minority ethnic carers experience with mainstream service provision but insofar as their particular needs have not been identified and thus not accommodated in the planning and provision of services, these carers have suffered the effects of indirect racial discrimination.

It is also worth drawing attention to the evidence that minority ethnic carers share many of the expectations of white carers with regard to services, that is, that services should ensure the well-being of the person being cared for, be consistent and affordable. However, the study also provides evidence of preferences which starkly highlight the limitations of the 'colourblind' approach. In order to ensure that the person receiving care is adequately and properly looked after, minority ethnic carers have demonstrated clear preferences for service delivery. which takes account of language, food and the need for contact with others from the same ethnic group. While the strength of the preferences varies with the individual carer, they should certainly be considered when tailoring existing services to meet the needs of minority ethnic carers and the people they look after.

The ability of service-providers to meet specific requirements may partly contribute to the relatively high uptake of services provided by MILAN and ECESA. Both agencies are staffed by people from the Asian and Chinese communities respectively, who speak the appropriate languages. Both organisations have premises which are popular with their target service users, and promote their activities within the community. Both offer food which is culturally familiar and organise activities such as talks on health-related matters and English classes. At MILAN, the practice of gender separation among some communities is respected by the presence of a screen across the room, while at ECESA, certain items of news and forthcoming events are always read out in Chinese. Both organisations thus provide service users with opportunities for social interaction in a safe and familiar setting.

It is clearly important that these, and other minority ethnic organisations should be adequately supported in the continued provision and expansion of their services, especially in light of the current low awareness of the Social Work Department among minority ethnic people. Forms of support may include the provision of finance and other resources, suitable premises for service expansion and staff development and training. It is equally clear that the Social Work Department should adopt a pro-active stance in making their services known through all the communities they serve. Improved collaboration between minority ethnic services and mainstream organisations such as the Social Work Department and other voluntary organisations is also necessary in order to increase the uptake of both services specifically targeted to the communities as well as appropriate mainstream services.

The evidence in the study also shows that thus far, the available services are clearly targeted towards older people rather than their carers. Although the importance of services such as meals on wheels, home helps, lunch club and day care provision in supporting carers indirectly cannot be under-estimated and some of the older carers may directly benefit from such services, a gap in service provision to carers clearly exists. In particular, none of the carers in this study were familiar with, or had experienced any form of service which offered them a break from caring. The study suggests that mainstream services offering residential respite care may not be attractive in their current form, due to the preference of carers for the people they are looking after to be in contact with other users from the same minority ethnic group. Initiatives in this area should consider the provision of culturally sensitive residential respite care for minority ethnic groups either in separate locations or as part of the services offered by selected existing centres. Other forms of respite care which are likely to be appropriate to the needs of minority ethnic carers are the provision of domiciliary sitter services by staff who are able to speak the appropriate language. Such services are currently being provided by voluntary organisations in Leicester, Nottingham and other parts of the UK.

While this study shows that the majority of minority ethnic carers look after older people within a domestic setting, the importance of planning for care to be provided within an institutional setting should not be under-estimated. It would be misleading to use the current low numbers of people who are using residential care as indicators of the demand for these services. On the contrary, the fact that a small number of minority ethnic people are using mainstream services which are not culturally familiar to them and which have not been designed to meet their needs points to the potential demand for such services if they are sensitive to the social and cultural needs of minority ethnic people.

While the needs of minority ethnic carers, like those of carers in general, are closely linked to those of the people they look after, it is important that they are considered in their own right, an opportunity which is legitimised by the passing of the Carers Recognition and Services Act, 1996. As with other carers, some of their needs may coincide with those of the cared for while others may be in direct conflict. Sensitively designed and conducted community care assessments would be alert to the potential for both consensus and divergence in service requirements between these two groups of users.

Furthermore, assessments should be carried out in full awareness of existing race equality strategies and cultural pluralism. This may be facilitated by prioritising increased service uptake among minority ethnic carers and the people they tend to, conducting staff training programmes in racism awareness and increasing the recruitment of people from these ethnic origins. However, thorough assessments of need are in themselves exercises in futility unless there is also a whole-hearted commitment to providing culturally sensitive services. Although much may be achieved at little or no cost through increased awareness and sensitivity among staff, the provision of certain required services is likely to involve additional expenditure. In the face of limited resources, ultimately, the extent to which the needs of minority ethnic carers and the people they tend to are prioritised in the political agenda will depend on the extent to which the communities they belong to are recognised and prioritised in community care policies.

10. Pakistani women, general practitioners and health visitors: communication and service access

Alison Bowes and Teresa Meehan Domokos

Background

General practitioners are often women's first point of contact with health services, and act as gate keepers for access to other areas of service, such as health visitors, community nurses, maternity care, hospital services, mental health care services. For women in general, there have been recent criticisms of general practitioner services (reviewed at length by Foster 1995). Women with young children are also inevitably in contact with health visitors, who implement programmes of health surveillance, as well as offering advice and support. In this chapter, we examine the key issue of communication with general practitioners and health visitors, a crucial element in women's initial and continuing access to health services, and consider, with reference to data collected in Glasgow in 1994-5[1], how far Pakistani[2] women are disadvantaged in this area, and how their

---

[1] The research discussed in this chapter was funded by the Chief Scientist Office, Scottish Office.

[2] The term 'Pakistani' is used to denote the ethnic background of one of the groups of women interviewed, and is a term they used themselves. The term 'South Asian' is used to denote people with origins in the Indian subcontinent as a whole. Other terms, such as 'Asian', appear where respondents or literature sources have used them. It should be noted that the terms 'Pakistani' and 'white' (used for the other group of women) do not imply ethnic uniformity within the categories.

experiences compare with the experiences of white women. We look at, and compare, the perspectives of both patients and professionals.

The issue of communication with health professionals as a key problem for Pakistani women using health services was raised by Pakistani women themselves, responding to an exploratory research project completed in Glasgow in 1991-2 (Bowes and Domokos 1993, 1995a). They referred repeatedly to communication problems with their GPs, and many attributed these to language difficulties. Others, without such difficulties, revealed communication problems more like those expressed by non-Pakistani women in other research (e.g. Roberts 1985). By contrast, the women we interviewed had not experienced communication difficulties with health visitors, who, in Glasgow, are not generally Punjabi-speaking. We suggested that language was almost certainly not the only barrier to effective communication and questioned assumptions about the cultural basis of Pakistani women's problems of access to health care. Relevant factors influencing communication, and therefore access to health care appeared to include gender, class, 'race', processes of negotiation of health care, and some elements of cultural differences, such as language (Bowes and Domokos 1995b).

Our recent work aimed to examine the issue of communication more fully, to compare communication with GPs and communication with health visitors, to include the perspectives of professionals, and to compare a sample of Pakistani women with a sample of white women. We aimed to identify factors which inhibit and promote communication, and to ascertain how far these factors are distinctive for Pakistani women. Our work was intended to provide a baseline for developing recommendations for better practice.

The research record on South Asian (including Pakistani) interaction with health services is limited and the findings rather contradictory, especially regarding South Asian women. Language is frequently stated to be an obstacle to communication (eg Wright 1983, Johnston, Cross and Cardew 1983, Donovan 1986), and, therefore, a factor restricting access to health care, although Bhopal and Samim (1988) argue that for pertussis vaccination, patients' lack of English may explain high uptake, due to non-understanding of negative publicity. Ahmad, Baker and Kernohan (1991) share our concern at the preoccupation with language, and note (p.52) that there has been little attempt to investigate 'factors such as social class, gender, ethnicity and doctors' attitudes towards patients'. Their study revealed rather negative attitudes towards Asian patients in 'Milltown'. Roberts (1985), Doyal (1994) and Foster (1995) are critical of GPs' views of women in general and Leys (1976) reflects an emphasis on the inadequacies of the patient including class-based inadequacies, in his review of attempts to improve doctor-patient communication. Regarding choice of practitioner, Ahmad, Kernohan and Baker (1991) found that South Asian women placed ethnicity (Asian) above gender (female) in importance; Donovan (1986) found South Asian women preferred good doctors, regardless of ethnicity and gender; McAvoy and Raza (1988) found strong preference for female doctors. Jain et al (1985) questioned the importance of ethnicity. Existing work therefore, raises interaction issues other than language, especially those of class, gender and GP attitudes, none of which has been satisfactorily investigated or resolved.

All these issues are relevant to the apparently more successful communication between South Asian women and health visitors, which may also be related to the particular commitment to identifying and satisfying special needs characteristic of the profession (Shepherd 1992). Whilst health visiting may formerly have been undervalued by GPs (Wright 1983), recent NHS reforms could increase its significance, due to health visitors' wide ranging qualifications (in nursing, midwifery, counselling etc) which make them an economical health care resource, and to their role in promoting preventative services. At the same time, health visiting is challenged by the reforms to justify its role more clearly (Twinn and Cowley 1992), and there have been significant cuts in the health visiting service in Glasgow in recent years.

There is extensive literature on relationships between health visitors and GPs, which reveals many structural and attitudinal problems (Hallett and Birchall 1992 give a comprehensive review). Full investigation of these was outside the scope of the research, but account was taken of the structure of practices which could facilitate or inhibit communication between health visitors and GPs and thus indirectly affect service delivery to Pakistani women.

Methods

Semi-structured interviews were completed with 62 women of Pakistani heritage who were mothers of at least one child under five, 68 similar white women, 50 health visitors and 25 general practitioners. All respondents were identified on the South Side of Glasgow, using random sampling methods. Samples of women were weighted to ensure representation of a range of socio-economic groups, using housing area type as a proxy. The Pakistani women were randomly sampled from the electoral roll, and the white women on the basis of random addresses in the same areas. A sifting survey was conducted, to identify women with a pre-school child, who were prepared to participate in the research. Pakistani women formed a representative sample. White women formed a comparator sample, and were not intended to be representative of white women in Glasgow generally. Twenty four interviews with Pakistani women were conducted in Punjabi/Urdu, with a bilingual interviewing assistant. Interviews with women and health visitors lasted at least one hour, and interviews with GPs lasted at least half an hour.

Women were asked about their contacts with and views about general practitioners and health visitors, particularly in the context of their experiences as mothers of pre-school children, and we aimed to collect specific examples of encounters as well as general evaluations of experiences. Women's suggestions for service improvements were also covered. The same schedule was used for both samples of women.

Health visitors and general practitioners were asked about their experiences with Pakistani women patients, their perceptions of their health, any relevant training they had received, any suggestions they had for improving services, and about inter-professional communication, especially between health visitors and general practitioners. There was also discussion of comparisons between their work with different sections of the population.

Professionals were not asked about particular patients, or women about particular health personnel, in order to maintain confidentiality, and to allow free expression of views.

All the interviews were transcribed, to produce approximately 6,000 pages of text. This was systematically indexed, the index being generated from the interviews themselves, to ensure emphasis on the perspectives of interviewees. Indexed transcripts were then sorted and explored using NUD.IST software. Basic quantitative data, particularly demographic data, were processed using SPSS.PC.

The data set covers the issues of communication which were the central focus of the work, and complements this with contextual material. From the outset, communication was conceptualised broadly, and the interviews were designed to be ethnographic, to cover the full range of contextual factors influencing communication. In presenting a broad overview of the data, we aim to identify the main areas of comment, and how both patients and professionals perceived communication problems, both generally, and specifically in relation to Pakistani women. We use illustrative quotations from the interviews: these represent the general spread of views revealed by systematic data analysis[3].

Findings

Health visitors and general practitioners: experiences, attitudes, training

All but one of the health visitors interviewed were women, and there were 19 male and six female GPs. The median years of experience of health visitors was 13 (range 1-26), and for GPs, 18 (range 4-40). Six South Asian professionals were included, five of whom spoke Punjabi. Caseloads of

---

[3] All quotations are attributed. GP denotes general practitioner, HV denotes health visitor, PW denotes Pakistani woman, and WW denotes white woman. The number is the interview number.

154

Pakistani mothers varied: 29 health visitors, working in areas of lower Pakistani population, had fewer than ten on their caseloads, whereas nine had fifty or more (227 was the highest). Eight GPs had fewer than ten mothers, 12 had between ten and 100, and five were working in practices with very large caseloads of up to 2000 Pakistani families. The level of experience of working with Pakistani families was therefore very varied.

White professionals identified language and difficulties of access to good interpreters as problems. Cultural differences and the need to understand and be sensitive to people's preferences, especially religious preferences, were also mentioned. GPs tended to emphasise language, showing varying degrees of sensitivity to language difficulties:

> Well, with the Pakistani women, obviously it is the language problems and the cultural differences. (GP401)

> I might see someone with an interpreter, and feel as if I have dealt with it quite well.....but the patient themselves might be thinking 'That was rubbish. I'm going to have to go somewhere else and start again.' (GP402)

> There is a tremendous communication barrier for those Pakistanis who don't understand English, so... the need is to improve communication or try to either make them understand English, or get some health visitor to understand their language. (GP419)

This GP did not feel that a GP could understand other languages. Health visitors also referred to these types of problem:

> The difficulty with an interpreting service...[is]...having to make appointments to get the person to come with you. Very often, you wanted reasonably quickly a service, and it wasn't reasonably quickly available. (HV345)

Another health visitor compared the problems of Pakistani women with those of white women, and felt that there were culturally based differences:

> The men folk are not nearly as willing to lend a hand to these girls, and I think that a lot of them...came over from Pakistan, and they were extremely isolated, and perhaps were staying with a mother-in-law who they didn't get on with, and I think there was a lot of unhappiness as far as that was concerned (HV304)

155

She went on to say that she felt problems like this were becoming less common, as more Pakistani women were born and brought up in Scotland.

Health visitors were less likely to speak about language as a key problem than were GPs:

> I think communication is much more than language, and people just get hung up on this language thing. (HV320)

In many respects, Pakistani women were perceived as different from white women. For example, GP401, who saw language as a key problem for Pakistani women, went on to say of 'others' with problems, by which he meant some white women

> I think more often, mothers of children, they tend to be people who are harassed, depressed, either single mothers, have unsympathetic husbands, alcoholic husbands or whatever, and they are pretty distraught, and they find it difficult to communicate because they are so frustrated with their responsibilities. (GP401)

These were not apparently problems restricting communication for Pakistani women. One health visitor, who also saw Pakistani women as different from white women, spoke of her positive experiences of Pakistani households:

> I enjoy very much visiting Asian families, very hospitable, very welcoming, and I've never had any problems. Much more welcoming than some Scottish families who have social problems. (HV301)

> There were also some negative views, particularly concerning excessive demands on services made by Pakistani families.

> I think communication with the older ones is one problem, and I find that this particular group are very demanding. (GP404)

> I don't want to sound racist, but they do seem to be looking for their rights, and everything they're entitled to, they're wanting. (GP416)

Asian people are very demanding, and if they want an appointment with the doctor, they want it, like, now. (HV303)

They are a bit more demanding...of your time, demanding of facilities to a certain extent. (HV306)

Several GPs spoke at length about communication with patients, including Pakistani women, and the need for it to be successful in order for their advice to be accepted, and for their job to be done. They nevertheless felt under considerable pressure in their work. One doctor expressed a widespread view:

There is no question, the busier you are, whether you do it consciously or subconsciously, you will shut people off from telling you things. Whereas if you are relaxed and open, and let them talk and bring out their problems, then they will certainly do that. I mean, that is your ideal consultation, which we should probably try and do every time. (GP403)

The most frequently discussed issue for GPs was housecalls, 50-95 per cent of which were felt to be unnecessary, especially for lower socio-economic groups, both white and Pakistani.

My feeling on house calls is that I think a lot of them are unnecessary. You have got your percentage where it is just absolute rubbish: there is let's say a third absolute rubbish, there is another third where you can sort of see where the patient was coming from really, but at the same time, the outcome of the house call is well, I will need to see you again down at the health centre. (GP402)

Families were felt not to understand when a call was necessary, and when an illness would not be affected by a trip to the surgery.

Well I think they demand home visiting when... particularly if they have a car, there's nothing whatsoever to stop them....wrapping the child up and bringing the child down. It would be seen an awful lot quicker. I mean if they phone just now and I say wrap him up and bring him down, I'm gonnae see him within half an hour, whereas I'm no gonnae see him until this evening now if I've to go there (GP416)

Some views were particularly negative:

> They [Pakistanis] are less inclined to deal with minor ailments on their own in the way that the local population round here are...I think they think it is their right, or the done thing, to call the doctor at the slightest sniffle. (GP419)

This was not a general view: indeed, several GPs felt that extended Pakistani families could support mothers in recognising a minor illness, which did not need GP attention.

Complaining about cases in which white families would call the doctor out at night, having failed to collect a prescription during the day, one GP continued the theme of unnecessary house calls and misuse of services:

> [They say] 'How can I go? I don't have the bus fare' And they are sitting there with ten cans of .....lager. You tend to ask people 'Where did you get the money for that? You don't have the money to get your prescription'. (GP409)

Another doctor saw two sides of the picture:

> There are medically unnecessary house calls but then, whether your role is strictly [to say] 'This is a viral infection, there is nothing I can do about that, goodbye'.... if you perceive your role that way then, yes, they are unnecessary . Or if you perceive your role as a wider one where you know, you are the drug, you come into the house and say 'Don't worry, everything is all right, you can go to sleep now, the kid's not got meningitis, okay'.(GP405)

Health visitors emphasised the need of families in lower socio-economic groups for their health education role. Health visitors valued home visiting highly, describing it as the basis of building good relationships with their clients, communicating information effectively, including information about use of health services, doing preventative work and detecting problems early.

It's all to do with trying to build up relationships, isn't it.
(HV347)

Several health visitors regretted that they had been obliged to cut down on home visiting:

> Unfortunately, over the last four years, we have been discouraged from doing as much visiting as we did in the past, and therefore we tend not to have the same rapport with families as we perhaps did in the past, because we don't get to know them as well. (HV304)

Several GPs echoed this, and valued the health visitors' home visiting role. For all professionals, working with all clients, especially Pakistani clients with whom they did not share a language, a major problem was time constraints, felt to be increasing to the point of becoming false economies: repeated short consultations allowed problems to remain unattended, whereas one longer consultation might have dealt with them. Paperwork was encroaching on the time available for consultation.

Within the constraints of time and pressure of work, many health visitors were making considerable efforts to improve their service to Pakistani families. Three had studied Punjabi, and several had attended relevant in-service training (often in their own time). Health visitors saw building relationships with Pakistani families as a crucial investment. Several GPs also spoke about the need to cross cultural barriers, and forge good relationships with Pakistani families. The South Asian GPs felt that their knowledge of relevant culture and language was an asset in their work with Pakistani families, and for increasing their general sensitivity towards patients. One in particular spoke about the difficulty that many health personnel saw when they felt there were language problems:

> ...This mind set comes across, 'What language, don't understand, difficult' and that happens with all nurses, doctors, everybody, clerks, so that the minute they [Pakistani patients] walk in the door, you get this sort of thing, and that itself is intimidating [for the patient]. (GP418)

> Most GPs were not seeking training or support in their work with Pakistani families.

The median age of the Pakistani women interviewed was 30, and the white women, 33. Pakistani women had more children than white women (median 3, rather than 2), they were more likely to live in an extended family (27 per cent, compared with 4 per cent of white women), less likely to have jobs outside the home (5 per cent as compared with 38 per cent), and more likely to have relatives living nearby, though 15 per cent of them did not, as compared with 27 per cent of white women. White women's housing circumstances were more varied, both worse and better, than those of Pakistani women: Pakistani households tended to be larger, and there was more pressure on living space.

In general, both Pakistani and white women interviewed confirmed the conclusion drawn from our previous work that communication was better with health visitors than with GPs.

> She's more important than the doctor, especially when you've got a baby...and we need someone really, really helpful and really, really understanding. (PW107)

> I found it easier to talk to my health visitor than I did to the doctor, to any of the doctors. I think I felt that they weren't interested. They are there for illnesses rather than for depression. (WW215)

Many Pakistani women spoke about language difficulties as an obstacle to effective consultation with GPs, and, to a lesser extent, health visitors. Access to Punjabi speaking professionals was greatly appreciated. Some women who had problems with English were avoiding consultations, sometimes because there was no interpreter, but also sometimes because inappropriate interpreters such as family members and other non-professionals were being used. One woman explained how a desperate stranger had asked her for help.

> I remember there was a time when there was a lady sitting there [in the doctor's waiting room], and she's had to say to me 'Would you come in with me to explain to the doctor exactly what I want to say?' And I felt very awkward, because I didn't know this lady, and I felt she shouldn't have to tell me, you know, her private matters. (PW129)

Another woman (PW107) explained how she had been made to feel by clinic staff that her English was not good enough, and how this made her reluctant to visit the doctor. Her interview for the research was conducted in English, without difficulty.

Translated leaflets for Pakistani women were often not culturally sensitive, and many women could not read them: written Urdu involves a level of education many of them did not have, and the Punjabi spoken in Glasgow is not a written language. For some white women too, leaflets were a problem: some had difficulty with reading, and others explained that they preferred someone to sit with them and go over the leaflets, so that they could better follow them.

> She was really good. She'd come back and sit with me for maybe about four hours. And she brought me these leaflets explaining what postnatal depression is and all that. But I said I'm not very good at reading, and I don't understand all this. (WW225)

Both white and Pakistani women discussed housecalls extensively. Many felt that GPs were unwilling to visit, and that visits to surgeries were unduly distressing for a sick child. Whereas GPs concerns, as previously outlined, focused on the seriousness of the medical condition, women spoke of distress to the child:

> My child he was vomiting right, and he [the doctor] thought it wasn't so necessary for him to call out just because he is vomiting, but I thought you know that he should come out and see him, because I mean you know you can't expect for a child, especially when you go into a surgery, then again you've got to wait. (PW106)

> They're saying to bring the baby in cause it won't affect them, it won't make them any more ill, they won't catch anything, it's just a virus that they've got, but it really is quite distressing for them sitting around for that length of time. If there's no appointment you're just down there waiting and waiting.(WW202)

Women also referred to physical difficulties of access to surgeries, and complained of the insensitivity of GPs who suggested the use of taxis.

> We phoned up the doctor and the doctor says well the
> surgery was closed so he says bring it [sick child] to the
> house. We sometimes don't have a car to go to the house.
> We need to jump in a taxi and we cannot afford sometimes
> £3 and £4 in taxis up and down you know.(PW162)

Women described reluctance to call out GPs, knowing how busy they were.

> You don't want to bother them unless you have to.
> (WW209)

Another spoke of the doctor's reprimand, when she had called him,
believing the visit to be really necessary:

> And doctor came, and they [the children] were both sitting
> in the sitting room, and they were watching TV, and
> doctor said 'They're fine, why do you call me?' And he
> really insult me. 'Do you have a doctor in ...your own
> country? And can you call a doctor in your country like
> this?' All this and that, he didn't check my sons, and he
> was ... really insult me. (PW127)

Women's views therefore showed a very marked contrast with the GPs'
views about unnecessary house calls, and misuse of services. Women's views
seemed to be reinforced by the use of deputising services, as deputies always
called, they did not reprimand women, and they usually prescribed: this
would confirm women's view that the visit had been necessary. In this area,
therefore, there were some clear differences of perception, and lack of
communication.

Health visitors' home visits were generally appreciated, and many women
spoke of good relationships with health visitors. Pakistani women were
particularly positive, and were asking health visitors' advice before
consulting GPs.

> She was very, very bad baby. It's a mother's nightmare,
> and [the health visitor], she saved my life, she really did.
> (PW114)

> She listens to you, and she tries to be helpful, giving you
> hints and advice. (PW126)

The health visitors seem to be more keen to spend time,
and will even follow up with a phone call a day or so later.
(WW217)

She wasn't like a health visitor, she was like a pal. It was
like somebody was trying to help you all the time.
(WW225)

There were some problems with health visitors for a few of the white
women, who felt they had been treated autocratically, and referred to a
potential for health visitors to take children away.

You do hear a lot about social workers taking your kids
away from you, and health visitors and social workers
taking your kids away if they don't think that they're well
looked after (WW206)

Interviewee WW225, who had spoken of one health visitor as a 'pal',
compared another, very unfavourably:

I says 'You've told me, you've promised me about getting
my wean into a nursery, and you've never done it, you
don't want tae dae it.' I says, 'And don't build my hopes
up like that again like that, because I'll never believe
anything you say tae me again.' I says, 'I'm no wanting
you as my health visitor.' (WW225)

Another felt that health visitors were somewhat threatening:

I think the health visiting is a load of rubbish, because I
don't think they're equipped to do their job...See they put
people in a tizzy 'That health visitor's coming'. I don't
think you should feel under duress in your ain hoose fae
nobody, do you know what I mean? (WW229)

In several cases, health visitors had helped women to be more assertive in
seeking treatment from their GPs, acting as advocates:

I took him [child] to the doctor, and he said 'No, there's
nothing wrong with him'...I came back and my health
visitor said 'No, take him back again. Keep on taking him
until the doctor listens'. (PW120)

This woman did return to the doctor, and her child was eventually diagnosed with anaemia. Other women described similar experiences:

> She [health visitor] says 'Tell the GP to send you, go to a hospital, where you can see a specialist'. (PW122)

In this case, the problem was unexplained chest pains. A white woman's health visitor was helpful with access to the doctor in a more general way:

> If you can't get an appointment with the doctor, if you phone and ask her [health visitor's] advice...she'll tell you to come down, and she'll actually even go and get the doctor for you when you're there. (WW258)

Women who spoke well of their GPs attached great importance to GPs' listening skills, and referred to informality in consultations, GPs' ability to interact with children, general friendliness and time. Describing her ideal GP, one Pakistani woman expressed the views of most respondents:

> Somebody who'll tell you without rushing. A doctor that'll sit down and explain things to you, that's the most important. And a nice pleasant attitude. (PW117)

A white woman explained how her doctor helped with communication:

> Just by listening....he lets you speak without rushing you along....I just don't feel under any pressure when I go. (WW112).

Others felt that time was not so much an issue as attitude:

> Although he's probably as rushed as the rest, he doesn't give that impression, he will listen. (WW202)

> It's not the time - I don't think the time is the point really. (WW219)

She went on to explain how the doctor appeared to understand her problems, and that therefore, communication with her was easier.

Women who were positive about their GPs were taking their advice much more readily, whereas those who were more negative were more likely to seek alternative advice and use alternative, not always appropriate treatment. Several women were not attempting to take GP advice:

[If] they can't be bothered to listen to you, then you won't
bother to tell them. (WW201)

I don't want to ask them [GPs in local practice], because
they are in always bad mood. I don't want to disturb them
to ask what is this medicine. (PW127)

The last women quoted had not understood her medicine, and was not
taking it correctly.

Some women described bad relationships with their GPs, and were not
taking their advice, following, for example disputes with GPs, and GPs'
shouting at them. A Pakistani woman who visited the GP with her sister-in-
law recounted

She [was] having pains in her stomach, and he wouldn't
let me explain at all. And he got really angry....he grabbed
the table like that [demonstrates] and I was really scared
of him....I thought he was going to hit me. (PW123)

A white woman told a similar story:

Doctor says 'There's nothing the matter with you. See
youse women, youse think, youse always think there's
something the matter with you.' And he started shouting
and bawling at me. (WW225)

Other women, both white and Pakistani, felt that their GPs were not
listening to them: there were many cases of repeated trips to the GP in
attempts to communicate problems which were only dealt with after
considerable time. Often, women felt they had tried to say things to the GP,
but had failed to communicate, partly because of their nervousness, and
partly because of the GP's 'inattention'. This could have consequences for
service use:

If I had known more, then maybe I would have gone
maybe just once a week or something, instead of going
three or four times a week. (PW125)

He was stand-offish. I didn't feel that I could go down and
talk to him. He put everything down to your weight or
your age or the fact that you smoked. You know, you
couldn't have any underlying problems. You had to lose
all your weight and stop smoking. (WW223)

165

About two thirds of both groups of women stated that they preferred women doctors. Of course, many practices recognised this, and offered the option of consulting a woman doctor. Where the option was available, however, women were often not aware of it, as practice information had not reached them in an accessible form. The reasons for this preference focused on the embarrassment of consulting a man, and, for many, the feeling that women doctors were more understanding of women's problems. For some of the Pakistani women, the preference was also explained in cultural terms

> For Asian women, it's different. We're not allowed for a man to check us up, so it has to be a woman. (PW103)

Both white and Pakistani women were likely to say:

> I just feel more comfortable talking to a lady doctor than I do to a man, especially if it's woman trouble....I get all embarrassed talking to men doctors. (WW207)

There were a few white women who expressed active dislike of women doctors:

> I think some female doctors can be very bitchy, especially if they don't have any children of their own. (WW224)

Conclusions and implications for health services

For many Pakistani women in Glasgow, language is certainly a factor restricting their access to and use of health services, in that service personnel generally use English, and Punjabi speaking professionals are not readily available. In several cases, we found inappropriate interpreters were being used, to the detriment of effective service provision. Where women were able to use English, but found it difficult, professionals frequently did not have time to let consultations take their full course, with the result that consultations would multiply. There was some evidence that professionals expected Pakistani women not to speak English, and were therefore using stereotypes, which were acting as barriers to communication.

There are two main ways in which the language issue can be tackled. Firstly, appropriate, professional language assistance can be made more easily available. Health training for such assistants is important, to ensure that information is given correctly. Professionals can also be trained in the use of interpreters. However, as several of the professionals we interviewed explained, even the best of interpreters can still be a barrier, and, where possible, direct communication with the patient is desirable. Thus, secondly, where patients can use English, given time, the investment of extra time by professionals is appropriate. In the long run, as many professionals recognised, one longer consultation may prevent many shorter ones, and ensure quicker and more effective treatment. It is very likely that women's perceptions of health visitors as better communicators than GPs were at least partly related to health visitors' ability to devote more time to the process.

One of the largest communication gaps revealed in the data concerned GP housecalls. Generally, from the point of view of the GPs interviewed, a large proportion of housecalls, especially from people in lower socio-economic groups, were unnecessary, and involved trivial problems, which either did not need a doctor's attention, or which could be dealt with easily or more effectively (as facilities would be available) at the surgery. Sometimes, GPs said, calling the GP to the house amounted to abuse of the health service. Many felt that the problem was getting worse. Women however, both Pakistani and white, felt that their callouts were justified, particularly for children, who were likely to be distressed by visits to the surgery. Their accounts suggested they were far more reluctant to call GPs than the GPs felt was the case. Some housecalls reflected women's difficulties in getting an appointment quickly, or their disappointment at not getting a prescription on a prior visit to the surgery.

The GPs' use of deputising services to cover housecalls at night appeared to reinforce women's views that visits were unnecessary. From 28 February 1996, the new General Practitioners' Emergency Services set up clinics which patients could attend at night, and replaced some of the use of deputies. Whilst such a service might relieve some of the pressures on GPs, it is doubtful whether it will do much to change the basic communication gap concerning housecalls.

GPs reported that the number of housecalls had increased in recent years, and health visitors that protocols were restricting their home visiting. Whilst we cannot say that these trends are interlinked, their observation draws our attention to the potential role of health visitors in helping to tackle the house calls issue. Health visitors interviewed frequently spoke of their role as health promoters, helping mothers assure their children's health, and as supporters, building greater confidence in women's own judgements. Part of these tasks certainly related to assessing when medical attention was needed, and when it was needed urgently. From health visitors' points of view, the better the relationship they were able to build with women, the more effective their activities would be, and being able to make home visits improved relationship building. It was clear from the interviews with women that health visitors were generally respected, and their advice valued. Many GPs valued the role of the health visitor highly. There are therefore two identifiable measures which might alleviate the pressure of housecalls on

GPs: firstly, the role of the health visitor as educator and supporter can be utilised, and, secondly, the threat to health visitors' home visiting can be re-evaluated.

Many of the professionals interviewed, especially the health visitors, emphasised the importance of professional communication skills. It was clear that where professionals were conscious of this, and worked to develop their skills, barriers of culture and class could be crossed successfully, and women would seek and accept professional advice. From women's points of view, good professional communication skills were noted and appreciated. Clearly, however, from women's point of view, there were professionals, especially GPs, who lacked skills of this kind, who were felt not to listen, to rush patients, and even to abuse them.

There is certainly a case for GP training to include a clearer focus on communication skills than in the past: several of the GPs interviewed described how they had acquired their skills through experience, and regretted that they had not received training. Several reflected that they were working constantly to improve their skills. Health visitors were much more likely to have been trained in communication skills, and many had taken up opportunities for further study later in their careers. Some of health visitors' relative success may be related to their training, but we strongly suspect that it is also related to the holistic nature of their work (which has echoes in the women's more holistic concerns for their children when discussing housecalls), the manner in which it is done (especially the longer consultations), and also to their predominant gender. It is unlikely that all GPs can acquire these qualities and ways of working, but further promotion of inter-professional co-operation in the primary health care team is appropriate. Our findings suggested that the quality of inter-professional communication between GPs and health visitors was variable, although there was evidence of efforts to improve it. Health visitors were more likely to complain of poor communication than were GPs. The formality or informality of means of communication among primary care teams varied. This is an area which merits further investigation, since the potential for communication breakdown appears considerable. GPs can certainly utilise health visitors' skills more effectively.

With regard to service access for both white and Pakistani women therefore, the role of the health visitor was strongly highlighted. For Pakistani women, who could face extra difficulties arising from language, the time allocation and methods of working used by health visitors appear especially important.

A further striking feature of the data is that there was rather little evidence of overt racism on the part of professionals. This contrasts with some previous work, such as Bowler's (1993a) study of midwives, which showed that it was very widespread. There were some examples of negative stereotyping, concerning Pakistani overuse of services and language problems, but these were not common. Also, women recounted few experiences of racism. These findings suggest that there is a good basis for improving communication. However, it should be noted that several accounts given by women who had changed GPs referred to negative experiences, and also that the GPs who agreed to be interviewed may over-represent those with more positive attitudes.

Previous work (e.g. Stubbs 1993) has argued that there is institutional racism in the NHS, which requires challenge. It can be argued, for example, that the lack of appropriate language assistance revealed in our study represents an institutionalised exclusion from access to health services of Pakistani women who need such assistance. We would not dispute these arguments, but would urge greater attention be paid to the very positive work being done by many of the professionals interviewed in Glasgow.

It is also important to note that other forms of potentially exclusionary stereotyping were revealed in the data, including the emphasis, as we noted, on the particular problems many professional felt were presented by people, both white and Pakistani, in lower socio-economic groups. Several women described how they felt professionals to be prejudiced against them on class grounds, assuming stupidity or ignorance in women living in certain parts of the city. An overemphasis on racism as a central exclusionary factor can obscure the role of class differences.

Similarly, the preference for female doctors, which was not always satisfied, might be seen as another factor restricting women's access to health care, and is undoubtedly related to the gendered division of labour in the NHS. Again, emphasis on racism can exclude consideration of this factor.

In conclusion, it appears that there are communication difficulties for Pakistani and white women using general practitioner and health visiting services in Glasgow, and that these seem to be greater for general practitioners. Apart from issues related to Punjabi language, and some evidence of racism, the problems of white and Pakistani women are remarkably similar: even where the explanations for problems such as preferences for GP gender differed, similar solutions were appropriate for both groups of women. The problems do not appear insoluble.

11. South Asian women's access to cervical cytology

Sheila Paul

Introduction

This chapter explores the issue of South Asian women's access to cervical screening, a preventative service provided for women to assist in the prevention of cervical cancer. It draws on findings from semi-structured interviews with 36 South Asian women in Edinburgh[1]. The example of cervical screening is used to

---

[1] It is acknowledged that the use of terminology denoting minorities is problematic. The term 'minority ethnic groups' is used as it refers to sections of the population and their experiences in relation to the 'majority ethnic' population and to those that may experience discrimination and inequality on account of skin colour, heritage, way of life, language or religion. It also signifies that ethnicity is possessed by everyone, not just those readily identifiable as belonging to some distinctive sub-population The term South Asian is used to refer to those from or who are descended from those who were born in the Indian subcontinent (i.e. India, Pakistan or Bangladesh). The term white is used somewhat interchangeably with 'majority ethnic population', it is recognised that the former scarcely represent a unitary ethnic identity, however, the terminology used in the studies cited is followed throughout.

challenge previous work on minority ethnic groups and healthcare: firstly, attempts to explain South Asian women's uptake of, experience of, and health behaviour in relation to, the service have drawn on constructions of South Asian culture. Secondly, relatively more attention has been paid to the attributes of South Asian women compared to the attributes of health services. Thirdly, this has occurred without adequate attention being paid to South Asian women's experiences of, and perspectives on, the service. Fourthly, where constructions of South Asian culture are commonly overplayed in understandings of access to cervical screening, the 'race' and gender dimensions of South Asian women's access to the service have been submerged. Having examined some of the women's attitudes to cervical screening and some of the strategies they use to maximise their access to the service, paying particular attention to the role of social support, the chapter then uses the women's accounts to examine the 'race' and gender dimensions of access to this service.

Background

There is a dearth of information on women's experience of cervical screening (McKie 1995, Gregory and McKie 1991), on the factors that encourage women to be screened, or on the views and experiences of women who have never had or rarely use cervical screening (Gregory and McKie 1992, Senior and Williamson 1990). Generally, existing literature has centred on measures of service uptake and on women's levels of knowledge of cervical screening, *rather* than on their perspectives on, and experience of, the service. In addition, insofar as the literature has identified differences in the uptake of cervical screening among different categories of women, it has concentrated on age and class differentials (Schwartz *et al* 1989, Bowling 1989). Few studies have been designed to explore access to cervical screening services for categories of women occupying other social positions, for example, minority ethnic women.

A number of studies on uptake point toward inequalities in access to cervical screening for South Asian women. The picture, however, is contradictory. Studies refer to the widespread assumption that South Asian women as a group have low uptake rates of cervical screening services and preventative health programmes (Bowes and Domokos 1995, 1993, NAHAT 1995, Bradley and Friedman 1993, Anon 1991, Baker *et al* 1984). Some studies have confirmed relatively low cervical screening uptake rates (Pilgrim *et al* 1993, Hoare *et al* 1992, Doyle 1991, McAvoy 1989, McAvoy and Raza 1988), especially among younger and older South Asian women (HEA 1994). Bradley and Friedman (1993), however, show similar rates of uptake between older non-Asian and Asian women in Oldham.

Other work shows that the opportunities for accessing the service may be different for South Asian women compared to other categories of women. Several

171

studies indicate that South Asian women have poor knowledge of cervical screening and that they are less likely to have been screened in the past than majority ethnic women (Bradley and Friedman 1993, Doyle 1991, Firdous and Bhopal 1989, McAvoy and Raza 1988). Bradley and Friedman (1993) suggest that South Asian women may have had fewer opportunities to attend in the past than non-Asian women (see also Firdous 1987, Firdous and Bhopal 1989).

Some epidemiological evidence shows differences in the rate of cervical cancer among groups of women. Although it must be stressed that information on the incidence of cancer among minority ethnic groups is limited (Harding and Allen 1995, Smaje 1995), of particular importance to this study is some tentative evidence (Donaldson and Clayton 1984, Matheson *et al* 1995) suggesting that cervical cancer appears more frequently in Asian compared to non-Asian women.

Other studies, (such as McAvoy, 1989, McAvoy and Raza 1988, Barker and Baker 1990) however, show no difference in the incidence of cervical cancer among South Asian compared to non-Asian women. Mortality from the disease may be lower in those born in the Indian subcontinent than in the general population (Harding and Allen 1995, Balajaran and Bulusu 1990), though the impact of factors such as generation or migration on incidence and mortality rates remain unknown.

Constructions of culture, 'race' and gender and South Asian women's access to cervical screening

Cervical screening provides a good example for illustrating themes in the wider literature on minority ethnic groups and healthcare. Research has paid relatively little attention to the points of view of minority ethnic healthcare users (Ahmad *et al* 1989). The focus has been on attributes of minority ethnic groups rather than on the attributes of services, or on minority ethnic groups' ideas about, and experiences of, services.

Cervical screening also allows exploration of 'race' and gender dimensions of access services. Some gender dimensions are immediately apparent. Cervical screening is a preventative health service which recognises the unique health needs of women and is commonly perceived as a women's health issue (McKie 1995). It has attracted mainstream support, policy responses and resources (DoH 1992, Scottish Office 1992). Cervical cancer is a growing problem for all women and current policy recommends that women undergo screening regularly for most of their adult lives.

Although commentators have debated the advantages and disadvantages of cervical screening (e.g. Foster 1995, Holland and Stewart 1990, Skrabanek 1990, 1988, McCormick 1989), the dominant view is that cervical screening presents a number of health benefits for women. It has a possible preventative effect, and helps to reduce morbidity and mortality through detection and treatment. Furthermore, it is seen to help women in the active management of their health and healthcare.

The issue of South Asian women's access to cervical screening demonstrates the influence of assumed South Asian cultures in explanations of access to healthcare. Constructions of minority ethnic culture are used in an uncritical way and contain a limited understanding of minority ethnic groups' health and life experiences (Douglas 1992, Phoenix 1992, Lawrence 1982). In contrast, some have argued that culture is a dynamic force that sustains and nurtures people (Ahmad 1993a). Its effects on access to healthcare must be investigated rather than assumed (Bowes and Domokos 1996a). South Asian culture is widely assumed to generate constraints which deter South Asian women from attending, mean that cervical screening is a cultural taboo (cf. Bowes and Domokos 1996a) and allow little understanding of cervical screening. This has meant that explanations of South Asian women's supposedly poor uptake rates and experience of the service centre on the widely held assumption that South Asian women do not comply with, or are not motivated to use, cervical screening services (McAvoy 1989, McAvoy and Raza 1988).

Where ideas about cultural constraints stemming from stereotypical constructions of culture are overemphasised, debates have submerged the influence of 'race' and gender difference.

The issue of South Asian women's access to cervical screening then reflects the construction of minority ethnic groups' concerns and the pathologisation of their culture, health beliefs and behaviours, where groups are seen to deviate from 'good' health and healthcare, and are then blamed for their health problems. Thus, South Asian women are seen as irresponsible, or are 'bad' patients who are a danger to their own health. In effect, the cause of access difficulties becomes located within the minority ethnic communities themselves. It is suggested that women would attend if they were educated out of their beliefs and anxieties, that they need to adapt to health services, and not that health services might need to adapt to the users of services.

It is clear that the effects of South Asian culture, 'race' and gender difference on South Asian women's access to cervical screening require more investigation. Research must be designed to examine and understand women's own views, rather than predetermine their concerns, assume their preferences or take for granted the existence of culturally based taboos in relation to this health service.

The study

The findings presented below are drawn from a wider qualitative study focusing on South Asian women's access to healthcare in Edinburgh (Paul 1996). This involved 36 semi-structured interviews with women from the four main South

Asian ethnic categories in Edinburgh (Pakistani, Bangladeshi, Indian (of Hindu heritage) and Sikh). Thirteen interviews involved the use of an interpreter. The women were aged between 23 and 66. All but five were born in the Indian sub-continent. The study aimed to provide a detailed understanding of access to healthcare which was sensitive to the perspectives and experiences of South Asian women. In order to do this, it focused on a range of healthcare areas including cervical screening. Women were asked about their perspectives on, knowledge and experiences of, cervical screening services, especially their first and most recent experiences. Of the women questioned, all but one had undergone one or more tests, 26 of the women had had their first test in their twenties. The findings, therefore, relate to the views and experiences of regular and irregular attenders rather than non-attenders.

Most women talked quite freely about their views and experiences. Only one woman seemed embarrassed to talk about her experiences and another, who had not been screened, was not asked about her experiences as it was felt by the interpreter to be inappropriate at the time of interview. These findings provide an initial challenge to the widespread assumption of constraints imposed by South Asian culture.

Women's attitudes to cervical screening

Beliefs upon which health actions are taken help us to understand how women use the service and why they use it in particular ways. The accounts showed a range of attitudes, with the majority of women generally positive about screening, its function, effectiveness and relevance to their own health. One woman was more negative. Most felt that cervical screening provision was a 'good idea' or 'good for you'. Some held more positive views than others. Their reasoning revolved around a 'need to know if they were healthy', to make sure 'nothing was wrong' and to ensure early treatment should any problems occur. Such ideas led women toward rather than away from screening:

> It's important for me, it's good to know if everything is OK. If something's wrong with you you've got to get it treated isn't it? (Sikh woman age 42, 0903[2])
> Yes they are good, you get, like they do smear test it's every three years I think, three to five years, yes that's good. Even though you can't be bothered like you don't like going for a smear test but end of the day it's good for you, it's better to be safe than sorry you know...You never know anything could

[2] All quotations are attributed. The number at the end of each attribution is the interview number.

have happened, anything can happen with you so it's good if you can have a few test and you can find out these thing so why not? (Indian woman age 27, 3501)

Others were positive about screening, and wanted to know if they were healthy and to ensure early treatment, but their attitude also involved a degree of obligation to participate in the service:

Good for us. That's why...for check-up no...They checks inside so if you've got anything wrong do something. SP: Did you ask some questions during the test? No. I thought the doctor knew better I just ask what for no?...They suggest me no? (Indian woman age 59, 1504)

Others were more neutral, mentioning an obligation to attend but omitting ideas about the health benefits of screening:

I don't know really, I have no experience, whatever the doctors did to me, I feel like is good for me. Because I don't know why, good with me. (Bangladeshi woman age 22, 2901)

Women's attitudes towards cervical screening showed variation rather than cultural consistency. They provided no indication that South Asian women's attitudes to cervical screening are totally distinct from other women or are dictated by conventional ideas about South Asian culture. In general, the views of those interviewed did not differ significantly from those of other categories of women revealed in other studies. They reflected a widespread understanding that cervical screening is diagnostic rather than preventative i.e. to detect cancer as a first step to treating it, rather than to prevent cancer (Gregory and McKie 1992, 1990). They perceived that attending is a positive health behaviour enabling women to find out about health problems and act on them, rather than to prevent cervical cancer.

Most women were sure about the need for regular screening. Eleven of the 15 women who said they had attended regularly and six of the nine women who had not attended regularly, knew that testing needs to be done every three years. Only a minority were seriously misinformed about the frequency of screening specified in policy. Other studies have identified women's misapprehensions about the need for regular screening, including studies on majority ethnic women (Gregory and McKie 1991, Posner and Vessey 1988) and on South Asian women (McAvoy 1989, McAvoy and Raza 1988), but the present findings suggest that the views of women interviewed are in line with positive health behaviours.

Other commonly cited barriers to uptake such as fear of cancer did not seem to dissuade attendance. This contrasts with other studies which suggest that screening uptake is constrained by women's anxiety, apathy and fatalism about cancer (Naithoo 1988), and that people's misconceptions about cancer make them delay obtaining medical treatment (Johnson and Meischke 1994). Gregory and McKie (1992) and O'Donoghue (1993) suggest that women may not want to be screened because they do not want to know of any problems that might be present. Although it may be true that among women who do not attend, fear of knowing about health problems inhibits uptake, the women in this study identified similar factors prompting them to take up screening. This was linked to a perception that health is uncertain. Three women felt that one 'can never be sure that one is fine' if diseases like cancer exist. This occurred despite a feeling, in the accounts of twelve women who talked about their beliefs about and attitudes toward cancer more generally, that the public is more aware of, and better informed about, cancer than in the past.

> They should get smear tests, I think all women should nowadays, because there's a lot of diseases about now and it's good that women should be checked...(Sikh woman age 38, 1002)

> So many this country...they are hearing television everybody die in cancer. If you don't want to check-up [have a smear test]. If tell earlier can go and do something you know. If you go later can't do anything no? (Indian woman age 59, 1504)

Social support and South Asian women's access to cervical screening

The concept of social support is poorly understood for minority ethnic groups. For South Asian women, non-professional support is often assumed to be supplied by the extended family (Carby 1982, Parmar 1982). This invokes stereotypes of minority ethnic culture, and assumptions about extended families can have negative implications for South Asian women's experiences of health services (Bowler 1993a, 1993b, Evers *et al* 1989).

It is clear from the present study that social support plays a number of roles in women's management of access to this service and affects women's attitudes to, and uptake of, cervical screening.

Although the women were discerning over who they talked to about screening, social support enabled access to cervical screening in a number of ways. Firstly, it helped women learn about cervical screening: it is notable that they felt they learned more about screening by word of mouth than from health promotion material such as leaflets and posters. Thirteen women emphasised the value of learning about cervical screening in informal learning environments such as women's voluntary groups. The interview data suggest that linkworkers (mentioned by two women), friends and relatives (16 women) and women's voluntary groups (seven women) enhanced the likelihood of attending, affecting decisions to attend and to keep on attending.

Secondly, social support helps to improve the quality of the screening experience for women. Eight women felt encouraged by friends and relatives who confirmed that screening 'is good for you' and helped to allay worries about the procedure. Others helped women to think positively, to rationalise fears, for example, about positive results, and helped them to 'talk out' their fears. Five women said they found it useful to talk to others if they had had similar experiences, for example, finding screening painful, receiving an abnormal result, or encountering the same language constraints. Some accounts illustrated the importance of social support for women new to the service and reluctant to approach a health professional. They stress the importance of knowing how the service works and that access is easier for women who are UK born or have lived in the UK for some time. These two women had lived in the UK for less than 10 years:

> Every woman is not, you know...experienced unless [there is] somebody to tell her, [like a] mother or sister but I don't have here, mother and sister. So I just tell to my husband 'I did this, I feel this like that' and go to doctor. (Pakistani woman age 27, 3101)

> She [sister-in-law] told me everything, what they going to do because she been there first. She been here twenty years, more than twenty years so she knows everything. She told me you don't have to scare yourself and nobody give [will cause] you any harm. (Indian woman age 32, 2202)

Some women (eight) described how they were concerned about the approachability of health professionals in relation to screening, others (11) were concerned about the pain and discomfort of screening, some (nine) described a sense of embarrassment, or were anxious to some degree about the implications of screening (20 women). Sources of social support play an important part in enabling access by providing advice, 'genuine concern', understanding and emotional support:

> She [friend] really genuinely cares about me so she is giving me good advice. Whereas the others it's just like a job for them...But having that support, genuine concern, does make you feel you should do it [attend for screening] really. (Pakistani woman age 33, 0303)

It's easier talking to women because they are same, they know, like what is happening to them and what's happening to us like. But talking to a professional I don't think so...I don't think they understand anymore, I think you're better talking like to a woman, like my friend... (Sikh woman age 38, 1002)

Well talking to people it would help me in a way to relieve my stress. Talking to professionals is helping me professionally about a problem. (Sikh woman age 37, 0202)

Social support could also provide practical assistance. Family and friends, especially other women, provided informal childcare, reminded women when screening was due (eight women), provided transport to use the service (two women) and provided language assistance (five women).

Social support therefore affects women's attitudes towards, uptake of and experience of, cervical screening. It assists with the social and psychological, informational and practical aspects of attending. Social support is an unseen but positive part of the service (Gregory and McKie, 1990). It is used both overtly and covertly to relay information and to provide support that is more immediate and personal than, for example, published health information. Social support enhances attendance and the likelihood that women will keep on attending, and is effective in persuading, reinforcing and reminding women to adopt healthy behaviours and to use the service.

Gender dimensions of access to cervical screening

Gender role obligations affected women's use of screening services in various ways. Six women were concerned about their family commitments and the lack of childcare provision when using the service. For example, they described instances of waiting in clinics with small children in tow. Some described how they had negotiated their way around commitments to others, including their families.

Another woman described how she negotiated demands on her time and the organisation of health services, and how both factors affected her use of the service. Her health needs must be seen against the needs of others. It was her feeling that she was able legitimately to go for screening in what she called her time, in this case when she was at work:

...when I have to cancel something for my children I am not very happy. Then I have to find the time that doesn't disturb my children that doesn't disturb my husband, I work in

178

between. As a working mother with a young family it is difficult to find time which is you know suitable for everyone. Sometime if the time is suitable for you it's not suitable for doctor. ...If they offer me the same thing...in my working time and things like that, yes I'll go. But if they offer me in the hospital which is far away...then I'll probably cancel...(Indian woman age 39, 0102)

Another woman's account illustrates the effects of gender role constraints on service uptake by women, especially those with young children. She was screened opportunistically and described how she felt able to have her one and only test because the children were not with her:

Yes it was a lady doctor that did it. I remember I went in for something else and it was on the notes where it said I was supposed to have one and because I didn't have the kids with me that day for some reason, she said 'You might as well, you have got a bit of time, why not get it over and done with'. It would save me having to come back again. (Pakistani woman age 23, 1301)

Gender role obligations also affect how women feel about being screened. For some, this was linked to a perception that health is uncertain and to the implications of screening. This woman recalled her feelings about a suspected positive result and considered the implications for her family including her school aged sons:

I was worried like anything because my children were so small, if anything happens to me, who's going to look after the children. Any time I get a little bit sick, I always worry about what's going to happen to my children. (Pakistani woman age 35, 3402)

Another woman recounted how her experience of screening was affected by attending with one nursery school age child, another primary school age child and her new baby:

I go with my [children] and I says I don't want to [in] this room...I tell the doctor when you smear test. She says 'they [children] are safe in the waiting room, they look after her if you don't want'. Because my husband is not with me and he can't come...[with] me and I have to do this smear test, I want to do this smear test but I don't want my daughter and the others to see. (Pakistani woman age 27, 3101)

She stressed that she wanted to be screened, and the relevance of screening to her health. Instead of declining her test, she clearly negotiated the service and 'made do'. It is easy to see how women may be distracted by their children and how this may mean they are unable to take in what the health professional is saying.

The accounts convey the effects of gender role constraints on access to the service at a number of levels, both in terms of going to the service and in women's experience of the service. They also show how constraints stemming from the obligations attached to gender roles may be reproduced in health services themselves, for example, where services do not provide for women with young children. Gender role obligations and associated time pressures may detract from the quality of the screening experience and affect women's patterns of use. The resources of time, transport and organisation needed to access health services are not available to all women (Pearson and Spencer 1990) or to women all the time. Health professionals have paid much attention to the 'failure' of women to attend for screening (Foster 1995, Eardley et al 1985). If a woman does not participate she forgoes the wider health benefits described above, is labelled a non-complier and is considered to be 'irresponsible' in terms of her own health. Women's health behaviour, however, is a negotiation of overarching demands on time resources and other commitments (Pearson and Spencer 1990). Given the complexity of women's lives, it is easy to see how, as for white women, South Asian women's own health may become a low priority (Gregory and McKie 1992, 1991, Pill and Stott 1982).

Two women described how they felt unable to ask questions about cervical screening given the intrusive nature of the procedure. This woman went on to say that by the time examination was over she had forgotten what she wanted to ask:

> ...Well I always have this thing like when the doctor says 'get up on the bed and take your trousers off and you know, lie down with your legs wide open' that's the uncomfortable part of thinking of it and then you think oh God what are they going to do now? And the actual test was a bit uncomfortable but it was over with, only a few minutes so I didn't think too much about it. (Pakistani woman age 23, 1301)

Thirteen women first learned about cervical screening as part of maternity care. Some stressed that they were 'used to this kind of thing' as they had experienced similar procedures in pregnancy and childbirth. Their accounts suggest that the experience of maternity care may mean that women learn not to question medical procedures, particularly those in body spaces involved in reproduction. As in other studies on white women, this may mean then that women see medical interventions associated with reproduction ambivalently (Gregory and McKie 1992). They may learn not to question the way cervical screening is offered to them, or not to ask for help when they feel dissatisfied or confused, or want to know more about what is happening to them.

One woman recalled that her experience led her to delay subsequent tests. Another recalled the difficulties in learning about screening after having a baby. She felt that, at the time, she was not in a position to question or learn about any medical interventions. These aspects of the interview data suggest that, in such circumstances, screening becomes a procedure rather than an entitlement to keep healthy:

> How often I used to get them? I really couldn't tell you but for the last 10 years now I get them every three years. I know that I got a letter to the house because my kids are all grown up. Maybe they used to do them after six weeks check-up, after the babies and things like that. You are so busy you don't ask, you never got the chance to ask these questions from your doctor. Why you are doing this? Why are you doing that? And what is happening? SP Why is it different now? 0903: Now maybe I got more time, the kids have grown up, you are worried you want to know what's going on in yourself. Maybe earlier on you were so busy...Now you want to know...(Sikh woman age 42, 0903)

She made sense of her feelings by linking her experience of health services to her level of knowledge of cervical screening. Health service experiences like these perpetuate the situation in which women feel that they do not know enough about screening and at the same time feel that they cannot ask about it.

These women emphasise constraints on access to cervical screening which stem from the attributes of health services, and which are linked with gender roles, rather than from constructions of South Asian culture.

There are a number of implications for access to the service. Firstly, medical environments and the messages that women receive from them, can reproduce confusion, anxiety, dislike and all the other concerns of the women referred to above. Secondly, in such circumstances women's knowledge about screening may be constrained. Thirdly, if medical environments constrain women's ability to make healthcare choices, the service may remain 'medically managed' rather than 'women centred', and the wider promotive healthcare benefits are thereby restricted.

Racism and cervical screening

The women's accounts showed that racism was a significant and persistent force in shaping their experiences of the service, and acted subtly to make cervical screening services less accessible.

Some accounts linked women's experiences of ideas about 'race' difference to the attitudes of health professionals. Interpersonal racism involved overt racial prejudice and discrimination by individuals, and might include the expression of stereotypical assumptions about South Asian women's health behaviours and needs. One woman recalled how stereotyping shaped her experience of screening. She went on to question the cultural stereotype:

> Yes she [nurse] said like 'some Asian women like they don't like getting it done, this smear test and then even they don't like getting, they bring their husband along with them'...so she was very surprised with me like I was so free about these things...and when she is doing it they [South Asian women] are being sissy, oh it's hurting when it's not hurting them. So she was very happy with me...It depends on person to person...like way of thinking...(Indian woman age 27, 3501)

Her account indicates that a practice nurse in effect made her feel different from other women because she was South Asian.

Another woman felt unable to ask about what was happening to her because she did not want to appear, in her words, 'stupid'. She was particularly confused and wondered if cervical screening screened 'for breast cancer'.

> ...I think our women tend maybe not to ask too many questions, they just let the doctor do what he has to do sort of like you know. They just see it as a thing that has to be done but they don't ask too many details about it. It's like you feel embarrassed to ask something. You shouldn't feel embarrassed obviously. If you can't talk to a female doctor then who can you talk to really?...

> I don't mean that they don't actually go for the test. The problem is that they don't know too much about it and that they don't ask much about it. Probably they have got a male doctor or they feel embarrassed asking questions or they felt they should know already about it. They feel that *they can't ask because people think they are stupid*...I feel as though I should know about it and I feel that I should know. I feel as though saying, I think it is for breast cancer, I feel as though I

have probably said the wrong thing (Pakistani woman age 23, 1301) [own emphasis]

Communication difficulties are part of the negative typification of South Asian women in their use of health services (Bowler 1993a). Language constraints in particular are commonly assumed and attached to all South Asian women as a catch-all explanation for constraints in access to healthcare provision. In common with other work on South Asian women, the two accounts above suggest that women may be disadvantaged by assumptions about, and stereotypes of, the health behaviour of South Asian women (Bowler 1993a, 1993b, Parsons et al 1993).

Assumptions about the health behaviour and culture of South Asian women may shape women's experiences of, and their responses to, screening. One of the effects of stereotyping is that it masks sensitivity to the individual and her needs and wishes. It is a way in which discrimination based on 'race' occurs without the actions involved appearing, at least on the surface, to be racist, and is a way of handling the common-sense racism in society in an everyday context (Ginsberg 1992). These findings support the small body of work which reports that health professionals may hold negative stereotypes of South Asian patients, and this has implications for provision and the quality of healthcare as well as for individual healthcare choices (e.g. Bowler 1993a, 1993b; Patel 1993; Ahmad et al. 1991; Evers et al. 1989).

Most women voiced their concerns about institutional racism, whether they said that they had experienced it or not. They talked about personal experiences, or empathised with other South Asian women and were concerned about the exclusion others might face in services.

The operation of institutional racism was particularly apparent in relation to language. Language difficulties affected women's health service choices and their ability to define needs, to learn about healthcare, and to understand screening procedures:

> Yes but I think I have got an advantage with communication, I think that way. You can say what you want to say and how you want to say it...(Indian woman age 33, 2002)

They also affect women's confidence in service use and the ability to 'fit in':

> ..other women, they have their own language, they are in their own country and I think that makes it easy for them to approach for anything...If you can't speak very good English, then you worry about doing anything you want to do, you feel you are not happy, your inside is not happy, you don't have the confidence that other women would have I would

say...Because you are coloured, you are not the same as they are and if you don't fit in their groups, they are not going to accept you and that is very important to be accepted by a foreigner...and you're different and if you start being different then it's so difficult to get into I would say. (Indian woman age 41, 2803)

To attend for screening, one must possess an understanding of how the health system operates. Eleven women felt that other categories of women had better access to the service because they spoke the 'language of services', knowing where to go, and who to see at the outset. One woman had been screened on registering with her GP surgery. She had been in the UK for only a few weeks and had limited fluency in English. She had not grown up in the context of a medical system where cervical screening is part of mainstream care. Her experience led to feelings of anxiety and distress because she did not fully understand what was going on and was not familiar with screening or the health system. On returning home she told her husband:

Interpreter: If that's what they do here, I want to go back to Pakistan! (Pakistani woman age 30, 0501).

Another woman depended on her school aged children to help her with language problems in daily life. Sometimes, she was able to use a linkworker, available through the women's voluntary sector, to assist her. She recounted her last screening experience very angrily:

Interpreter: Now is little bit easier because they write the letter to go there to the clinic and nurse and check and they did not ask anything, they didn't make any question or anything just...SP: When Mrs K. went they said nothing? Interpreter: Yes...Then report [results] they send by post. (Bangladeshi woman age 31, 2402)

She felt unsure of the precise benefits of cervical screening. Staff did not appear to have taken the trouble to ensure that she understood the process or the nature and implications of the examination. Her experience of screening did not allow her to improve her knowledge, to attend actively for screening or to make a considered decision to attend because the health professionals made no effort to communicate with her. Even though a female health professional took the test, as she wanted, her interaction with the service was faceless and negative.

The accounts suggest that a lack of information may be perpetuated by the system, not via the operation of a cultural taboo. It is not that health messages and benefits were not heard or fell on 'deaf ears' on account of South Asian culture, but that health messages may not be conveyed by health professionals to users appropriately or at all, and women were effectively prevented from expressing views or asking questions.

In conclusion, poor access to healthcare through the operation of racism, can be reproduced and reinforced by the actions of health services and health professionals. Health services and health professionals can play a role in defining groups as 'different' and in making women aware of their marginality and making them feel different. At the same time, health services are ostensibly blind to the presence of different ethnic groups. For example, failure to provide for language needs can create and maintain barriers affecting access to health services. One of the main damaging effects is that the actions of health services and professionals can reinforce the stereotyped view that South Asian women are uninterested in preventative healthcare described above. It follows that women can be blamed for their health service experiences and are seen as a danger to their own health. The pathologisation of South Asian women's health behaviours is thus reproduced, and for South Asian women as a group, it means that women's needs are left unmet and are not a priority.

Ideas about 'race' difference compound the effects of ideas about gender difference in restricting access to healthcare. This means that South Asian women, as a racialised group, experience pressures and constraints in addition to those experienced by majority ethnic women.

Conclusion

This chapter has emphasised that understandings of South Asian women's experiences of cervical screening should not be confined to ideas about service uptake, the attributes of women or women's levels of knowledge about the service. A focus on South Asian women's experiences and perspectives of the service has enabled me to challenge explanations using culturally based arguments both to deny and explain South Asian women's access to this preventative service. The widely-held assumptions that South Asian culture generates constraints which deter South Asian women from attending, and they have little enthusiasm for preventative services, lack knowledge about screening and experience constraints stemming from cultural taboos are not supported by this study. By focusing on women's own views, the chapter has also highlighted a range of factors affecting South Asian women's screening experiences that are not normally flagged in explanations of South Asian women and cervical screening. They include women's positive preventative health behaviours, social support and the 'race' and gender dimensions of access to cervical screening.

The study has also identified a number of constraints on access to the service. Ideas about 'race' and gender difference run right through women's decisions to attend, their attitudes toward screening and their experience of the service. This provides another challenge to explanations of South Asian women's screening experiences that draw on constructions of South Asian culture. The women negotiate these constraints so that they are not rendered passive in their experience of the service. A number of factors are shared with other categories of women identified in other studies. These have included constraints on the use and experience of the service posed by obligations attached to gender roles, beliefs about screening and cervical cancer and the medicalisation of women's bodies. Other factors are specific to members of racialised groups. Stereotyping South Asian women's health behaviours in relation to the service, and institutional racism, both detract from the quality of women's screening experience and make women inactive in their healthcare. Ideas about 'race' and gender difference have also been shown to contribute to the processes preventing women from being active in their healthcare and rendering them unable to make their needs known or express their concerns.

Finally, the practices of health professionals and the attributes of services are included among the constraints on women's access to the service. Screening presents a number of access difficulties including communication with health professionals and constraints on women's ability to increase their knowledge about, and attend actively for, screening. Importantly the accounts have revealed ways in which the assumed health behaviours of South Asian women persist. The manner in which the service is provided can help to reproduce and support the negative social constructions of South Asian women, help define South Asian women as 'different' and emphasise their assumed pathological health behaviours.

Acknowledgements

The author would like to thank all the women who were interviewed, the women's voluntary sector in Edinburgh as well as Shamshad Rahim and Nila Joshi for their help with translation and the study. Also Dr Alison Bowes and Professor Susan Smith for their help throughout the project.

This study would not have taken place without a Research Studentship from the ESRC.

An earlier version of this paper was presented to a meeting in Sheffield, YRGH organised by the Department of Geography, Sheffield University.

12. Understanding depression in young South Asian women in Scotland

Eddie Donaghy

Introduction

Successive studies have identified life events as playing a significant part in the onset of depression in women. This chapter addresses the diverse nature and impact of life events in a selection of second-generation South Asian[1] women living in Edinburgh and Glasgow some of whom were depressed and some not depressed. It aims firstly to highlight research findings, particularly those of Brown and Harris (1978), on the impact and nature of severe life events and their part in the social origins of depression in women in the UK. Secondly it alerts the reader to some of the issues relating to mental health studies in second-generation South Asian women, including the use of the term 'culture conflict', which is often used as an explanation as to why some young South Asian women develop mental health problems. Thirdly it gives an account of the author's study and its

---

[1] This term shall be used throughout the chapter to refer to the interviewees who participated in this study and those who have been the focus of other similar studies referred to in this work. In using the term South Asian, I refer to those people whose parents were born or they themselves were born in the Indian subcontinent, i.e., India, Pakistan and Bangladesh. The term does not suggest a homogeneous grouping of people and acknowledges the variations in language, culture, religion, class and caste that exist.

findings on the nature and impact of severe life events in a sample of 46 South Asian women in Scotland, with particular emphasis on why some of the women in the sample became depressed. Fourthly, it discusses the applicability of the Brown and Harris model to those women who took part in the study and second generation South Asian women generally.

Research in the UK into the mental health of minority ethnic communities in general and the South Asian community in particular, was, until relatively recently, restricted either to quantitative work, for example statistical analysis of compulsory admissions for specific mental illnesses by ethnic origin, or to specific issues such as the high incidence of schizophrenia or depression. Recent research has noted that, as with the white indigenous communities, a wide variety of mental health problems exist, including depression, anxiety, eating disorders and various psychotic disorders (Mumford 1991b, Ineichen 1990). A number of recent studies of depression (Beliappa 1991, Fenton and Sadiq 1993, 1996), eating disorders (Raleigh 1989, Merrill and Owens 1986, Merrill 1988, 1989, Merrill et al 1990), and parasuicide (Merrill and Owens 1986, Merrill 1988, 1989, Merrill et al 1990), have identified several factors believed to influence a range of mental disorders. In some studies 'culture conflict' has been seen as the key factor, especially in eating disorders and parasuicide in young South Asians.

In the wider literature, it has been argued that the experience of severe life events can increase the risk of mental illness: studies, particularly research on depression, indicate that experiencing severe life events, in the absence of social support, can increase the risk of depression in women. They suggest an approach to the study of depression in South Asian women which moves away from the emphasis on culture conflict, and stresses individual biography and circumstances.

Following their study of life events and depression among working class women in Camberwell (London), the approach of Brown and Harris (1978) became established as a major contribution to understanding the role of life events in the development of depression. Brown and Harris (1978) and Brown (1989) describe life events essentially as re-adjustments in thoughts provoked by an event, or series of events over time, which affect how a person views the world. This is usually paralleled by a change in outlook and behaviour. The link between life events and depression has been confirmed by several studies, particularly those adopting the Brown and Harris approach, such as Costello (1982), Campbell et al (1983), Martin (1982), Parry and Shapiro (1986), Bebbington et al (1984).

Brown and Harris (1978) note loss and disappointment to be the central features of a majority of severe events bringing about depression. There is general consensus regarding the role of loss in the development of depression (e.g., Paykel 1974, Brown and Finley-Jones 1981, Miller and Ingham 1983, Dohrenwend et al 1978). In such circumstances, a person with depression has usually lost an important source of value and/or reinforcement of value, which may be derived from a person, a social role or aspiration (Brown 1989). The greater a person's desire and involvement with an aspiration, role or person, the greater the impact of loss and failure is likely to be (Brown 1987). In the same vein, Craig and Brown (1984) and Hammen *et al* (1985) noted that when a severe life event disrupts that aspect of an individual's life domain in which the person has major goals, concerns and commitments, such an event is more likely to have an adverse effect on mental health.

The work of Brown and Prudo (1981) among Hebridean women extended the knowledge of variables involved in depression across different social and cultural contexts, suggesting the importance of examining cultural context in detail. Greenglass *et al* (1988), Poole and Langan-Fox (1991) have contributed to the increasing recognition of the gendered nature of depressive illness. Family experiences may also affect mental health. Shaw (1988) and Ballard (1990), studying South Asian families, identified factors in the traditional roles of women and family loyalty that also arose in the work of Brown and Prudo (1981) and Brown et al (1981). Shaw noted that the concept of *izzat* (male and family honour) was of central importance in many South Asian families. Anything that challenged *izzat* and/or *biraderi* (the wider family network) was often conceived by the male heads of the family as bringing dishonour on to that family (Shaw 1988, Ballard 1990). The demand for women to conform to individual roles and family expectations is often strong, and deviation from this, in whatever form, can often lead to conflicts and distress. Merrill (1988, 1989), Merrill *et al* (1990) and Mumford (1991) reported that role conflict correlated highly with feelings of hopelessness and suicidal intent among young South Asian women, and that conflicts over traditional behaviour and dress for South Asian girls led to eating disorders. Beliappa (1991), found that South Asian women who were dissatisfied and in conflict over their perceived roles constituted a group at high risk of developing depression. The social role of women resulted in conflict and, since female roles were linked fundamentally to the family, women were more vulnerable to psychological distress arising out of role conflicts between them and their family.

The literature thus suggests that Brown and Harris's model may enable us to reach a better understanding of young South Asian women and depression. The factors they identify as significant in causing depression, namely severe life events combined with lack of social support, may occur for young South Asian women as for other women, though their specific manifestation may vary (as it did for the Hebridean women as compared with the women in Camberwell). The model involves a focus on individual biography and experience, rather than collective phenomena such as culture. The emphasis on 'culture conflict' as the key factor in depression and other mental health problems of young South Asian women appears misguided in the light of these strong suggestions that the Brown and Harris model can be applied. On this basis, this study examines how and why second generation South Asian women living in Britain can become depressed, and uses the Brown and Harris model.[2]

The study

The study focused on severe life events among second-generation South Asian women living in Glasgow and Edinburgh. Women interviewed were aged between 16 and 35, and were married with children. They were either born in Scotland, had moved to Scotland from another part of the UK, or had arrived into Scotland from India or Pakistan aged five years or under. A total of 46 women took part in semi-structured, in-depth interviews on a range of issues from primary/secondary schooling experiences, adolescence, employment, through marriage and motherhood to the present day. All three major religious groupings were interviewed, the samples being constructed to be as representative as possible, with a majority being Pakistani Muslims, followed by Indian Hindus, and Indian Sikhs.[3]

One half of the interviewees had been diagnosed by a GP or psychiatrist as having depression and were receiving treatment for this condition. The remaining 23 had no history of mental illness. The depression/ anxiety scale HADS, which has been used in depression studies on South Asians in the UK and in the Indian subcontinent was used to give a rough estimation of the presence and absence of depression in both groups. (For a wider discussion on the validity of HADS and other depression/anxiety scales and their use in South Asian populations see Chaturvedi 1990, Mumford 1990, 1991b, Nayani 1989).

In attempting to cover women's diversity of experience and beliefs, an ethnographic approach was seen as the best means of data collection. In attempting to gain an insight into the life experiences, hopes, goals, values and aspirations of the women, the researcher was investigating key factors implicated in depressive illness (Brown and Harris 1978). Drawing on Brown and Harris, the study aimed to investigate the likely meaning of events for each interviewee by assessing their place in the 'person's biographically determined circumstances'. To achieve this, it was necessary to gain an insight into the women's social and personal environments as perceived and described by the women themselves.

---

[2] A full account of the study, including a review of methodological issues, is given in Donaghy 1995a and 1996.

[3] In preparing the ground for and carrying out the study, a range of methodological issues arose, not least the issue of gender and ethnicity particularly in relation to the research and the interviewees.

Thus, the approach was designed to investigate the likely meaning of an event for an individual by assessing its place within her personal history and current situation (Brown and Harris 1978). An assessment of the strength of a particular life event was made by the author, following lengthy discussions with the women.

A semi-structured interview schedule was developed, to cover educational experiences, employment, marriage, parenthood, social contacts, aspirations and personal goals, but the interviews were open-ended and flexible enough to allow the women the freedom to describe a range of life details and experiences not contained in the schedule but relevant to themselves. If, as studies such as Merrill's (1989, 1990) suggest, culture and tradition were factors, the researcher wanted the women to bring these issues out themselves. This in fact happened, as the women frequently referred to their life experiences at certain stages by saying 'it's the tradition' or 'it's a cultural thing'. The researcher would then ask the interviewee what they meant by this. This led in turn to definitions of tradition, culture and religion and the similarities and differences between these areas as perceived by the women. Where the women felt it necessary, their own perceptions of religion, culture and tradition were in turn related to specific areas of their past and present life experiences, outlook and personal goals. The interview schedule addressed the issue of racism and provided the women with an opportunity to discuss racism generally and specifically in relation to their own life experiences.

The interviewees determined when and where the interview took place, the majority being in the respondent's homes, where familiar territory built confidence and the researcher was invited in as a guest. Where interviews took place in centres, the researcher was a guest of the women's group or community group and they, in conjunction with the interviewee, determined when and where the interview took place.

Findings

This section looks at the events which have played major roles in women's lives and classifies women according to dominant kinds of life events they have experienced. Among depressed women interviewed, three categories of event emerged, firstly, severe events involving loss, secondly severe event without loss, and thirdly, on-going major difficulties. Some of the non-depressed interviewees had experiences not dissimilar to the depressed interviewees and the differences between the two groups will be explored.[4]

---

[4] All the quotations are attributed, as follows: gmd = Glasgow Muslim Depressed: ehd = Edinburgh Hindu Depressed: gsd = Glasgow Sikh Depressed: emd = Edinburgh Muslim Depressed: ghd = Glasgow Hindu Depressed: esd = Edinburgh Hindu Depressed. Where nd is stated, this refers to non-depressed.

Severe events involving loss

Loss through role conflict

The twelve women in this category experienced strong forms of conflict involving three areas of their lives; educational aspirations, boyfriends/marriage, and employment/careers. In four instances the conflict began with the women's parents and continued into their marriage with their husband. Four cases involved husbands only, three cases involved husband and mother-in-law, and one case involved husband and husband's family.

Conflict centred on the expected roles, behaviour and attitudes of women before they were married, on the question of marriage, and continued into their marriages. Many of these women did not agree with, were dissatisfied with or had difficulty conforming with their parents'/husband's/mother-in-law's expectations of what their role should be and, consequently, how they should act. The values and intended roles of the women were at odds with those promoted by their parents'/husband/mother-in-law as well as their community generally. Many of the women expressed concern at the way they were expected to uphold the 'honour' of the community and family and felt that, as well as being unfair in that it did not apply to men to the same extent, it could and did place restrictions on the way they led their lives.

Three interviews exemplify some of these conflicts. The experience of role conflict was also found with the non-depressed interviewees and some of their comments are included to contrast their situation with the depressed sample.

One Glasgow Muslim woman (gm6d) had hoped to go to university, but her parents had wanted her to leave school at 16. She had maintained her desire to enter further education but this conflicted with her husband's views of her role as wife and parent.

> I received very little affection from my parents, I was the eldest and it was always do this, do that, do the housework, it was awful. I had no encouragement, no support, I was there to do as they said...... It was getting frustrating, even if I did go out it had to be with someone. The first time I was in a post office I was 18 years old. On TV even in Asian films, women had more freedom. I was angry, always arguing, no give and take at all. It was very frustrating. It was like a brick wall, there was no movement.
>
> I was told I had to get married because I was getting old. My God I was 22. I didn't want to get married and especially to the man who is now my husband. He has very strict ideas on how women should act... I don't share them. We live near

192

where all his family live, all his sisters and sisters-in-law go along with things but I know from talking to some of them that they feel the same as me. I spoke out once when we were all together and I was scolded by my husband in front of them all. (gm6d)

A second example is an Edinburgh Muslim (em1d) who had been in dispute with her husband over her wish to hire a childminder to look after their children while she went out to work. She was also very conscious of not being able, or willing, to meet the requirements of a 'good housewife'.

When I got married I thought this was the person for me. I had been married before and it was a disaster. I wanted a family and a husband that loved me. We worked hard, bought a small shop where my husband still works. I gave him my savings. I fell pregnant, then my husband called his brother over from Pakistan. When he came over things changed completely between my husband and myself. I became a second-class citizen, his family were number one. Part of the problem was that I didn't know all the cultural things like how to act towards my brother-in-law. My husband expected me to act in a certain way.... he had come over from Saudi Arabia and it was his first time in a country like Britain. I agreed at the time that his brother could come and stay with us but I really had no say at the time.

He expected me to look after the two of them, I was seven months pregnant- he should have been looking after me. My son was born. I had no time with him, I had to look after two men. I had no support in bringing up my son. Living all the time in the house.. I tried to go back to work and I did for about 6 weeks. We got a child-minder in. But my husband said 'no more childminder: only mothers can look after their children'.... I gave up working, I was really upset about that..... work gave me a sense of satisfaction, a sense of achievement, it gave me time off from the baby. ....l look back at how it was in the past and compare it to now..now it is nothing. (em1d)

One Glasgow Hindu woman was in dispute with her husband and mother-in-law over her behaviour not meeting their expressed wishes.

Me and my husband had a really lovable, good relationship. But it started to go all wrong when his mother came over from India. Her husband died and she wanted to come and stay for good. She didn't respect any privacy, she wanted to dominate all the time.....I think it was her personality. She started interfering all the time One time she went through my handbag. She found the pill [birth control pill] and asked my sister-in-law what they were. She was annoyed when she found out. Then I knew the times that she had been in my room looking for things. I couldn't take it any more, my husband was never in, he started to go out all the time.

I think I'm different from Indian women in that I drink a wee bit wine and go out, I'm more open. But I am Indian. He's blaming my Scottish friends for me being so outspoken and going out... He and his mum think I should be a certain person. It has gone downhill completely now, my husband has left and taken his mother with him, thank God,......I think why?. Why can't he accept who I am? (gh1d)

The woman was determined to 'be herself'. Following failed attempts to patch up their marriage, the couple separated. She found the separation very difficult, because of a lack of support.She could confide in her sister who lived in Dundee but she did not like to 'burden her'.

These interviews represent the women in the 'role conflict' category. They had very specific, and in most cases deeply held, aspirations but had found them blocked. This process had often resulted in conflicts with parents, husbands and/or in-laws. The women found themselves performing tasks and duties they disliked, which were significantly removed from their own personal goals, values and aspirations. Generally, they had weak support, and therefore bore the conflicts alone. This is important, because there were women in the non-depressed group who experienced role conflicts, but who had support throughout the experience. In general, however, depressed interviewees had a much higher incidence of strong role conflict, many experiencing it from more than one source. For non-depressed women, strong role conflict was much less common.

A non-depressed interviewee, em3nd, experienced strong role conflict on upbringing/schooling, boyfriends and marriage. She did not, however, develop depression. This is a Muslim woman of Pakistani parents, born in Edinburgh and married with one child. When aged 18, she fell in love with a young man who, like herself, was born in Edinburgh of Pakistani parents. They wanted to marry. Her parents were totally opposed to this 'love marriage'. She felt that her parents were 'trying to decide my life for me'. She wanted to continue working and marry the person she loved, but her parents wanted her to stop working and get married.

For her, the central issue was 'Me deciding who I wanted to be and what I wanted to do'. She went ahead with her own plans, and had great support from her friends. Subsequently:

> My parents' outlook changed because of what I did. They realised they'd have to compromise. I think respect is the key, but I left home to get what I wanted. It's what I want that's key. Parents realise that girls will leave home if they are forced to do things. They try to condition you to be the person they want, but things happen - life changes you. My mum is more compromising now. (em3nd)

> This woman, apart from having strong support from her friends, was also a member of an Asian women's group which gave her 'great help and encouragement'. Her parents did not take long to change, and she was re-united with her mother and father. Her sisters had supported her through all the turmoil. Therefore although she had experienced strong role conflict, she had strong support throughout it, and the conflict was resolved when her parents came round to her way of thinking.

Loss through specific events

The second sub-group in the loss category involves five depressed interviewees who experienced loss through separate and specific events, namely loss through death (2), loss through miscarriage, loss through separation and loss through family dispute. Two examples are given here.

A Glasgow Muslim woman, gm2d, became depressed following the death of her sister to whom she was 'very close'. The death was sudden, had come as a major surprise and was a devastating blow.

> I'm still trying to cope with the death of my sister. With the way things had been going, she was the only really close person I had, we used to see each other every day as she only lived up the street. She was the closest person I had and now she's gone there's a big gap.... I've never really been able to talk with my husband the way her and me used to talk. When things were difficult we could always laugh at things but now I can't... my husband, he works all day and night so we don't get the chance to talk..... ....we still have time to argue, though. (gm2d)

The woman's closeness to her sister meant that she could enjoy her company, as well as talking about problems, which she found a big help. The woman was still grieving seven months after the death, had not spoken to anybody about it, and was having to cope with the loss on her own. Her sister had been her only confidant, a source of support, and also, apparently, her closest friend. To lose all of this without warning overburdened the woman with grief. That she had no outlet for this grief seemed to make the loss harder to cope with.

Another woman (gm10d) had had a recent dispute with members of her family after hearing that her father had been having an affair with another woman whilst married to her mother. She had confronted him and had argued with other members of her family. This led to some of her family not speaking to her, and, being very much family-orientated, she was in distress over the whole situation.

> It was so difficult, we used to be such a happy family, my brothers and sisters got on so well. But now we are split, the bond is no longer there, it's not the same now. I seemed to have reacted to it worst of all in my family. My mother has lost interest in her children- she sees me as an enemy. That's what the problem has been.

> I can't really go to anyone. Because the problem is between my parents and it is known between my in-laws, I can't turn to them to talk about it. I feel ashamed. I feel ashamed because of my parents- my father. ....Family is important- the head of the family are your parents. They are seen as the pillars of the family, if one pillar is bad it disturbs the whole building. Because of the conflict the family has been scattered. (gm10d)

She could see no way of overcoming her difficulties, although she had thought about moving to Pakistan to live. But her children were becoming settled in school in Glasgow, and she felt if she didn't go soon, a move would be unfair on her children. She felt awkward about talking regularly to her husband about her own parents. All contact with previous confidants had been broken, as had her social network which had previously been quite active.

Severe event without loss

One woman explained that on a recent trip to Pakistan she had been sexually harassed by a relative. In addition to finding the whole event deeply upsetting, the situation became worse when the mother of the harasser claimed that she must have led the young man on. This led to an argument, and the holiday ended abruptly and disastrously.

> When I was abroad in Pakistan a relative made advances to
> me and sexually harassed me. ... It was my husband's youngest
> brother. He is young and immature... I didn't tell my husband
> but he kept asking me 'what's wrong' eventually I told his
> mother and she blamed it on me, she said that he would never
> do that and if he did I must have been leading him on, it was
> total rubbish. I felt very guilty about the whole thing and
> eventually told my husband. He said that he would never
> speak to his brother again and his family accused me of
> breaking up their family... it was terrible. He has relations
> over here and they know about what happened and I know
> they have said things about me. When I was younger I was a
> bit of a rebel so they think... you know... there's no smoke
> without fire (gm8d).

The woman was unable to discuss the problem with anyone. Although able to
confide freely in her husband, she did not discuss this event with him as it caused
both of them too much distress.

On-going major difficulties

The final category of depressed women were five who had experienced on-going
major difficulties. In addition to severe events, Brown and Harris (1978) also
found that in a minority of cases a restricted class of long term difficulties -
termed major difficulties- appeared to be of critical importance for depression.
Brown and Harris (1989) noted that although the process by which major
difficulties contribute to depression is less intuitively clear than the role of severe
events, these major difficulties embody many similar features found in severe
events i.e. they are the same in terms of meaning, comprising aspects of
disappointment and loss.
The first example of ongoing major difficulties involved a woman working in a
business owned by her husband and brother-in-law, who had financial
disagreements on the running of the business which became personal and
involved other family members.

> In the shop with the family there are a lot of pressures,
> working with your brother-in-law can create difficulties. My
> husband's brother always thought he was the boss although he
> only owned 25% of it. Things in the shop started to go wrong
> and that's when all the family problems started.

> I was close to his family but problems started when my sister-
> in-laws came to live with us. The problem was that we had a

197

crisis in our business then things started to go wrong in our family relationships. They wanted too much money from the shop.

[Later] they were moving out of the house, my husband put the house up for sale. That's when they started talking about us. They were mixing things saying that we were kicking them out of the house. I didn't know I was depressed. I was losing weight and I couldn't sleep at night. When my mother-in-law died everybody would come to our house especially my sister-in-law. We were very close but she stopped talking, I don't know why. We needed a bigger house. I was very upset.......When I look back I was too soft, I didn't know how to be tough. I look back and say 'how did I let him get away with that'?

Two of his brothers stopped talking to me. I don't know why, a lot of things happened. Probably the thing with my brother-in-law. I felt the world had ended. There was a lot of gossip going around. My husband says 'forget about everything, get on with your life' but its hard when you are so down. The family can stress me out, I worry a lot about it. (gs1d)

The trauma described by gs1d had begun over two years ago. She went through this trauma unsupported, both in terms of confiding and social network support. As she said herself in the interview :

I couldn't talk to my husband about it because he was suffering as well, although not as bad as me. I had no one, which made it worse. When I tried no one would listen.

Eh1d, who also fell into this category, had weak confiding relationships:

My husband works away from home all the time..... It means that I have to bring up the kids totally on my own. His family offer to help but I don't want their help.... because they take his side all the time. We had this big argument because I thought he was up to something... you know seeing another woman. He keeps telling me I'm off my head but I don't know about him. His family said that I was wrong and that I was being ungrateful because he was out all the time working and here was me giving him a hard time. They were telling *me* how I should talk to my husband. That was typical though... they try and interfere, his mum and sisters, telling me where my kids should go to school and all that. When they go out they always expect me to go with them.... when I don't I'm some kind of bad person, they get their nose in at every excuse. Who needs that? I just find it too much at times I end up losing the head and shouting. I mean what I say, but after it I wish I'd kept my mouth shut. (eh1d)

There was no confidant regularly available with whom she could discuss her dilemma, and her husband's family, she felt, 'always took his side, no matter what'. The pressures of her deteriorating relationship with her husband and his family were exacerbated by what she saw as 'interference' in her own personal family life. This situation had lasted for 'over a year'.

The women in the depressed group spoke about their family disputes as a central, very negative feature of their lives. They saw no obvious or easy way out of their dilemma, other than the rather drastic step of moving house or leaving the country. The non-depressed group of women referred to the family disputes as an occasional irritant. There are, therefore, significant differences in the strength, duration and impact of the family disputes when comparing the two groups of women. The other critical difference is that the depressed women had weak confiding relations (and a poorly developed social network preventing them from meeting potential confidantes) which militated against them coping with the disputes they found themselves involved in. As one of the depressed women commented, this made matters worse.

Discussion

In understanding the nature and influence of life events in this sample of second-generation South Asian women, their varied social experiences, as well as the interview data reproduced in this chapter, have to be taken together, particularly when addressing and understanding the question of social roles and role conflict. As this chapter has attempted to show, Brown and Harris and Brown's insistence on taking account of the social and cultural context as well as a person's biographical account of their circumstances is particularly relevant. The notion of loss and disappointment were the central features of most events in second-generation South Asian women interviewed in this study. From the study it appears that social roles are implicated in life events among these women, in particular the loss of a valued goal or aspiration, which led to conflict over an existing role.

By no means all the women experienced role conflict in this study, and by no means all who did experience it went on to develop depression. This testifies to the varied experiences of second-generation South Asian women and the different ways such role conflicts manifest themselves. One of these, role conflict involving loss, can be a stressful life event, and where there is no support and where the conflict is unresolved, this can have a debilitating effect on the mental well-being of the women, as happened in this study.

As for the other two categories in the depressed group, severe events without loss and on-going major difficulties conspired (in the absence of social support) to have a negative impact on the women's mental health and led to depression, as has been found in a range of previous studies.

The findings suggest that a person's values, goals and aspirations, and how these manifest themselves in a person seeking a desired social role, are a key element in understanding the social origins of depression among those women interviewed in this study. This approach helps us to understand how and why social roles can, under certain circumstances, become associated with stressful events. Such a scenario can develop where a role is unwanted, where a person is bound in one role while wishing to play another, and where a person is unable to engage in role change as a result of various social pressures. Comments made by the depressed women indicated quite strongly that loss and disappointment were critical factors in their depression. The notion of loss does include loss of a person and material/financial loss, but, critically, loss of a cherished idea, loss of aspiration concerning cherished ideals and values, and loss of a valued goal emerged as the most critical factors in the aetiology of depression. This is so because such a loss can lead to role strain/conflict which can, in the absence of a confiding relationship, increase the risk of depression in women.

The significance of gender in contemporary social life applies to all sections of society, not least the South Asian community in Britain. South Asian women are not immune from the type of influences that their white counterparts face. And some of these influences can result in a clash of values and aspirations. In redefining their cultural identity, many second generation South Asian women do so differently from their parents, and stress values such as the equality of the sexes, greater freedom of choice in matters relating to marriage and occupation, and freedom to express dissent. In many instances, clashes are resolved by discussion. However, such clashes can and do result in conflicts for some South Asian women. As this study indicated, some women find that roles assigned solely on the basis of gender can be restricting; these may then be challenged, and new roles that better suit the individual's own values and outlook are sought. This process does not automatically result in a depressive illness, as social supports can buffer such stressful events. Nevertheless, the stresses of the acculturation process for second-generation South Asian women are an important variable when considering aetiological factors implicated in the onset of depressive illness.

Whilst the concept of loss is of critical importance, there are a number of situations where a severe event not involving loss is a factor in the onset of depression. These tend to be acute, unexpected events such the sexual harassment expericnced by gm8d. There is also a restricted class of difficulties called major difficulties, which also appear to be involved in the onset of depression in some of the women. As with loss, such events do not automatically lead to depression, the availability of a strong confiding relationship being a key determining factor. In this study, chronic difficulties leading to depression were present in five cases, mainly related to family disputes. Although not fundamentally dissimilar to chronic difficulties like those found in Brown and Harris's studies, there are factors particularly pertinent to South Asian families. One is the pooling together of resources in business, house ownership/occupation, and child care that existed in a number of families. Although not as common as in the past, this pooling did lead to chronic difficulties in some cases such as gs1d where two families living in the same house constantly argued over the running of the house and their small business.

Whilst family members, especially sisters, can be and are a source of support for second- generation South Asian women, they can also serve as a stressor, adversely affecting the women's situation. Whilst for many of the women interviewed in this study confidants were of the same sex, (unlike in the Brown and Harris studies), regular availability was often a problem because of sisters moving to different parts of the country following marriage. An additional feature, given the tight-knit nature of many of the communities, was a reluctance to divulge personal problems except to very close people, for fear that this would be openly discussed in the wider community.

Conclusion

The study lends support to the notion that loss associated with personal aspirations and goals can, in the absence of a strong confiding relationship, increase the risk of depression for second-generation South Asian women. At the same time, on-going major difficulties, in the absence of a strong confiding relationship, can also increase the risk of depression in the same group of women. Lastly, severe event without loss, in the absence of strong confiding relationships, also increases the risk of depression. A significant difference in relation to Brown and Harris's model was that confiding for the overwhelming majority of South Asian women in this study was with someone of the same sex, usually a sister or friend (unlike Brown and Harris's studies where it was usually a husband or boyfriend).

The study questions the wisdom of using the term 'culture conflict' as a reason why second-generation South Asian women experience mental health problems such as depression. Most cultures are not homogeneous, watertight packages. When the author addressed the question of identity, and attitudes to cultural and religious traditions in this study there was significant diversity of attitudes and opinions within and between Muslim, Hindu and Sikh interviewees (for details relating to questions of identity and attitudes towards cultural and religious traditions, see Donaghy 1995b).

There is as much diversity in 'South Asian culture' as there is in 'British culture' or even 'European culture'. The term 'South Asian culture' is reductive and potentially discriminatory, as it identifies the South Asian 'culture' as the problem. The 'culture conflict' approach fails to look at the individual's own personal situation or to give them as individuals the opportunity to describe, in their own words, what their problems are and, with their co-operation, and opinions taken into account, what is the most effective way of assisting them. There is an implication that cultural problems are unique to South Asian communities, which a wide-range of health and social studies have shown to be clearly not the case.

In conclusion, the author's study identified a range of experiences in second-generation South Asian women. The desire to change, to move away from traditional expectations of women's roles in an attempt to achieve one's goals is one factor increasing the risk of depression, but by no means a global representation of risk. There are other factors such as chronic housing difficulties and the chronic effects of poverty and racism. Loss in relation to miscarriage and divorce are also factors increasing the risk of depression. It is important to note that some women do change and do not get depressed, some try to change, do not succeed and do not get depressed. Some women who are traditional do not want to change but still become depressed, as a result of experiencing a severe life event and having no social support. Recognising the diversity of experience among young South Asian women is fundamental in attempting to understand and address mental health problems such as depression in second-generation South Asian women.

13. Conclusion: minority ethnic groups and health and social care

Alison Bowes and Duncan Sim

Introduction

The contributions to this book have explored a wide range of substantive, theoretical, methodological and policy issues which have general implications for future research and policy relating to minority ethnic groups, both within and outside Scotland. In this final chapter, we will be exploring some of these implications, with particular reference to the current policy climate, and the development of community care policy and practice. In doing so, we aim to contribute to the small body of work on community care and minority ethnic groups. We will be addressing the three central themes identified by Ahmad and Atkin (1996) which are firstly, the tendency for service provision to ignore the needs of minority ethnic groups, secondly, the preoccupation with cultural differences which is characteristic of service providers, and, thirdly, the issue of racism, which they see as central in restricting minority ethnic access to services. Research has an important contribution to make towards tackling these barriers to access, but can only do so by working reflexively so as not to reproduce the barriers it is investigating. Researchers face a number of challenges: there is undoubtedly a need for specialised research on minority ethnic groups in this field, as conclusions from other work cannot readily be generalised; researchers have to move away from the preoccupation with cultural explanations which has served to explain all the experiences of minority ethnic groups by their minority ethnicity, as though other factors do not come into play; and the operation of racism remains to be fully understood at institutional and interpersonal levels.

Key issues in housing

Scottish housing agencies, especially the housing association sector, have become committed in recent years to looking at the housing needs of minority ethnic groups, and there is some evidence that they are altering their practices to improve access (Scottish Homes 1994, Glasgow City Housing 1994). These moves have used research findings in formulating policy, and have also responded to community and other pressure from outside (such as the CRE (1993) investigation into housing associations, and the campaigning work of Positive Action in Housing, formerly the Housing Equality Action Unit). The UK wide experience has shown parallel policy changes, especially regarding access to social rented housing. Nevertheless, many issues remain.

Firstly, there are areas of housing need in which little research has been done, and where there have been few policy initiatives. These include housing for older people from minority ethnic groups, an area in which there are many myths about lack of demand, as Carlin's work suggests. Her review of research, and her study of minority ethnic older people, indicates demand which is likely to increase in the near future. Her study of housing providers revealed very little awareness of the needs of minority ethnic elders, and few moves to ascertain them or meet them. Very commonly, lack of articulated demand, or a purported small population was given as a reason for inaction, and lack of reflection.

Secondly, although there have been policy changes, it is clear that there is a need for further work. The sequence of research projects outlined by Third and MacEwen not only informed policy development, but also identified further issues of research and policy as the level and depth of knowledge and understanding increased, Thus, while the early work indicated that the housing association sector was not tackling issues, later work at the local level (in Leith) began to indicate how local conditions might affect policy responses, and the national study of owner occupation began to see the whole picture of minority ethnic housing in Scotland, and consider ways in which Scottish Homes' policy could be more effective on a wider scale.

Thirdly, it is important to understand, in the context of more general policy changes, what form the housing careers of minority ethnic groups take. This is particularly necessary, in the light of the continuing pattern of disadvantage in housing faced by minority ethnic groups throughout Britain, despite policy designed to improve access to better housing. There are suggestions in the work of Bowes, Dar and Sim that housing strategies pursued by Pakistanis at least may perpetuate this disadvantage, at the same time as, for some individuals, they find ways through the difficulties of finding housing in an environment of constraint.

There is some evidence that developments in community care policy in Scotland are taking account of housing, and that the particular needs of minority ethnic groups in this respect are being recognised. Brailey (1991) for example notes that there appears to be a view that minority ethnic groups in Scotland would be better served by ethnically sensitive mainstream services, rather than specialist minority provision, with the possible exceptions of women leaving the marital home, and elderly people, especially, she feels, Chinese elderly people. There exist, in Scotland, specialist services for South Asian women leaving violent situations (Gryffe Women's Aid in the west and Shakti in the East), and also specialist housing provision for Chinese elderly people, in the form of sheltered housing in Dundee and Edinburgh, built by Cleghorn and Fountainbridge Housing Associations respectively. A third scheme in Glasgow is now planned. Furthermore, Glasgow City Housing's strategy for special needs and community care (Glasgow City Housing 1994) takes into account the particular issues for minority ethnic groups throughout the document. In many respects here, the policy initiatives are ahead of the research, in that the small amount of work that specifically addresses community care issues for minority ethnic groups fails to consider housing (e.g. Ahmad and Atkin 1996). There is clearly more work to be done in this area.

Key issues in social work

All the papers relating to social work services focused on elderly people, and there was a particular emphasis on the perspective of users, a perspective which has been lacking in much previous research (cf Blakemore and Boneham 1994). Although social work is a field in which considerable attention has been paid to issues of racism, it became clear from all four papers that there is still further work to be done if service access is to be improved.

One of the strongest themes to emerge from this section was that minority ethnic elderly people often lack knowledge of the services available to them: this issue was addressed in all the papers. Lack of knowledge was seen by all the contributors as a significant barrier to access. They pointed out however that lack of knowledge was an issue which social work departments themselves must tackle, by becoming involved in more creative ways of communicating with local minority ethnic populations, by, for example, an active programme of contacts with community organisations. Bowes and Dar's work included a discussion of some models for contact with community organisations, and suggested that these were not necessarily being well managed in the context under investigation. Netto, and Brownlie and Anderson also referred to the need for services to maintain contact with minority ethnic organisations. Chakrabarti and Cadman, whose research was carried out in an area of more sparse minority ethnic population, and fewer community organisations, recommended that social work services use the possibility of contacts through health clinics, and develop means of providing information such as videos, rather than the more conventional translated leaflets.

These chapters also emphasised the need for services to be culturally sensitive, and focused on the point of view of the minority ethnic clients, who frequently felt that services were not appropriate for them. The social workers interviewed in Bowes and Dar's work felt themselves to be deficient in the skills necessary to offer an ethnically sensitive service, Brownlie and Anderson argued from their case studies that staff had not been able to deal with minority ethnic dementia sufferers, and both Netto and Chakrabarti and Cadman noted that carers also believed services to be inappropriate for them. The need for ethnically sensitive services is thus very strongly stated by the clients and potential clients who were interviewed in this range of research.

In the literature however, the issue of ethnically sensitive services and how to provide them has been little discussed in recent years, as commentators have concentrated their efforts on identifying racism in social work practice, and on developing anti-racist practice. This could explain why professionals felt ill-equipped in their efforts to provide appropriate services. There is undoubtedly more work to be done here: on the research side, to identify the needs of clients as they perceive them, and on the policy side, the development of ethnically sensitive practice, and ways of allowing professionals to pursue it are essential. The difficulties inherent in the notion of 'ethnically sensitive practice' must be recognised in these processes: one reason for the emphasis on anti-racism in social work has undoubtedly been the former tendency for professionals to operate with cultural stereotypes of minority ethnic groups (see e.g. Patel 1990), to look for lists of cultural 'tips' which would form a recipe for good practice. This could amount to a form of racism, as it entailed the assumption that the service needs of minorities were wholly dictated by their minority status, and that no other factors came into play, or that the issues were all on the client side, and professionals did not need to reflect on or change their own practice.

The social work chapters also raised the important issue of who should provide services for minority ethnic groups, as they examined the role of the voluntary sector. All the papers, as mentioned, saw a potential role for community groups, though there were suggestions that this might be problematic, in terms of the relationship between the groups and the statutory services, and in terms of the availability of groups in different areas: as Blakemore and Boneham (1994) argue, it is in the nature of community groups in the voluntary sector that their coverage is patchy, and that they cannot therefore readily provide comprehensive services. As community care policy develops, the role of the voluntary sector is to become more significant, and this is likely to be especially so for minority ethnic groups because of the failure of the statutory sector to deliver appropriate services, and because of its lack of confidence that it can do so. The ability of the voluntary sector to respond to the challenge of bidding for services is not clear, nor is the ability of the statutory sector to evaluate services thus offered.

Within statutory services, there are issues relating to the role of minority ethnic staff. All the contributors stressed the need for staff to be able to communicate effectively with minority ethnic clients, and the clients expressed a preference for staff who could use their languages. There is a clear danger that minority ethnic staff are designated to work only with minority ethnic clients, thus creating a kind of ghetto, restricting the career options of minority ethnic staff, and perpetuating the current situation in which white staff do not have, and cannot get, experience of work with minority ethnic clients. There can be no guarantee, furthermore, that bilingual staff will be available at all times to deal with clients from minority groups, and it is inevitable that the vast majority of staff in social work departments will not be bilingual. Therefore, there is a need to look closely at the possibilities for training non-bilingual staff in the effective use of interpreters, especially in areas where the minority population is small, and bilingual social work staff few. At the same time, the position of bilingual staff requires careful monitoring, to ensure that attempts to offer ethnically sensitive services are not at the expense of minority ethnic staff.

Key issues in health and health services

The three chapters on aspects of health all focused on women's health. There was a strong emphasis in all of them on the need to question the use of culturally based explanations for women's patterns of well- and ill-being and health care use. Both Paul and Bowes and Domokos argued that explanations which looked at the nature of health services were essential, and Donaghy that factors which operated in the case of white women also operated in cases of South Asian women diagnosed with depressive illness. All criticised perspectives which explained the experiences of women through their ethnicity, without taking into account factors which would be assumed relevant for other women, such as poverty, or bad housing conditions, or severe life events, and without looking at racism and stereotyping operating in the wider society. The emphasis on culture in many explanations could in fact be seen as a form of racism in itself, blaming women for their own health problems and difficulties of access to health services.

The emphasis on culture has also been detrimental to the development of adequate theoretical frameworks for the study of minority ethnic health. Where it has been challenged, commentators have stressed the importance of racism as a factor affecting minority ethnic health, and there has been a tendency for culture or racism to appear alternative explanatory factors. By raising questions about a wider range of factors, the writers in this section are opening debates about the contribution of, for example, class and gender to minority ethnic health and health service use.

In putting forward suggestions for improving services, Paul and Bowes and Domokos argued that the services themselves needed to work at being more ethnically sensitive, and at removing barriers to access which resulted from a failure to consider the particular needs of South Asian women. Examining the perspectives of professionals, Bowes and Domokos identified marked gaps between their views and the views of their clients, whilst also noting that the efforts of many professionals to improve communication between themselves and their clients was a considerable resource for any attempts to improve services.

All the contributors emphasised the importance of looking at women's health care in the context of their lives as a whole, and not considering it the purely specialist province of health care experts. Thus Paul wrote of the informal support networks which women used, as they sought preventative services. These came from family members, and from other women in the community, as well as community groups. Donaghy, using the model developed in previous studies of depression, examined the role of social support in maintaining mental health, and especially in preventing depression. Bowes and Domokos discussed, for example, how, in seeking health care for their children, mothers considered not only the illness, but also the whole welfare of the child.

There is very little research on minority ethnic health which attempts to take the broad, contextual view adopted in the accounts presented here, and which involves a particular focus on the point of view of health service users. Thus there appears to be very considerable scope for further research in this area, and questions can easily be raised about the health care and use of health services of other sectors of the minority ethnic population, and about other areas of health services. This is one area in which it is especially important that research issues are carefully prioritised, lest studies simply multiply to no particular end. It is very clear, for example, both from the work presented here, and from the wider literature (e.g. Ahmad 1993) that health service practice includes the use of ethnic stereotypes, and that health worker training could usefully include some work challenging this. It is also clear that there have been considerable problems with the use of interpreters in South Asian consultations with health service personnel, and that there are barriers to access to health care which exist because services are not ethnically sensitive, or because people feel that they are not so, and are therefore reluctant to use them. Here, research and practice could form useful alliances to explore the effectiveness of recent policy and practice initiatives, such as the Health Action Project of Community Service Volunteers in Glasgow, which is developing a linkworker scheme, and Greater Glasgow Health Board's ethnic minority health group, which involves peripatetic clinics going out to community groups.

Methodological issues

The research carried out for the various chapters in the book adopted a considerable variety of methodologies, and illustrates that there is no one 'correct' methodology for research with minority ethnic groups. Indeed, we would argue that the use of a variety of methods is desirable and necessary, especially in fields where there has been relatively little work.

For example, Brownlie and Anderson's exploratory work involved a focus on case studies, in the absence of more systematic data on minority ethnic sufferers from dementia, and enabled them to identify issues requiring further investigation, Similarly, they carried out exploratory work on professional perspectives, complementing the results from the case studies, which had indicated the lack of knowledge and awareness the professionals then showed.

Wider scale, survey based work, such as in some of the studies by Third and MacEwen, Chakrabarti and Cadman, can give a broader picture of the needs and views of a group, provided it is informed by an appreciation of what are relevant issues: it is worth noting that all the survey work discussed in this book involved consultations with minority ethnic community groups before it was carried out, to ensure that the research instruments developed were effective and relevant.

Much of the work discussed in the book has used qualitative methods, which are especially appropriate for the investigation of issues in depth, and for studying people's own points of view. They are useful for looking at ideas in relation to behaviour, exploring in detail with an interviewee first their in-principle views on some issue, then their actions: thus, for example, in Bowes and Dar's study of elderly people and the social work service, widespread misinformation about the service existed, and yet people did manage to use it, especially by attending the community groups. Such an approach therefore allows detailed investigation of people's routes into service use, which could not be ascertained from knowledge of their information alone.

Qualitative work is especially appropriate for studying areas which may be difficult to approach, either for researcher or for interviewee. Paul and Donaghy were both involved in researching areas of some sensitivity, and both found relatively open-ended interviews to be effective in exploring often very personal areas of their interviewees' lives. It was possible to go into these issues in considerable depth.

Qualitative approaches are also classically used in exploratory work, to identify issues for investigation, where the research record is limited. Bowes, Dar and Sim for example used the life history technique initially to try and identify what the issues might be for Pakistani householders attempting to find housing in a constrained environment, and to develop a fresh perspective on what factors were coming into play. Similarly, Brownlie and Anderson used qualitative investigation to open the issue of dementia, and to raise many questions for further investigation.

Several of the chapters refer to studies which have used a combination of methods of data collection, and used these to build a comprehensive picture. The series of studies completed by Third and MacEwen involved both more quantitative and more qualitative methods at different stages, and each successive study was used to inform both the research questions and the methodology of the next. Carlin also used more qualitative work with older people, and more quantitative, formal survey work when looking at local authority practices throughout Scotland.

There has been an extended debate in the literature about the social characteristics of researchers who work with minority ethnic groups, principally concerning the desirability of shared ethnicity between researcher and researched. This volume includes people who shared ethnicity with the people whom they researched, and people who did not. There were also other dimensions of shared or not shared social identities, including class, gender, status, age, parenthood and others. Some contributors to the book (Bowes and Domokos 1996b, Donaghy 1995a) have been involved in the more general debate, and have argued for a reflexive approach to research which takes account of the role of shared or not shared social identities in the research process, rather than for the establishment of principles about who should be conducting research.

A further, related issue concerns the purpose of research. The contributors to this book were all involved in work aimed at informing policy and practice in each of the three areas. It was common practice for them to attempt to include in their work the points of view of those who would be receiving services, and often, those staff who would be delivering them. They have attempted to consider issues recognisable and relevant to service users and service providers.

General implications

The specific issues raised by each set of papers can be seen to apply in the other areas, and build into a general picture of recommendations for further research and policy development.

Knowledge and information

Though lack of knowledge and information about services was a particularly strong theme in the chapters on social work, it was clear throughout the book that services still have much to do to communicate successfully with minority ethnic groups. This reflects a national, UK wide picture, whereby minority ethnic groups, especially those using minority languages, generally have less knowledge of services than do majority groups. With recent changes in the organisation of health and social care services, including the increased emphasis on community care, the development of the contract economy of care and, in Scotland, the local government reorganisation of 1996, issues of communication with all clients have come increasingly to the fore, and commentators are beginning to explore more effective means (e.g. Tester and Meredith 1992, Allen Hogg and Peace 1992, Atkin Cameron Badger and Evers 1989, Rickford 1995). The levels and breadth of knowledge needed to use services effectively are probably greater following recent developments in community care, as clients are intended to be more fully involved in developing their own care packages, and, in some cases, in buying their own support.

Interagency collaboration

There was little discussion in the papers about interagency collaboration, except with reference to relationships between the statutory and voluntary sectors. Statutory services have been slow to develop collaboration in community care in general (see e.g. Stalker 1996), and, given the problems with their record in providing services to minority ethnic groups, it is not surprising that researchers have not been able to address the issue of collaboration. There is clearly scope for further work here: it is likely that a particularly important area concerns the role of housing agencies. A further issue here is likely to be related to the relatively small numbers of minority

211

ethnic clients seeking access to services which might entail interagency working. Where such clients have very particular needs, requiring ethnically sensitive services, the challenge of interagency working is likely to be greater, because staff's lack of experience of working with minority ethnic clients, which emerges from several of the papers in the book, is likely to be compounded by the general problems of interagency cooperation. Furthermore, access by purchasers to ethnically sensitive services is likely to involve wider contacts, since these are fewer and further between than services generally. We suspect that local government reorganisation will have increased these difficulties, as many of the teams working on initiatives to promote services for minority ethnic groups have been broken up, and some services (such as the Central Region Interpreting Service) have simply disappeared, through lack of funding from the new authorities.

Staff training and status

Several of the papers addressed the issue of staff training and status. Among white staff in all three areas, there was evidence of lack of experience and expertise in working with members of minority ethnic groups. Where minority ethnic staff were to be found, they were generally concentrated in low status jobs, rather insecure, often without training or support in their work. Many of these people were working in the voluntary sector. Clearly, lack of expertise and recognition of staff are problematic for agencies attempting to improve their provision for minority ethnic groups, and several of the papers urged that these issues be addressed. This cannot be simply a question of calling for more minority ethnic staff to work with minority ethnic clients, though there are certainly areas (such as the provision of home helps) in which this is recommended. If minority ethnic staff were recruited to deal with minority ethnic clients, this could serve to marginalise both the staff and the clients, and to sideline the issues attached to working in multi-ethnic Scotland, which are issues for all staff. In any case, it is unlikely that the smaller authorities, with relatively small minority populations would feel the appointment of specialist staff to be economically justifiable.

Resources already exist to improve training, and the three sets of provision covered in this volume can learn from one another. For example, in the housing field, there has been extensive work on means of dealing with racial harassment, and challenging racism in staff practices (Love and Kirby 1994) In the field of social work, there has for several years now been a focus on anti-racist working and the development of bodies of anti-racist practice, as well as anti-racist philosophy built into training programmes. In the health field, there have been attempts to help staff working with clients from various cultural backgrounds to do so in a sensitive way (Henley 1979, Mares Henley and Baxter 1985, Shukla 1991). Whilst we would not wish to suggest that any of these precedents offer ideal ways forward, it would seem eminently sensible for any reviews of training in the community care field to learn from the experiences of the various contributing services.

The role of the voluntary sector

It is a marked feature of much of the specialist provision for minority ethnic groups in Scotland that it emanates from the voluntary sector. According to Atkin and Rollings (1993a, 1993b), the voluntary sector is especially significant for minority ethnic groups throughout the UK, at least partly due to the deficiencies of statutory services, and its importance will increase as the 'contract economy' of care develops. However, there are problems attached to reliance on the voluntary sector, linked firstly with poor resourcing (Atkin and Rollings 1993a, 1993b), including instability of funding and insecurity of staff. Secondly, the patchy nature of voluntary provision, whereby some sectors of the community will have no access to services, whilst others will be amply supported (Blakemore and Boneham 1994) has been identified as problematic. For the mainstream sector, surveys such as MacLeod's (1988) of the Scottish voluntary sector, Field and Jackson (1989), Rooney and McKain (1990), have found that, like statutory services, it has widely failed to develop sensitive, non-discriminatory practice which would allow minority access to services. In Scotland, this view has recently been confirmed by a small, sample survey conducted by the Scottish Council for Voluntary Organisations (SCVO 1996).

Several of the contributions to the book have discussed voluntary sector service provision, notably for elderly people in relationship to care and housing services, and this has also been raised in connection with health. But throughout, though the role of the voluntary sector and the potential for this to increase have been noted, there is a marked lack of systematic research in this area, alongside potential warning signs which parallel those identified by other commentators. Bowes and Dar in particular noted that their data indicated problems with the system of referrals between the voluntary sector and statutory services. Several contributors, including Brownlie and Anderson and Chakrabarti and Cadman emphasised the important role of the voluntary sector, but saw this as operating in conjunction with statutory services, therefore suggesting a need for the relationship between the two sectors to be better understood.

Historically in Scotland, the role of the voluntary sector in the housing field has been perceived by some as especially important for facilitating access to statutory housing services (e.g. Murray 1991, MacLeod 1988). In this field the role of the voluntary sector, especially, though not exclusively, groups which have grown out of initiatives within the minority communities themselves, has been partly one of gatekeeper, providing information, and guiding clients in their quest for services. Recent work in the health field, such as the linkworker projects already mentioned, suggests that a similar role may be developing there. Thus, the voluntary sector may be a key factor if the issues of lack of information and restriction of access which have been raised throughout the book are to be addressed. Its problems therefore are problems for the general provision of services, not only for the sector itself.

Racism and cultural stereotyping

Issues of racism continue to be important in any examination of the relationship between minority ethnic groups and health and social services. In this book, they have appeared mainly in the operation of cultural stereotypes, which falsely predict, for example, people's housing preferences, the causes of depression, or lack of demand for services. These stereotypes appear in the work of professionals, though many are now trying to challenge them, and in the explanatory tools of researchers. They thus impede access to services, and prevent proper understanding of the needs of minority ethnic groups.

Cultural stereotyping, and explanations which emphasise culture as an explanatory factor were most emphasised in the chapters on health, in which assumptions about people's cultures could obstruct their access to health services. In the work on elderly people, it was also clear that assumptions about the nature of minority ethnic families could lead professionals to the misguided view that social work and housing services were not needed. And the assumed preference of Scottish minority ethnic families for owner occupation came into question in the work on housing histories. Thus, the need for vigilance in identifying need and supplying services was stressed throughout.

It is also important for services to recognise that, for many minority ethnic clients, racism is a matter of everyday experience, and may affect service needs. So in housing, widespread experience of harassment in certain neighbourhoods will quickly turn people against choosing such areas for their homes. Racism can also affect people's health, as well as their access to health care. And it may affect social service need, in that the general services are not seen as appropriate, and clients prefer to have separate services, shared with fellow minority group members.

Throughout the book, we have presented and discussed various perspectives on the need for services, the nature of appropriate services, and minority ethnic users' experiences of services. These have come from clients, professionals and policy makers. That they are not always shared has often been clear, and some of the disagreements identified are undoubtedly important for any attempts to improve services. Where service providers are racist or colourblind, or where they feel ignorant of minority needs, effective service provision is unlikely. Where potential clients believe services to be wholly inappropriate, they will not apply for them. Where policy makers ignore minority ethnic groups, and tailor policy specifically for white groups, powerful processes of exclusion are at work. But these incompatible perspectives, whilst they did appear in the work we have discussed, are also being challenged in all three sets of services, by policy makers, professionals and clients.

Housing policy, especially in connection with Scottish Homes and some local authority providers, is attempting to give specific attention to minority ethnic issues. Health care providers are beginning to develop services specifically designed for minority needs. Social work services have long been involved in anti-racist work, training issues, and the development of specialist projects. And the minority ethnic voluntary sector in Scotland continues to be very active in promoting minority issues.

As the contributors have argued, none of this work is perfect, many problems and issues remain, and there are no grounds for complacency. Whilst in 1991, we echoed the Association of Directors of Social Services' (1978) view that services for minorities were 'patchy, piecemeal and lacking in strategy' (Bowes and Sim 1991), we might now say that they remain more patchy than thorough in their coverage, more piecemeal than wholly successful, but that the issues are now being more widely discussed, and some strategic moves are being made. Because of this, we have been able, by bringing together this diverse research and representing these diverse perspectives, to identify areas of potential improvement. There is still much work to be done, but we can see the bases for doing it.

Bibliography

Age Concern Scotland, (1994), *Growing Old in Multicultural Europe*, Conference Report: Edinburgh.

Age Concern/Help the Aged, (1984), *Housing for Ethnic Elders*, Age Concern/Help the Aged Housing Trust: London.

Ahmad, B. (1990), *Black Perspectives in Social Work*. Venture Press: Birmingham.

Ahmad, W. I. U. (ed.), (1992), *The Politics of 'Race' and Health*, RRRU/University of Bradford: Bradford.

Ahmad, W. I. U. (1993a), 'Making black people sick: 'race', ideology and health research', in Ahmad, W. I. U. (ed.), *'Race' and Health in Contemporary Britain,* Open University Press: Buckingham.

Ahmad, W. I. U. (ed.), (1993b), *'Race' and Health in Contemporary Britain*, Open University Press: Buckingham.

Ahmad, W. I. U. and Atkin, K. (eds.), (1996), *'Race' and Community Care*, Open University Press: Buckingham.

Ahmad, W. I. U., Baker, M. R. and Kernohan, E. E. M. (1991) 'General Practitioners' perceptions of Asian and non-Asian patients', *Family Practice*, 8:1, pp.52-56.

Ahmad, W. I. U., Kernohan, E. E. M. and Baker, M. R. (1989), 'Health of British Asians: a research review', *Community Medicine*, 11, 1, pp.49-56.

Ahmad, W I U., Kernohan, E. E. M. and Baker, M. R. (1991), 'Patients choice of General Practitioner: importance of patients and doctors' sex and ethnicity', *British Journal of General Practice*, 41, 330-331.

Allen, I., Hogg, D. and Peace, S. (1992), *Elderly People: Choice, Participation and Satisfaction*, Policy Studies Institute: London.

Alzheimer's Disease Society, (1995), *Right from the Start: Primary Health Care and Dementia*, ADS: London.

Anon, (1991), 'Inner-city GP practices struggling to hit targets', *Medical Monitor*, 4, 5.

Arie, T. (1985), 'Dementia in the elderly: management', in *Medicine in Old Age*, British Medical Association: London.

ASHIA (Asian Special Housing Initiative Agency), (1992), *The Evidence, Survey of the Asian Community's Housing Needs*: Rochdale.

Asian Elderly Group of Merton, (1993), *Annual Report (1992-3)*, AEGM: London.

Askham, J. (1983), 'Policies and perception of identify: service needs of elderly people from black and minority ethnic backgrounds', in Arber, S. And Evandrou, M. (eds), *Ageing, Independence and the Life Course*, Jessica Kingsley: London.

Askham, J. et al, (1995), *Social and Health Authority Services for Elderly People from Black and Minority Ethnic Communities*, HMSO/Age Concern Institute of Gerontology: London.

Association of Directors of Social Services/Commission for Racial Equality, (1978), *Multi-Racial Britain:The Social Services Response*, CRE: London.

Assocation of Metropolitan Authorities, (1988), *A strategy for Racial Equality in Housing: 3. Allocations*, AMA: London.

Atkin, K. (1991), 'Community care in a multiracial society: incorporating the user view', *Policy and Politics*, 19,3, pp.159-166.

Atkin, K. (1992), 'Black Carers - The Forgotten People', *Nursing the Elderly*, March/April, pp.8-9.

Atkin, K., Cameron, E. Badger, F. and Evers, H. (1989), 'Asian elders' knowledge and future use of community social and health services', *New Community* 15,3, pp.439-445.

Atkin, K. and Rollings, J. (1992), 'Informal care in Asian and Afro-Caribbean communities: a literature review', *British Journal of Social Work*, 22,4: pp.405-418

Atkin, K. and Rollings, J. (1993a), 'Community care and voluntary provision: a review of the literature', *New Community*, 19,4, pp.659-667.

Atkin, K. and Rollings, J. (1993b), *Community Care in a Multi-racial Britain: a Critical Review of the Literature*, HMSO: London.

Badger, F., Cameron, E. and Evers, H. (1989), 'The nursing auxiliary service and care of elderly patients', *Journal of Advanced Nursing*, 14, pp.471-477.

Bailey, N., Bowes, A. and Sim, D. (1995) 'Pakistanis in Scotland: census data and research issues', *Scottish Geographical Magazine*, 111,1, pp.36-45.

Baker, R. R., Bandaranayke, R. and Schweiger, M. S. (1984), 'Differences in the rate of uptake of immunisation among ethnic groups', *British Medical Journal*, 288, pp.1075-1078.

Balajaran, R. and Bulusu, L. (1990), 'Mortality among immigrants in England and Wales', 1979-1983, in Britton, M., *Mortality and Geography: A Review in the mid 1980s*, OPCS Series DS No. 9, OPCS: London.

Ballard, R. (1990), 'Migration and kinships: the differential effects of marriage rules on the process of Punjabi migration to Britain', in Clarke, C. Peach, C. Vertovec, S. (eds.), *South Asians Overseas: Migration and Ethnicity*, Cambridge University Press: Cambridge.

Ballard, R. (1992), 'New clothes for the Emperor?: the conceptual nakedness of the race relations industry in Britain', *New Community*, 18,3, pp.481-492.

Bang, S. (1983), *We Come as a Friend: Towards a Vietnamese Model of Social Work*, Refugee Action: Leeds.

Barker, J. (1984), *Research Perspectives on Ageing: Black and Asian Old People in Britain*, (Manchester and London Survey). London: Age Concern Research Unit.

Barker, R. M. and Baker, M. R. (1990), 'Incidence of cancer in Bradford Asians', *Journal of Epidemiology and Community Health*, 44, pp.125-129.

Bebbington, P. (et al), (1984), 'Misfortune and resilience: a replication of the work of Brown and Harris', *Psychological Medicine*, 14, pp.347-363.

Begum, N. (1992), *Something to be Proud of* ... London Borough of Waltham Forest: Race Relations and Disability Unit: London.

Beliappa, J. (1991), *Illness or Distress? Alternative Models of Mental Health*, CIO: London.

Benski, T. (1976), *Interethnic Relations in a Glasgow Suburb*, Unpublished PhD. thesis, University of Glasgow: Glasgow.

Benski, T. (1980), 'Group goals, goal congruency and mutual perceptions: the case of Jews and non-Jews in a middle class suburb in Scotland', *Plural Societies*, 11,4, pp.31-40.

Benski. T. (1981), 'Identification, group survival and inter-group relations: the case of a middle class Jewish community in Scotland', *Ethnic and Racial Studies*, 4,3, pp.307-319.

Beresford, P. and Croft, S. (1986), *Whose Welfare: Private Care or Public Services*, The Lewis Cohen Urban Studies Centre: Brighton.

Berry, S. et al, (1981), *Report on a Survey of West Indian Pensioners in Nottingham*, Social Services Department: Nottingham.

Bhalla, A. and Blakemore, K. (1981), *Elders of the Minority Ethnic Groups*, Birmingham Survey, AFFOR.

Bhatnagar, A. (1994) *Milan (Senior Welfare Council) Report on Information and Advice Needs of Older People from Indian, Pakistani, Bangladeshi and Mauritanian Communities*, Milan: Edinburgh.

Bhopal, R. S. and Samim, A. K. (1988), 'Immunization uptake of Glasgow Asian Children: paradoxical benefit of communication barriers?', *Community Medicine*, 19,3, pp.215-220.

Black Carers Forum, (1992), *What do Black People Say?*, Black Carers Forum: Gloucester.

Blakemore, K. and Boneham, M. (1994) *Age, Race and Ethnicity: a Comparative Approach*, Open University Press: Buckingham.

Blieszner, R. and Shifflett, R. (1988), 'Stigma and Alzheimer's Disease: behavioural consequences for support groups', *Journal of Applied Gerontology*, 7,2, pp.147-160.

Boneham, M. (1989), 'Ageing and Ethnicity in Britain: the case of elderly Sikh women in a Midlands town', *New Community*, 15.3, pp.447-459.

Boneham, M., Saunders , P. Copeland, J. Wilson, K. (1994), 'Age, race and mental health: Liverpool's elderly people from ethnic minorities', *Health and Social Care in the Community*, 2.2, pp.113-116.

Bonnerjea, L. and Lawton, J. (1988), '*No racial harassment this week': A Study Undertaken in the London Borough of Brent*, Policy Studies Institute: London.

Bowes, A. M. and Dar, N. S. (1996), *Pathways to Welfare for Pakistani Elderly People in Glasgow*, HMSO: Edinburgh.

Bowes, A. M. and Domokos, T. M. (1993), 'South Asian women and health services: a study in Glasgow', *New Community*, 19,4, pp.611-626.

Bowes, A. M. and Domokos, T. M. (1995a), 'Key issues in South Asian women's health: a study in Glasgow', *Social Sciences in Health* 1,3:1, pp.45-157.

Bowes, A. M. and Domokos, T M, (1995b), 'South Asian women and their GPs: some issues of communication' *Social Sciences in Health* 1,1, pp.22-33.

Bowes, A. M. and Domokos T. M. (1996a), '"Race", gender and culture in South Asian women's health: a study in Glasgow', McKie, L. (ed.), *Researching Women's Health*. London: Mark Allen Press pp.67-101.

Bowes, A, M. and Domokos, T. M. (1996b), 'Pakistani women and maternity care: raising muted voices', *Sociology of Health and Illness*, 18,1, pp.45-65.

Bowes, A. M., McCluskey, J. and Sim, D. F. (1989), *Ethnic Minority Housing Problems in Glasgow*, Glasgow City Council: Glasgow.

Bowes, A. M., McCluskey, J. and Sim, D. F. (1990a), 'The changing nature of Glasgow's ethnic minority community', *Scottish Geographical Magazine*, 106,2, pp.99-107.

Bowes, A. M., McCluskey, J. and Sim, D. F. (1990b), 'Racism and harassment of Asians in Glasgow', *Ethnic and Racial Studies*, 13,1, pp.71-91.

Bowes, A. and Sim, D. (eds.), (1991), *Demands and Constraints. Ethnic Minorities and Social Services in Scotland*, SCVO: Edinburgh.

Bowler, I. (1993a), '"They're not the same as us?" midwives' stereotypes of South Asian maternity patients', *Sociology of Health and Illness*, 15,2, pp.157-178.

Bowler, I. (1993b), 'Stereotypes of women of Asian descent in Midwifery some evidence', *Midwifery*, 19,3, pp.7-16.

Bowling, A. (1989), 'Implications of preventive health behaviour for cervical and breast cancer screening programmes: a review', *Family Practice*, 6.3, pp.224-231.

Bradley, S. M. and Friedman, E. (1993), 'Cervical cytology screening: a comparison of uptake among Asian and 'non-Asian' women in Oldham', *Journal of Public Health Medicine*, 15.1, pp.46-51.

Brailey, M. (1991), 'Ethnic minorities and special needs housing provision', in Bowes, A. and Sim, D. ,(eds.), *Demands and Constraints. Ethnic Minorities and Social Services in Scotland*, SCVO: Edinburgh.

Brown, C. (1984), *Black and White Britain: The Third PSI Survey*, Heinemann/Policy Studies Institute: London.

Brown, G. W. (1987), 'Social factors and the development and course of depressive disorders: a review of the research programme', *British Journal of Social Work*, 17, pp.615-634.

Brown, G. W. (1989a), 'Aetiology of depressive disorder', in Bennet, D. and Freeman, H. (eds.), *The Practice of Social Psychiatry*, Churchill Livingstone: London.

Brown, G. W. (1989b), 'Life events and measurement', in Brown, G. and Harris, T. (eds.), *Life Events and Illness*, Unwin Hyman: London.

Brown, G. W. and Finley-Jones, (1981), 'Types of stressful life events and the onset of anxiety and depressive disorders', *Psychological Medicine*, 11, pp.803-815.

Brown, G. W. and Harris, T. (1978), 'A Study of psychiatric disorder in women', *Social Origins of Depression*, Tavistock: London.

Brown, G. W. and Prudo, R. (1981), 'Psychiatric disorder in a rural and urban population: 1. Aetiology of depression', *Psychological Medicine*, 11, pp.581-599.

Brown, S. and Riddell, S. (1992), *Class, Race and Gender in Schools: a New Agenda for Policy and Practice in Scottish Education*, Scottish Council for Research in Education: Edinburgh.

Brownlie, J. (1991) *A Hidden Problem? Dementia Amongst Minority Ethnic Groups*, Dementia Services Development Centre, University of Stirling: Stirling.

Cadman, M. and Chakrabarti, M. (1991), 'Social work in a multi-racial society: a survey of two Scottish local authorities', from, *One Small Step Towards Racial Justice*. CCETSW: London.

Campbell, E. (et al), (1983), 'Social factors and affective disorder: an investigation of Brown and Harri's' *British Journal of Psychiatry*, 143, pp.548-553.

Carby, H. V. (1982), 'White women listen! Black feminism and the boundaries of sisterhood', in Centre for Contemporary Cultural Studies, *The Empire Strikes Back: Race and Racism in 70s Britain*, Hutchinson: London.

Carlin, H. (1994), 'The housing needs of older people from ethnic minorities: Evidence from Glasgow', *Occasional Papers on Housing No. 6*, Housing Policy and Practice Unit, University of Stirling: Stirling.

Cashmore, E. (1992), 'The new black bourgeoisie' *Human Relations*, 45,12, pp.1241-1258.

Central Council for Education and Training in Social Work, (1983), *Teaching Social Work for a Multi-Racial Society*, (Paper 21), CCETSW: London.

Central Council for Education and Training in Social Work, (1991), *Rules and Requirements for the Diploma In Social Work*, (Paper 30), CCETSW: London.

Central Council for Education and Training in Social Work, (1995), *Rules and Requirements for the Diploma in Social Work*, (Paper 30), (Revised Edition, 1995), CCETSW: London.

Chakrabarti, M. (1991), 'Anti-racist perspectives in social work', in Bowes, A. M. and Sim, D. F. *Demands and Constraints: Ethnic Minorities and Social Services in Scotland*, pp.95-112, SCVO: Edinburgh.

Chakrabarti, M. and Cadman, M. (1994), *Survey of Needs of Minority Ethnic Elders and Carers for Social Work Support in Tayside*, University of Strathclyde: Glasgow.

Chalmers, K. I. (1992), 'Giving and receiving: an empirically derived theory on health visiting practice, *Journal of Advanced Nursing* 17,11, pp.1317-1325.

Chalmers, K. I. (1993), Searching for health needs: the work of health visiting', *Journal of Advanced Nursing*, 18,6, pp.900-911.

Chalmers, K. I. (1994), 'Difficult work: health visitors' work with clients in the community', *International Journal of Nursing Studies* 31,2, pp.168-182.

Chan, P. (1991), *The Housing Needs of the Chinese Community Within Central Region of Scotland*, Unpublished dissertation, Diploma in Housing Administration, University of Stirling: Stirling.

Chartered Institute of Housing in Scotland, (1994), *Community Care - The Early Experience*, CIH: Edinburgh.

Chaturvedi, S. K. (1990), 'Asian patients and HADS', *British Journal of Psychiatry*, 156, pp.133.

Cheetham, J. (1982) 'Positive discrimination in social work: negotiating the opposition', *New Community*, 10,1, pp.27-37.

Clapham, D. and Munro, M. (1988), *The Cost-effectiveness of Sheltered and Amenity Housing for Older People*, Scottish Development Department, Central Research Unit: Edinburgh.

Clapham, D., Kemp, P. and Smith, S.J. (1990), *Housing and Social Policy*, Macmillan: Basingstoke.

Coles, J. (1990), *The Needs of Elderly Black People, Carers and People with Disabilities*, Lambeth Social Services: London.

Commission for Racial Equality, (1987), *Living in Terror: A Report on Racial Violence and Harassment in Housing*, CRE: London.

Commission for Racial Equality, (1989), *Racial Equality in Social Services Departments: A Survey of Equal Opportunities Policies*, CRE: London.

Commission for Racial Equality, (1991), *Race Relations Code of Practice in Rented Housing*, CRE: London.

Commission for Racial Equality, (1992), *Race Relations Code of Practice in Primary Health Care Services*, CRE: London.

Commission for Racial Equality, (1993), *Housing Associations and Racial Equality*, CRE: London.

Cooper, J. (1979), 'Elderly West Indians in Leicester, 1978' in Glendenning, F. (ed.), *The Elders in Ethnic Minorities*, Beth Johnson Foundation: London.

Costello, C. G. (1982), 'Social factors associated with depression: a retrospective community study', *Psychological Medicine*, 12, pp.329-339.

Cox, C. (1995), 'Comparing the experiences of black and white caregivers of dementia patients', *Social Work* 40,3, pp.343- 349.

Cox, C. and Monk, A. (1990), 'Minority caregivers of dementia victims: a comparison of Black and Hispanic families', *Journal of Applied Gerontology*, 9,3, pp.340-355.

Craig, T. K. and Brown, G. W. (1984), 'Goal frustration and life events in the aetiology of painful gastrointestinal disorder', *Journal of Psychosomatic Research*, 28, pp.411-421.

Cranny, K. C. (1988), *The Lack of Provision for People with Special Needs Within the Black Community in Glasgow*, Glasgow Special Housing Group: Glasgow.

Crook, A. D. H. (1992), 'Private rented housing and the impact of deregulation', in Birchall, J. (ed.), *Housing Policy in the 1990s*. London: Routledge, pp.91-112.

Delacuesta, C. (1993), 'Fringe work: peripheral work in health visiting', *Sociology of Health and Illness* ,15.5, pp.665-682.

Denney, D. and Ely, P. (1987), *Social Work in a Multi-Racial Society*. Gower: Aldershot.

Department of Health, (1989), *Caring for People: Community Care in the Next Decade and beyond*, HMSO: London.

Department of Health, (1992), *The Health of the Nation. A strategy for Health in England*, HMSO: London.

Dex, S. (ed.), (1991), *Life and Work History Analyses: Qualitative and Quantitative Developments*, (Sociological Review Monograph 37), Routledge: London.

DHSS, (1980), *Inequalities in Health: Report of a Research Working Group*, DHSS: London.

Dohrenwend, B. S. and Dowrenwend, B. P. (1978), 'Some isues on research in stressful life events', *Journal of Nervous and Mental Disease*, pp.166, 7-15.

Dominelli, L. (1991), 'An uncaring profession? An examination of racism in social work', in Braham, P. Rattansi, A. and Skellington, R. *Racism and Antiracism: Inequalities, Opportunities, Policies*, pp.164-178, Sage: London.

Donaghy, E. (1995a), 'A study of depression in second generation South Asian women in Scotland: some methodological reflections', *Social Sciences in Health* 1, 2, pp.80-94.

Donaghy, E. (1995b), 'Identity, maintenance and change: second generation South Asian women in Scotland', in Fenton, S. (ed.), *The Family, Minorities and Social Change Place?*, Policy Press.

Donaghy, E. (1996), *A Study of Depression in Second Generation South Asian Women*, Unpublished PhD thesis, University of Edinburgh: Edinburgh.

Donaldson, L. and Clayton, D. G. (1984), Occurrence of cancer in Asians and non-Asians, *Journal of Epidemiology and Community Health*, 38, pp.203-7.

Donaldson, L. J. (1986), 'Health and social status of elderly Asians: a community survey', *British Medical Journal*, 293, pp.1079-1082.

Donovan, J. (1986), *We Don't Buy Sickness, It Just Comes*, Gower: Aldershot.

Douglas, J. (1992), 'Black women's health matters: putting women back on the research agenda', in Roberts, H. (ed.) *Women's Health Matters*, Routledge: London.

Dowd, J. J. and Bengston, V. L. (1978), 'Ageing in minority populations - an examination of the double jeopardy hypothesis', *Journal of Gerontology*, 33, pp.427-436.

Dowie, D. R. (1995), *Ethnic Minority Housing in Glasgow. Scottish Homes Glasgow District Office Development Funding Strategy*, Scottish Homes: Glasgow.

Doyal, L. (1994), 'Changing medicine? Gender and the politics of health care', in Gabe, J. Kelleher, D. and Williams, G. *Challenging Medicine*, pp.140-159, Routledge: London.

Doyle, Y. (1991), 'A survey of the cervical screening service in a London District, including reasons for non-attendance, ethnic response and views on the quality of the service', *Social Science and Medicine*, 3,2, pp.953-7.

Eardley, A., Elkind, A. K., Spencer, B., Hobbs, P., Pendleton, L. L. and Haran, D. (1985), 'Attendance for cervical screening - whose problem?', *Social Science and Medicine*, 20,9, pp.955-62.

Ecob, R. and Williams, R. (1991), 'Sampling Asian minorities to assess health and welfare', *Journal of Epidemiology and Community Health*, 45, pp.93-101.

Evers, H., Badger, F., Cameron, E. and Atkin, K. (1989), *Community Care Project Working Papers*. Department of Social Medicine, Birmingham University: Birmingham.

Farrah, M. (1986), *Black Elders in Leicester: An Action Research Report on the Needs of Black Elderly People of African Descent from the Caribbean*, SDD: Leicester.

Fenton, S. (1987) *Ageing Minorities: Black People as They Grow Old in Britain*, Commission for Racial Equality: London.

Fenton, S. and Sadiq, A. (1993), *The Sorrow in my Heart: Sixteen Asian Women Speak about Depression*, Commission for Racial Equality: London.

Fenton, S. and Sadiq, A. (1996), 'Culture, relativism and the experience of mental distress: South Asian women in Britain', *Sociology of Health and Illness*, 18,1, pp.66-85.

Fernando, S. (1988), *Race and Culture in Psychiatry*, Croom Helm: London.

Field, S. and Jackson, H. (1989) *Race, Community Groups and Service Delivery*, HMSO: London.

Finch, J. (1989), *Family Obligations and Social Change*, Polity: Cambridge.

Firdous, R. (1987), *The Reproductive Health of Asian women, a comparative study to analyse factors which affect reproduction*, unpublished MPH Thesis, University of Glasgow: Glasgow.

Firdous, R. and Bhopal, R. (1989), 'Reproductive health of Asian women: a comparative study with hospital and community perspectives', *Public Health*, 103, pp.307-15.

Ford, J. (1988), 'Personal social services', in English, J. (ed.), *Social services in Scotland*, Scottish Academic Press: Edinburgh.

Ford, R. (1988), 'Health services', in English, J. (ed.), *Social Services in Scotland*, Scottish Academic Press: Edinburgh.

Foster, P. (1995), *Women and the Health Care Industry: an Unhealthy Relationship?*, Open University Press: Buckingham.

Ganguli, M. and Ratcliff, G. (1995) 'A Hindi version of the MMSE: the development of a cognitive screening instrument for a largely illiterate rural population in India', *International Journal of Geriatric Psychiatry*, 10, pp.367-377.

General Household Survey, (1990), *1990 Report*, HMSO: London.

Ginsberg, N. (1992), 'Racism and housing, concepts and reality', in Braham, P. Rattansi, A. and Skellington, R. (eds.), *Racism and Antiracism*, Sage: London.

Glasgow City Council, (1993a), *Ethnic Minority Residents' View of Council Services*, Glasgow City Council Market Information Team: Glasgow.

Glasgow City Council, (1993b), *Glasgow's Housing Plan for the 90's. A sharper focus*, Glasgow City Housing Department: Glasgow.

Glasgow City, (1994), *Special Needs and Community Care Strategy*, Glasgow City Housing Office: Glasgow.

Glendenning, F. (1990), 'The health needs of black and ethnic minority elders', *Generations Review* 14, Autumn.

Goel, K.M., (1981), 'Asians and rickets', *The Lancet* 2:405-6 (and other articles)

Goodlad, R. (1993), *The Housing Authority As Enabler*, Longman: Harlow.

Green, H. (1985), *Informal Carers*, HMSO: London.

Greenglass, E. R. (et al), (1988), 'A gender role perspective on role conflict', *Journal of Social Behaviour and Personality*, 3,4, pp.317-328.

Gregory, S. and McKie, L. (1990), 'Smear tactics', *Nursing Times*, 86.19, pp.38-40.

Gregory, S. and McKie, L. (1991), The smear test: women's views, *Nursing Standard*, 5.33, pp.32-36.

Gregory, S. and McKie, L. (1992), 'Researching cervical cancer: compromises, practices and beliefs', *Journal of Advances in Health and Nursing Care*, 2,1, pp.73-84.

Griffiths, K. (1992), *Reports of Consultations with Asian and Chinese Carers from 1991-1992*, Birmingham Social Services: Birmingham.

Griffiths, R. (1988), *Community Care: Agenda for Action*, HMSO: London.

Gunaratham, Y. (1991), *Call for Care*, Health Education Authority and King's Fund Centre: London.

Gunaratnam, Y. (1993), 'Breaking the Silence: Asian Carers in Britain', in J. Bornat et al. *Community Care: a Reader*, Macmillan/Open University: London/Buckingham.

Hall, A. S. (1974), *The Point of Entry*, Allen and Unwin: London.

Hallett, C. and Birchall, E. (1992), *Coordination and Child Protection: a Review of the Literature*, HMSO: Edinburgh.

Hammen, C. (et al), (1985), 'Depressive self-schemes, life stress and vulnerability to depression', *Journal of Abnormal Psychology*, 94, pp.308-319.

Harding, S. and Allen, E. (1995 in press), *Sources and uses of data on cancer among ethnic groups*, Cancer Research Campaign/Department of Health Symposium on Ethnic Minorities and Cancer, Regents Park College: London, 4 May 1995.

Hart, D. and Chalmers, K. (1990), *The Housing Needs of Elderly People in Scotland,* Scottish Office, Central Research Unit: Edinburgh.

Health Education Authority, (1994), *Black and Minority Ethnic Groups in England, Health and Lifestyles*, Health Education Authority: London.

Health Education Board for Scotland, (1996), *Coping with Dementia*, HEBS: Edinburgh.

Henderson, J. and Karn, V. (1987), *Race, Class and State Housing: Inequality and the Allocation of Public Housing in Britain*, Gower: Aldershot.

Henley, A. (1979), *Asian Patients in Hospital and at Home,* King Edward's Hospital Fund: London.

HMSO, (1976), *The Race Relations Act.*

HMSO, (1990), *The National Health Services and Community Care Act.*

Hoare, T. A. Johnston, C.M. Gorton, R. and Alberg, C. (1992), 'Reasons for non-attendance for breast screening by Asian women', *Health Education Journal*, 51,4, pp.157-161.

Holland, D. and Lewando-Hundt, G. (1986), *Coventry's Ethnic Minority Elderly Survey*, Coventry City Council: Coventry.

Holland, W. W. and Stewart, S. (1990), *Screening in healthcare: benefit or bane*, Nuffield Provincial Hospitals Trust: London.

Housing Finance, 30, (May 1996), Table 2, p.48.

Ineichen, B. (1990), 'The mental health of Asians in Britain', *British Journal of Psychiatry* 300, pp.1669-1670.

Institute of Race Relations, (1993), *Community Care: The Black Experience*, IRR: London.

Jackson, H. and Field, S. (1989) *Race, Community Groups and Service Delivery*, HMSO: London.

Jain, C., Narayan, N., Narayan, K., Pike, L. A., Clarkson, M. E., Cox, I. G. and Chatterjee, J. (1985), 'Attitudes of Asian patients in Birmingham to general practitioner services', *Journal of the Royal College of General Practitioners* 35, pp.416-418.

Jeffrey, J. and Seagar, R. (1993), *Housing Black and Ethnic Elders*, FBHO: London.

Johnson, J. D. and Meischke, H. (1994), 'Women's preferences for cancer related information from specific types of mass media', *Healthcare for Women International*, 15, pp.23-30.

Johnson, M. R. D. Cross, M. and Cardew, S. A. (1983), 'Inner city residents, ethnic minorities and primary health care', *Postgraduate Medical Journal* 59, pp.664-667.

Jones, H. (1994), *Health and Society in Twentieth-Century Britain*, Longman: Harlow.

Jones, H. R. and Davenport, M. (1972), 'The Pakistani community in Dundee. A study of its growth and demographic structure', *Scottish Geographical Magazine*, 88,2, pp.75-85.

Julienne, L. (1995), Conference speech, published in *Testing Good Intentions*, pp.16-17, Housing Equality Action Unit: Glasgow.

Kalsi, K. (1993), *Asian Elderly Carers: Their Needs in the London Borough of Greenwich*, Greenwich Social Services: London.

Karn, V. (1978), 'The financing of owner-occupation and its impact on ethnic minorities', *New Community*, 6,1 and 2, pp.49-63.

Kearsley, G. W. and Srivastava, S. R. (1974), 'The spatial evolution of Glasgow's Asian community', *Scottish Geographical Magazine*, 90,2, pp.110-124.

Khan, V. S. (1976), 'Pakistanis in Britain: perceptions of a population', *New Community*, 5,3, pp.222-9.

Killeen, J. (1991), *Dementia in Scotland: Agenda for Action 1991-1995*, Scottish Action on Dementia and the Mental Health Foundation: Edinburgh.

Kings' Fund Centre, (1989), *10 Point-Plan*. King's Fund Centre: London.

Kitwood, T. (1989), 'Brain, mind and dementia: with particular reference to Alzheimer's Disease', *Ageing and Society*, 9, pp.1-15.

Lambeth Social Services, (1993), *The Care Needs of Asian Older People in Lambeth: Working in Partnership for racial equality*, Lambeth Social Services: London.

Lawrence, E. (1982), 'In the abundance of water, the fool is thirsty: sociology and black "pathology"', in Centre for Contemporary Cultural Studies, *The Empire Strikes Back: Race and Racism in 70s Britain*, Hutchinson: London.

Lear, A. (1987), *Black Access to Housing Association Stock*, Unpublished project, Diploma in Housing Studies, University of Glasgow: Glasgow.

227

Ley, P. (1976), 'Towards better doctor-patient communications. Contributions from social and experimental psychology', in Bennet, A.E. (ed.), *Communication Between Doctors and Patients*. Oxford University Press: Oxford for the Nuffield Provincial Hospitals Trust, pp.75-98.

Li, P-L. (1992), 'Health needs of the Chinese population', in Ahmad, W. I. U. (ed.), *The Politics of 'Race' and Health*, Race Relations Research Unit, University of Bradford: Bradford.

Love, A. M. and Kirby, K. (1994), *Racial Incidents in Council Housing: the Local Authority Response*, HMSO: London.

Maan, B. (1992), *The New Scots. The Story of Asians in Scotland*, John Donald Publishers: Edinburgh.

MacEwen, M. (1991), *Race, Housing and Law: the British Experience*, Routledge London.

MacEwen, M. (1994), *'Race' and Housing in Scotland: A Literature Review and Bibliography*, SEMRU, Heriot-Watt University: Edinburgh.

MacLeod, L. (1988), *'Irrespective of Race, Colour or Creed?' Voluntary Organisations and Minority Ethnic Groups in Scotland*, Scottish Council for Voluntary Organisations: Edinburgh.

MacLeod, L. (1988), *Irrespective of Race, Colour and Creed*, SCVO: Edinburgh.

Manthorpe, J. (1994), 'Reading around: dementia and ethnicity', *Journal of Dementia Care*, 2,5, pp.22-24.

Manthorpe, J. and Hettiaratchy, P. (1993), 'Ethnic minority elders in the UK', *International Review of Psychiatry*, 5,2-3, pp.171-178.

Mares, P. Henley, A. and Baxter, C. (1985), *Health Care in Multi-racial Britain*, Health Education Council and National Extension College: Cambridge.

Marshall, M. (1990a), *Social Work with Old People*. BASW/Macmillan: London.

Marshall, M. (1990b), *Working with Dementia: Guidelines for Professionals*, Venture Press: Birmingham.

Martin, C. J. (1982), *Psychosocial Stress and Puerperal Psychiatric Disorder*, Paper Presented at the Meeting of the Marce Society: London.

Matheson L. M., Dunnigan, M. G., Holt, D. and Gillis, C. R., (1985), 'Incidence of colorectal, breast and lung cancer in a Scottish Asian population', *Health Bulletin*, 45, pp.245-9.

McAvoy, B. R. (1989), *Attitudes to and use of contraception and cervical cytology services amongst Asian women*, Unpublished P.h.D. Thesis, MD, University of Leicester: Leicester.

McAvoy, B. R. and Raza, R. (1988), 'Asian women: (i) contraceptive knowledge, attitudes and usage (ii) contraceptive services and cervical cytology', *Health Trends* 20, pp.11-17.

McCalman, J. (1990), *The Forgotten People*, King's Fund Centre: London

McCluskey, J. (1991), 'Ethnic minorities and the social work service in Glasgow', in Bowes, A. and Sim, D. (eds.), *Demands and Constraints: Ethnic Minorities and Social Services in Scotland*, pp.113-132, SCVO: Edinburgh.

McCormick, J. (1989), 'Cervical smears: a questionable practice', *Lancet*, 2, pp.207-9.

McFarland, E., Dalton, M. and Walsh, D, (1986), *Personal Welfare Services and Ethnic Minorities - A Study of East Pollokshields (Glasgow)*, SEMRU/Glasgow College: Glasgow.

McFarland, E., Dalton, M. and Walsh, D. (1989), 'Ethnic minority needs and service delivery: the barriers to access in a Glasgow inner city area', *New Community* 15,3, pp.405-415.

McKie, L. (1995), 'The art of surveillance or reasonable prevention? The case of cervical screening', *Sociology of Health and Illness*, 17,4, pp.441-57.

McLennan, J. et al, (1993), *Dementia Touches Everyone: a guide for trainers and trainees in general practice*, Dementia Services Development Centre, University of Stirling: Stirling.

Means, R. and Smith, R. (1994), *Community Care Policy and Practice*, Macmillan: Basingstoke.

Merrill, J. (1988), 'Self-poisoning by Asians', *Update* 37, pp.931-934.

Merrill, J. (1989), 'Attempted suicide by deliberate self-poisoning in Asians', in Cox, J. (ed.), *Racial Discrimination and the Health Service*, Croom Helm: London.

Merrill, J. and Owens, J. (1986), Ethnic differences in self-poisoning: a comparison of Asian and White groups, *British Journal of Psychiatry*, 148, pp.708-712.

Merrill, J. et al, (1990), 'Asian suicides', *British Journal of Psychiatry*, 156, pp.748-749.

Miles, R. (1980), *Racism and Migrant Labour*, Routledge and Kegan Paul: London.

Miles, R. and Muirhead, L. (1986), 'Racism in Scotland: a matter for further investigation', in McCrone, D. (ed.), *Scottish Government Yearbook*: Edinburgh.

Miller, P. and Ingham, J. G. (1976), 'Friends, confidants, and symptoms', *Social Psychiatrist*, 11, pp.51-58.

Modood, T. (1994), 'Political blackness and British Asians', *Sociology*, 28,4, pp.859-876.

Mohan, J. (1995), *A National Health Service? The Restructuring of Health Care in Britain Since 1979*, Macmillan: London.

Mumford, D. B. et al, (1991a), 'Sociocultural correlates of eating disorders among Asian schoolgirls in Bradford', *British Journal of Psychiatry*, 158, pp.222-228.

Mumford, D, B. et al, (1991b), 'The translation and evaluation of an Urdu version of HADS', *Acta Psychiatrica Scandinavica*, 83, pp.81-85.

Mumford, D. B. (1990), 'Asian patients and HADS', *British Journal of Psychiatry*, 156, pp.589.

Munday, E. (1996), *An Evaluation of the Process of Housing Need Assessment for Minority Ethnic Elders: A Case Study of 'Cathay Court' Sheltered Housing Scheme for Chinese Elders*, Unpublished project, Diploma in Housing Studies, Edinburgh College of Art: Edinburgh.

Murphy, C. (1993), *Community Support Project: North East Glasgow*, Dementia Services Development Centre, University of Stirling: Stirling.

Murray, C. (1991), 'Ethnic minorities and community work: the experience of Crossroads Youth and Community Association', in Bowes, A. M. and Sim, D. F. (eds.), *Demands and Constraints: Ethnic Minorities and Social Services in Scotland*, SCVO: Edinburgh.

Naithoo, V. (1988), 'Investigation of non-responders at a cervical screening clinic in Manchester', *British Medical Journal*, 296, pp.1041-2.

National Association of Health Authorities and Trusts, (1995), *1995/6 NHS Handbook, 10th Edition*, JMH Publishing: Tunbridge Wells.

Nayani, S. (1989), 'The evaluation of psychiatric illness in Asian patients by HADS', *British Journal of Psychiatry*, 155, pp.545-547.

Norman, A. (1985) *Triple Jeopardy: Growing Old in a Second Homeland*, Centre for Policy on Ageing: London.

O'Donoghue, M. (1993), *Barriers to Cervical Screening Amongst Women Who Have Never Had a Smear*, Scunthorpe Community Health Council: Scunthorpe.

Oakley, A. (1986), *The Captured Womb: A History of the Medical Care of Pregnant Women*, Blackwell: London.

Office for National Statistics (1996), *Focus on Ethnic Minorities*, HMSO: London.

Parmar, P. (1982), 'Gender, race and class: Asian women in resistance', in Centre for Contemporary Cultural Studies, *The Empire Strikes Back: Race and Racism in 70s Britain*, Hutchinson: London.

Parry, D. and Shapiro, D. A. (1986), 'Life events and social support in working class mothers: stress-buffering or independent effects', *Archives of General Psychiatry*, 43, pp.315-323.

Parsons, L., MacFarlane, A. and Golding, J. (1993), 'Pregnancy, birth and maternity care', in Ahmad, W. I. U. (ed.), *'Race' and Health in Contemporary Britain*, pp.51-75, Open University Press: Buckingham.

Patel, N. (1990), *A 'Race' Against Time? Social Services Provision to Black Elders*, Runnymede Trust: London.

Patel, N. (1993), 'Healthy margins: black elders care-models, policies and prospects', in Ahmad, W. I. U. (ed.), *'Race' and Health in Contemporary Britain*, Open University Press: Buckingham.

Paul, S. (1996), *South Asian Women's Access to Healthcare in Edinburgh*, unpublished PhD Thesis, University of Edinburgh: Edinburgh.

Paykel, E. S. et al, (1969), 'Life events and depression', *Archives of General Psychiatry*, 21, 753-760.

Pearson, M. and Spencer, S. (1990), *Only Superwomen need apply? Problems of Access to Well women clinics in Liverpool*, Paper to the Institute of British Geographers, Medical Geography Study Group, 4 January, University of Glasgow: Glasgow.

Petch, A., Stalker, K., Taylor, C. and Taylor, J. (1994), *Assessment and Care Management Pilot Projects in Scotland: An Overview*, Social Work Research Centre, University of Stirling: Stirling.

Pharoah, C. (1995), *Primary Health Care for Elderly People from Black and Minority Ethnic Communities*, Age Concern Institute of Gerontology/HMSO: London.

Pharoah, C. and Redmond, E. (1991), 'Care for Ethnic Elders', *The Health Service Journal*, 16 May.

Philp, I. et al, (1995), 'Community Care for demented and non-demented elderly patients: a comparison study of financial burden, service use, and unmet needs in family supporters', *British Medical Journal*, 310, pp.1503-1506.

Phoenix, A. (1992), 'Narrow definitions of culture: the case of early motherhood', in McDowell, L. and Pringle, R. (eds.), *Defining Women: Social Institutions and Gender Divisions*, Polity in association with Open University: Cambridge.

Pilgrim, S., Fenton, S., Hughes, T., Hine, C. and Tibbs, N. (1993), *The Bristol Black and Ethnic Minorities Health Survey Report*, Departments of Sociology and Epidemiology, University of Bristol: Bristol.

Pill, R. and Stott, N. (1988), 'Invitation to attend a health check in a general practice setting: the views of a cohort of non-attenders', *Journal of the Royal College of General Practitioners*, February, pp.57-60.

Pollitt, P., O'Connor, D. and Anderson, I. (1990), 'Mild dementia: perceptions and problems', *Ageing and Society*, 9, pp.261-275.

Pollitt, P. (1996), 'Dementia in old age: an anthropological perspective', *Psychological Medicine* 26, pp.1061-1074.

Poole, M. E. and Langan-Fox, J. (1991), 'Conflict in women's decision-making about multiple roles', *Australian Journal of Marriage and the Family*, 13.1, pp.2-18.

Posner, T. and Vessey, M. (1988), *Prevention of Cervical Cancer: The Patients' View*, Kings' Fund Centre: London.

Qureshi, B. (1991), 'Ethnic elders and the general practitioner', in Squires,

A. (ed.) *Multicultural Health Care and Rehabilitation of Older People*, London: Edward Arnold.

Qureshi, K. and Walker, A. (1989), *The Caring Relationship*, Macmillan: Basingstoke.

Rack, P. (1983), *Race, Culture and Mental Disorder*, Tavistock: London.

Ram, M. (1992), 'Coping with racism: Asian employers in the inner city', *Work, Employment and Society*, 6,4, pp.601-618.

Report of the Royal Commission on the National Health Service, (1979), Cmnd. 7615, HMSO: London.

Richards, M. and Brayne, C. (1996), 'Cross-cultural research into cognitive impairment and dementia: some practical experiences', *International Journal of Geriatric Psychiatry*, 1,4, pp.383-387.

Rickford, F. (1995), 'Nursing new needs', *The Guardian*, 25 October: 25.

Roberts, H. (1985), *The Patient Patients: Women and their Doctors*, Pandora Press: London.

Robinson, V. (1980), 'Asians and council housing', *Urban Studies*, 17, pp.323-331.

Robinson, V. (1986), *Transients, Settlers and Refugees: Asians in Britain*, Clarendon Press: Oxford.

Rooney, B. and McKain, J. (1990), *Voluntary Health Organisations and the Black Community in Liverpool*, Report of a survey by Health and Race Project, Department of Sociology, Liverpool University: Liverpool.

Rowlings, C. (1978), 'Duty - the response to referrals', in Department of Health and Social Security, *Social Service Teams: the Practitioner's View*, HMSO: London.

Sage, J. and Sangavi, C. (1992), *An Equal Voice: The Needs of Minority Ethnic Elders and Carers in the Medway Towns*. Medway and Gillingham Race Equality Council.

Sarre, P., Phillips, D. and Skellington, R. (1989), *Ethnic Minority Housing: Explanations and Policies*, Avebury: Aldershot.

Schwartz, M., Savage, W., George, J. and Emohare, L. (1989), 'Women's knowledge and experience of cervical screening: a failure of health education and medical organisation', *Community Medicine*, 11,4, pp.279-89.

Scott, H. (1994), 'It's time to wake the "sleeping giants"', *Elders: the Journal of Care and Practice* 3, 2.

Scottish Council for Voluntary Organisations, (1996), 'Research into Racial Equality in the Scottish Voluntary Sector', *Connect*, 14 June, p4.

Scottish Development Department, (1975), *Housing and Social Work: A Joint Approach*, (the Morris Report), HMSO: Edinburgh.

Scottish Homes, (1993a), *Scottish Housing Condition Survey 1991: Report*, Scottish Homes: Edinburgh.

Scottish Homes, (1993b), *Housing the Elderly in the 1990's. A Discussion Paper*, Scottish Homes: Edinburgh.

Scottish Homes, (1993c), *Ethnic Minority Housing. A Consultation Paper*, Scottish Homes: Edinburgh.

Scottish Homes, (1994), *Action for Race Equality: Policy Document*, Scottish Homes: Edinburgh.

Scottish Homes, (1995), *Removing the Barriers: Housing for Older People. A Scottish Homes Policy Statement*, Scottish Homes: Edinburgh.

Scottish Office, (1983), *Ethnic Minorities in Scotland*, Scottish Office Central Research Unit: Edinburgh.

Scottish Office, (1991a) ENV8/1991: *Community Care in Scotland: Housing and Community Care*, Scottish Office: Edinburgh.

Scottish Office, (1991b), *Ethnic Minorities in Scotland*, Central Research Unit: Edinburgh.

Scottish Office, (1992), *Scotland's Health, A Challenge to Us All*, HMSO: Edinburgh.

Scottish Office, (1994), *Community Care: The Housing Dimension*, Scottish Office: Edinburgh.

SEMRU, (1987), *Ethnic Minorities Profile: A Study of Needs and Services in Lothian Region and Edinburgh District*, Scottish Ethnic Minorities Research Unit: Edinburgh.

Senior, M. L. and Williamson, S. M. (1990), 'An investigation into the influence of geographical factors on attendance for cervical cytology screening', *Transactions of the Institute of British Geographers New Series*, 15, pp.421-434.

Shaw, A. (1988), *A Pakistani Community in Britain*, Basil Blackwell: Oxford.

Shepherd, M. (1992), 'Comparing need with resource allocation', *Health Visitor* 65.9, pp.303-306.

Shukla, K, (1991), 'Nutrition and dietetics', in Squires, A. (ed.), *Multicultural Health Care and Rehabilitation of Older People*, Edward Arnold: London.

Skrabanek, P. (1988), 'The debate against mass mammography in Britain, the case against', *British Medical Journal*, 297, pp.971-2.

Skrabanek, P. (1990), 'Why is preventative medicine exempted from ethical constraints', *Journal of Medical Ethics*, 16, pp.187-190.

Smaje, C. (1995), *Health 'Race' and Ethnicity: Making Sense of the Evidence*, Kings' Fund Centre: London.

Smith, S. (1989), *The Politics of 'Race' and Residence*, Polity Press: London.

Social Services Inspectorate, (1986), *Social Services for Ethnic Minorities - Policy and Practice in the North-West*, DHSS.

Social Services Inspectorate, (1987), *Race and Culture in Social Services Delivery*, DHSS.

Solomon, A. (1992), 'Clinical diagnosis among diverse populations: a multicultural perspective', *Families in Society: the Journal of Contemporary Human Services*, June, pp.371-377.

South Glamorgan Race Equality Council and South Glamorgan Social Services Department, (1994), *Towards a Good Old Age? Action research into the health and social care needs of ethnic minority older people and their carers in South Glamorgan*, South Glamorgan Racial Equality Council: Cardiff.

Squires, A . (ed.), (1991), *Multicultural Health Care and Rehabilitation of Older People*, Arnold: London.

Stalker, K. (1996), *Supporting Disabled People in Scotland: an Overview of Social Work and Health Services*, Scottish Office: Edinburgh.

Stevenson, O. (1989), *Age and Vulnerability: a Guide to Better Care*, Edward Arnold: London.

Strathclyde Regional Council, (1986), *Forward in Understanding*. Strathclyde Regional Council Community Development Committee, Sub-Group on Ethnic Minorities: Glasgow.

Stubbs, P. (1993), '"Ethnically sensitive" or "anti-racist"? Models for health research and service delivery', in Ahmad, W. I. U. (ed.), *'Race' and Health in Contemporary Britain*, pp.34-47, Open University Press: Buckingham.

Tester, S. (1992), *Common Knowledge: a Coordinated Approach to Information-Giving*, Centre for Policy on Ageing: London.

Tester, S. and Meredith, B. (1987) *Ill-informed? A Study of Information and Support for Elderly People in the Inner City*, Policy Studies Institute: London.

Third, H., Wainwright, S. and Pawson, H. (1997), *Constraint and Choice for Minority Ethnic Households in the Home Ownership Market in Scotland*, Scottish Homes: Edinburgh.

Tibbs, M. (1996), 'Amos: a self lost and found', *Journal of Dementia Care*, March/April.

Townsend, P. (1962), *The Last Refuge,* Routledge and Kegan Paul: London.

Turnbull, A. (1985), *Greenwich's Afro-Caribbean and South Asian Elderly People*, Greenwich Social Services Department, London.

Twigg, J. (1992), *Carers: Research and Practice,* HMSO: London.

Twigg, J. (ed.), (1992), *Carers: Research and Practice,* HMSO: London.

Twigg, J. and Atkin, K. (1994), *Carers Perceived*, Open University Press: Buckingham.

Twinn, S. and Cowley, S. (1992), *The Principles of Health Visiting: A Re-examination*, Health Visitors Association, United Kingdom Standing Conference on Health Visitor Education.

Wainwright, S., Murie, A. and MacEwen, M. (1994), *The Experience of Households from Minority Ethnic Groups in the Scottish Housing System*, Research Report No.29, Scottish Homes: Edinburgh.

Wainwright, S., Pawson, H. and Third, H. (1997 forthcoming), *Housing Needs and Preferences of Minority Ethnic Households in Leith*, Scottish Homes: Edinburgh.

Walker, R. and Ahmad, W. (1994a), Windows of opportunity in rotting frames: care providers' perspectives on community care and black communities, *Critical Social Policy*, 40, pp.46-69.

Walker, R. and Ahmad, W. (1994b), 'Asian and Black Elders and Community Care: a Survey of Care Providers', *New Community*, 20.4, pp.635-646.

Ward, L. (1993), 'Race equality and employment in the National Health Service', in Ahmad, W. I. U. (ed.), *'Race' and Health in Contemporary Britain*, pp.167-182, Open University Press: Buckingham.

Wardhaugh, J. (1991), Asian women: campaigning for self-help, in Bowes, A. M. and Sim, D. F. (eds.), *Demands and Constraints: Ethnic Minorities and Social Services in Scotland*, pp.153-169, SCVO: Edinburgh.

Watson, J. L. (1977), 'The Chinese: Hong Kong villagers in the British catering trade', in Watson, J, L. (ed.), *Between Two Cultures. Migrants and Minorities in Britain*, Blackwell: Oxford.

Wenger, G. C. (1984), *The Supportive Network: Coping with Old Age*, Allen and Unwin: London.

White, I. and Kaur, R. (1995), *A Health Field Trip to the Panjab and Delhi, March 1995*, Unpublished: Glasgow.

Williams, J. (1990), *Elders from Black and Minority Ethnic Communities*, from The Kaleidoscope of Care, NISW.

Wright, C. (1983), 'Language and communication problems in an Asian community', *Journal of the Royal College of General Practitioners* 33, pp.2101-104.

Yee, L. (1996), *Improving Support for Black Carers: A Source Book of Information, Ideas and Service Initiatives*, King's Fund Centre: London.

Yee, L. and Blunden, R. (1995), *General Practice and Carers: Scope for Change?*, King's Fund Centre: London.

Index

joint housing and social work
 departments 4, 10

Kings Fund Centre 136
Kirkcaldy 19
knowledge of services 39, 48, 71-
 72, 81-82, 96, 125-126, 129-130,
 205, 211

Leicester 70, 71, 73, 149
Liverpool 73
local government structure 4, 11
London 32, 73, 188
Lothian Region 32, 135-150
Lothian Racial Equality Council
 137, 138

Midlothian 4
MILAN (Welfare Council) 138,
 140, 145, 148
minority ethnic staff 93, 95, 114,
 126, 147
Moray 4
Morris Committee 10

National Health Service 11-14, 23,
 102
National Health Service and
 Community Care Act (1990)
 102, 119, 135
neighbourhood 60, 62
New Towns 5
Nottingham 149

Pakistanis 17-34, 35-50, 80-82, 83-
 98, 120-122
 carers 139
 women 151-169
Positive Action in Housing 7, 133,
 204

racism 87, 104-106, 168-169, 182-
 185, 206, 214

religion 87-88
residential care 127, 145-147
Royal Commission on the National
 Health Service (1979) 11

Scottish Council for Voluntary
 Organisations 213
Scottish Ethnic Minorities Research
 Unit 51, 53, 137
Scottish Federation of Housing
 Associations 7
Scottish Homes 3, 5, 6, 7-8, 29, 52-
 55, 63, 65, 75-77, 133, 204, 215
Scottish Office 10, 16-17
Scottish Parliament 4
Scottish Special Housing
 Association 3
sheltered housing 30, 71-73, 76, 81,
 205
Social Services Inspectorate 118-
 119
social work departments 3, 8-11,
 75, 89-90, 93-95, 115, 120, 123-
 124, 126-131, 144, 149, 205-
 207
Social Work (Scotland) Act (1968)
 8, 131
South Ayrshire 4
Stirling 4, 18-19
Strathclyde Region 11, 17, 83-84,
 96
Strathkelvin 17-19

Tai Cymru 3, 5
Tayside 84
training 97, 112, 116, 133, 212-213
translation 131, 141, 161, 166-167

Urban Aid 113

Vietnamese 17
voluntary organisations 102, 213-
 214